THE VOICE OF GOD
————— IN THE —————
TEXT OF SCRIPTURE

PROCEEDINGS OF THE LOS ANGELES THEOLOGY CONFERENCE

This is the fourth volume in a series published by Zondervan Academic. It is the proceedings of the Los Angeles Theology Conference held under the auspices of the School of Theology at Fuller Theological Seminary, in January 2016. The conference is an attempt to do several things. First, it provides a regional forum in which scholars, students, and clergy can come together to discuss and reflect upon central doctrinal claims of the Christian faith. It is also an ecumenical endeavor. Bringing together theologians from a number of different schools and confessions, the LATC seeks to foster serious engagement with Scripture and tradition in a spirit of collegial dialogue (and disagreement), looking to retrieve the best of the Christian past in order to forge theology for the future. Finally, each volume in the series focuses on a central topic in dogmatic theology. It is hoped that this endeavor will continue to fructify contemporary systematic theology and foster a greater understanding of the historic Christian faith amongst the members of its different communions.

LOS ANGELES
THEOLOGY
CONFERENCE

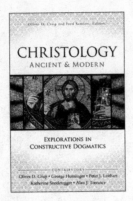

CHRISTOLOGY, ANCIENT AND MODERN:
Explorations in Constructive Dogmatics, 2013

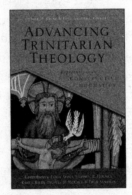

ADVANCING TRINITARIAN THEOLOGY:
Explorations in Constructive Dogmatics, 2014

LOCATING ATONEMENT:
Explorations in Constructive Dogmatics, 2015

Oliver D. Crisp and Fred Sanders, Editors

THE VOICE OF GOD
——— IN THE ———
TEXT OF SCRIPTURE

Explorations in
CONSTRUCTIVE DOGMATICS

CONTRIBUTORS: William J. Abraham • Stephen E. Fowl
John Goldingay • Amy Plantinga Pauw • Daniel J. Treier

 ZONDERVAN®
LOS ANGELES
THEOLOGY
CONFERENCE

ZONDERVAN

The Voice of God in the Text of Scripture
Copyright © 2016 by Oliver D. Crisp and Fred Sanders

This title is also available as a Zondervan ebook.

Requests for information should be addressed to:
Zondervan, *3900 Sparks Dr. SE, Grand Rapids, Michigan 49546*

ISBN 978-0-310-52776-3

Cover design: Matthew Van Kirk / Increto
Cover photo: Gianni Dagli Orti / The Art Archive at Art Resource, NY
Interior design: Matthew Van Zomeren and Ben Fetterley

Printed in the United States of America

16 17 18 19 20   DHV   10 9 8 7 6 5 4 3 2 1

To Richard Hays

CONTENTS

ACKNOWLEDGMENTS

THE EDITORS WOULD LIKE TO THANK Professor Joel Green as Dean of the School of Theology, and the faculty and administration of Fuller Theological Seminary for their support for the Fourth Los Angeles Theology Conference (LATC) in January of 2016, out of which these published proceedings grew. Without the assistance of the Events Team at Fuller Seminary, and of Roger Overton the Research Assistant who oversaw the practical running of the event, this conference would not have run as smoothly as it did. We are grateful to them. Thanks too to Biola University for its ongoing support of LATC. This is now the fourth time that we are able to record grateful thanks to our editor and colleague, Katya Covrett, for her invaluable assistance before, during, and after the fun and frolics of conference proceedings. Thanks too to the Zondervan Team (aka "The Z Team")—Stan Gundry as editor-in-chief, Jesse Hillman, Kari Moore, Josh Kessler, and Nancy Erickson.

We had hoped to have Professor Richard Hays at the conference, but he was unable to attend due to health concerns. We dedicate this book to him as a token of our gratitude and esteem for the way in which he has stimulated truly theological reading of Holy Scripture.

LIST OF CONTRIBUTORS

William J. Abraham—is Albert Cook Outler Professor of Wesley Studies and Altshuler Distinguished Teaching Professor at Perkins School of Theology, Southern Methodist University. He earned his BA from the Queen's University, Belfast, his MDiv from Asbury Theological Seminary, and his DPhil from Oxford University. He also holds a DD (h.c.) from Asbury Theological Seminary.

Stephen E. Fowl—is professor of theology at Loyola University, Baltimore, MD. He holds the BA and MA degrees from Wheaton College, and a PhD from the University of Sheffield.

John Goldingay—is David Allan Hubbard Professor of Old Testament, in the School of Theology, Fuller Theological Seminary in Pasadena, CA. He earned his BA from Oxford University, and a PhD from the University of Nottingham. He also holds a Lambeth DD (h.c.), awarded by the Archbishop of Canterbury.

Myk Habets—is Head of Carey Graduate School and lecturer in theology at Carey Baptist College, Auckland, New Zealand. He holds a Bachelor of Ministries and an MTh from Bible College of New Zealand, a Graduate Diploma in Tertiary Teaching from AUT University, and a PhD in theology from the University of Otago, New Zealand.

Erin M. Heim—is assistant professor of New Testament at Denver Seminary. She earned her BMus from the University of Minnesota, her MA from Denver Seminary, and her PhD in New Testament from the University of Otago, New Zealand.

Daniel D. Lee—is Director of the Asian American Center and adjunct assistant professor of Asian American Ministry at Fuller Theological Seminary. He earned his MDiv from Princeton Theological Seminary and his ThM and PhD degrees from Fuller Theological Seminary.

Jason McMartin—is associate professor of theology, Rosemead School of Psychology and Talbot School of Theology, Biola University. He holds the BA and MA from Biola University and a PhD from Claremont Graduate University.

Ryan S. Peterson—is assistant professor of theology, Talbot School of Theology, Biola University. He holds a BA from Moody Bible Institute, an MA from Biola University, a MTh from the University of Edinburgh, and a PhD from Wheaton College.

Timothy H. Pickavance—is associate professor of philosophy and Chair of the Philosophy Department in Talbot School of Theology, Biola University. He holds a BS from the University of North Texas, an MA from Biola University, and a PhD in Philosophy from the University of Texas at Austin.

Amy Plantinga Pauw—is Henry P. Mobley Jr. Professor of Doctrinal Theology at Louisville Presbyterian Seminary, KY. She holds a BA from Calvin College, an MDiv from Fuller Theological Seminary, and a PhD from Yale University.

Daniel J. Treier—is Blanchard Professor of Theology at Wheaton Graduate School in Wheaton College, Wheaton, IL. He earned his BA from Cedarville College, his MDiv and ThM degrees from Grand Rapids Theological Seminary, and his PhD from Trinity Evangelical Divinity School.

ABBREVIATIONS

BBR	*Bulletin for Biblical Research*
BibInt	Biblical Interpretation Series
BSac	*Bibliotheca Sacra*
CBQ	*Catholic Biblical Quarterly*
DTIB	*Dictionary for Theological Interpretation of the Bible*
HTR	*Harvard Theological Review*
Int	*Interpretation*
JETS	*Journal of the Evangelical Theological Society*
JTI	*Journal of Theological Interpretation*
LNTS	The Library of New Testament Studies
Neot	*Neotestamentica*
NICNT	New International Commentary on the New Testament
NIGTC	New International Greek Testament Commentary
NPNF	*Nicene and Post-Nicene Fathers*
NRSV	New Revised Standard Version
NTL	New Testament Library
NTS	*New Testament Studies*
OTE	*Old Testament Essays*
ProEccl	*Pro Ecclesia*
RelS	*Religious Studies*
SBLDS	Society of Biblical Literature Dissertation Series
SJT	*Scottish Journal of Theology*
SNTSMS	Society for New Testament Studies Monograph Series
ThTo	*Theology Today*
TS	*Theological Studies*
WBC	Word Biblical Commentary
WTJ	*Westminster Theological Journal*

INTRODUCTION

"BIBLIOLOGY" IS SUCH AN UNLOVELY WORD that most self-respecting theologians simply will not use it, even though it is etymologically obvious, has been around for a couple of centuries, and provides a much-needed label. It certainly would be handy to have a single word for referring to the Christian doctrine about Scripture. Instead, we get by with the phrase, ambiguously genitive though it is, "the doctrine of Scripture." The doctrine of Scripture occupies an important place in Christian theology, and so it is no surprise that after having devoted previous conferences to the three core doctrines (Trinity, incarnation, and atonement) the Los Angeles Theology Conference turned its attention now to this one, bibliology, with or without that handy name.

The two terms "text of Scripture" and "voice of God" indicate something of the range that a well-functioning doctrine of Scripture needs to cover. Text can be quite mundane. We read texts all the time, from browsing websites on our computers to leafing through the latest magazine, journal, or novel. Sometimes, we even read *old books*. Reading and understanding texts is a complex process, and much has been written on how to be a virtuous, and charitable, reader, as well as on trying to understand the meaning of a given text (if we think there is a meaning in the text at all). This includes the reading of multi-authored texts, the supreme example of which is surely the Bible.

Reading, pondering, attempting to understand—these are central to engagement with written texts. But how often do we allow the text to speak *to us*? How often do we expect to find the author of a text addressing us by means of the text in front of us? Of course we often find in texts wisdom that is as true today as it was when the text in question was originally inscribed, even if that was many centuries ago. But the question of letting the author of a text speak to us by means of the text is not quite the same sort of thing. There is something about it that is more immediate, the address of one person to another, or a group of others across time and space.

When the ultimate source of a text is God (even when that divine source is understood to be the author behind the author), we find ourselves stretched far beyond the mundane phenomena of texts-in-general. In this case, we stand before a theological claim of the first order, and one of the right responses is to develop a doctrine of Scripture adequate to its divine authorship. Somewhere in the mix between text and voice, a doctrine of Scripture that recognizes both the written text and the holy voice will need to call on the expertise of systematic theologians, biblical studies scholars, and philosophers. That is what we did for the 2016 Los Angeles Theology Conference, and the results are before you in this volume.

Though interdisciplinary collaboration is not a panacea for all ills, it does offer unique opportunities, and enables a project like this to avoid certain besetting problems. Doctrines of Scripture have often suffered from a lopsidedness that results from a lack of resources in one of these domains. Systematic theologians working without exegetical expertise often produce statements about Scripture which, profound and sagacious as they often are in their own right, seem to hover ethereally just a few feet above the actual documents which they are describing. Biblical scholars without an instinct for doctrine are often so close to the documents—or more typically, to one tiny sub-section of the documents—that they are unwilling to hazard anything like a global statement about the nature of the Bible as a whole. Philosophers generally have a difficult time construing the claims of either of these neighboring disciplines, since they are set forth in drastically different idioms than are current in analytic philosophical work.

But when practitioners of these disciplines manage to come together over a common task, they find interesting new ways of approaching perennial subjects that had been considered either completely settled in advance, or intractably unsettled in perpetuity. Some of those topics include the nature of the Bible's authority and truthfulness (Is it a community-norming document like a constitution and by-laws settled by those whom it governs, or is it an external word that norms or canons the community that looks to it?); the mode whereby the divine author communicates through the human authors (Is it by verbal inspiration, providential oversight, endorsement and authorization, or concurrence?); the unity and diversity of the biblical materials (How different are the constituent elements of Scripture? Is there a single biblical theology, or as many theologies as there are authors? What techniques of interpretation are appropriate to this differentiated unity of discrete texts?); and the character of the statements made in Scripture (Is the basic unit of intelligibility the word, the image, or the complete book? How do propositional and non-propositional elements relate to each other?). Looming above all these concerns is the question of the dogmatic location of the doctrine of Scripture within an overall theological system: Is the doctrine about Scripture simply one doctrine among many, or is it uniquely foundational for the others because it is an account of the source material for all the other doctrines? Is the doctrine of Scripture a sub-field of the doctrine of revelation, or does it belong within ecclesiology, or perhaps with an account of the progress of salvation history? What, finally, are the limits of a doctrine of Scripture? How do we know when we have said enough in this field of doctrine?

In the following chapters, each author comes to the task of describing a doctrine of Scripture from their own angle of approach, from their own areas of expertise, and in dialogue with a variety of conversation partners. The chapters are organized in a way that arcs from first principles to final purposes, so that the book as a whole suggests the overall shape of a doctrine of Scripture. Daniel Treier's chapter offers the broadest overview of the field, serving both as a substantive proposal for deriving the Christian doctrine of Scripture from "the Bible's own hermeneutical self-presentation," and also as a helpful map of themes that are handled in more detail by later chapters. As a systematic theologian attending to how "God has incorporated a particular collection of texts . . . into the Word's saving divine self-communication by the Spirit," Treier frames the doctrine of Scripture as something that must be shared among the theological disciplines.

Stephen Fowl's chapter also takes up very large methodological concerns, but does so in the genre of theological commentary on selected passages from Hebrews. Fowl is ultimately concerned with the formation of readers who can hear God, so he interrogates the book of Hebrews on this subject in order to sketch the character of such a hearer of the word. On this topic, Hebrews has much to say.

John Goldingay writes as a veteran of the long methodological battles over historical-critical scholarly inquiry into the Old Testament, and one who freely admits that historical method has militated against theological understanding. But Goldingay is not eager to see the pendulum swing to an ahistorical theological reading; instead he advocates "a theological historical reading, which will be a fuller historical reading because it articulates the text's own theology."

Amy Plantinga Pauw's chapter performs the thought experiment of starting the theology of Scripture with the wisdom literature, especially Proverbs and Ecclesiastes. If the dominant tradition has started with prophets and apostles, and thus highlighted an oracular model of speaking and hearing, Pauw's attention to sages makes new connections.

Myk Habets returns to the book of Hebrews to learn from its own retrospective hermeneutic, whereby it "treats biblical quotations not as the Word written but as the spoken Word of the tripersonal God." Habets argues that this transformation of text to voice deserves greater recognition as a characteristic of all Scripture, and should guide our own interpretive practice.

In her chapter, Erin Heim attends to the nature of metaphor in Scripture, venturing the proposal that God is rightly understood as the metaphor maker behind the text, rendering the metaphors in the text a special kind of conduit of divine self-revelation. What metaphors can uniquely do is convey information from a certain perspective, enabling the reader to see a truth from the speaker's perspective, to see it as something.

Jason McMartin and Timothy H. Pickavance enter the controversial territory where historical biblical criticism clashes with the theological interpretation of Scripture, but they bring with them the analytic tools of recent discussions in the philosophy of disagreement. By determining criteria for when an interpreter should suspend judgment or assent to expert testimony, they shed new light on vexed questions.

If McMartin and Pickavance use philosophy to adjudicate the old dispute between biblical studies and theology, William Abraham takes more the role of an observer and reporter in his chapter. He recounts the way postmodern thought has sought to relativize historical studies in general, and then points out the opportunities that are available for Christians who cannot see their own interests quite represented by either side of the debate. As Abraham reads the current scene, the old alliances and conflicts are passing away, and now is the time for a new approach to Scripture.

Daniel Lee's chapter considers the questions of contextual readings of Scripture in conversation with the Swiss theologian, Karl Barth. Following Barth, he argues that understanding Scripture involves a "double particularity." On the one hand, Scripture is established upon the particularity of that one historical event of God's self-revelation. On the other hand, Jesus Christ is the *living* God, not merely a figure of history. He speaks by means of Scripture into our particular and varied contemporary contexts.

Scripture "becoming the Word of God" means encountering God in our particularity in dialogue with particular biblical texts.

Ryan Peterson concludes the volume with a proposal that the telos of Scripture, the purpose toward which it directs readers, must be understood in terms of the relationship between God's identity and human identity. He retrieves, as a guiding image, Augustine's analogy of a journey through Scripture into the knowledge and love of God, and then shows how that analogy relates to some traditional attributes of Scripture.

May these essays extend discussion of the doctrine of Scripture, and our hearing of its various voices today, *ad maiorem dei gloriam.*

Oliver D. Crisp and Fred Sanders, April 2016

CHAPTER 1

THE FREEDOM OF GOD'S WORD: TOWARD AN "EVANGELICAL" DOGMATICS OF SCRIPTURE

DANIEL J. TREIER

DOGMATIC THEOLOGY PARTICIPATES in the church's effort to discern, develop a detailed account of, and defend its authoritative teaching. History demonstrates that these tasks intermingle: Defending Christian teaching is often the occasion of freshly discerning the truth and detailing its meaning. Here I cannot offer a full dogmatic account of Scripture, but I sketch a framework for developing such an account in today's complex environment. In that framework, the first task—discerning the church's traditional commitment—is fairly straightforward: The biblical texts together comprise one unified (form of the) Word of God. The second task—developing a detailed doctrine of Scripture—involves acknowledging important contemporary trends, which can help us to recover and reform the faithful hearing of God's Word in Scripture. Yet a third task—defending the church's traditional commitment—is also necessary, since theological challenges have arisen concerning the Bible's oral contexts and moral integrity.

This third, more defensive, task prompts a consistent operative principle throughout: focusing on the Bible's hermeneutical self-presentation. Whereas some believe that contemporary approaches to Scripture are necessarily beholden to general hermeneutics, others nearly reject such hermeneutics out of hand for binding us to human subjectivity and obscuring divine action.[1] In response to both concerns, however, theological accounts of Scripture must attend carefully to what God has actually done: God has incorporated a particular collection of texts—along with our hearing and understanding of them—into the Word's saving divine self-communication by the Spirit. Moreover, God has provided reflection in the texts themselves about their writing, reading, hearing, and understanding. Given this biblical material, neither merely hermeneutical generalizations (about texts being occasions for human understanding) nor dogmatic generalizations (about the divine voice being the occasion of judgment and grace) will suffice. Without being naïvely inductive or phenomenological, a dogmatic account of Scripture should reflect this concreteness of its self-presentation.

The resulting dogmatic framework will reflect the following claims: The Bible itself authorizes the church's traditional identification of Scripture as God's Word; the Bible itself acknowledges the dynamism and diversity of such divine speech, as reflected in certain contemporary trends; and the Bible itself addresses theological challenges regarding its oral aspects and moral authority.

THE CHURCH'S TRADITION

So, first of all, a dogmatic account seeks to discern the church's traditional commitment, honoring its past as a source of wisdom with which to pursue plausible continuity. Concerning Scripture, little controversy emerges in the church's orthodox tradition: The biblical texts together comprise one unified (form of the) Word of God. Given creedal generality and churchly division, this near unanimity may be counterintuitive, but only

---

1   See, e.g., the dogmatic concerns over hermeneutics in John Webster, "Hermeneutics in Modern Theology: Some Doctrinal Reflections," in *Word and Church: Essays in Christian Dogmatics* (Edinburgh: T&T Clark, 2001), 47–86, and the modest counterproposal regarding theological use of general hermeneutics in Francis Watson, "Hermeneutics and the Doctrine of Scripture: Why They Need Each Other," *International Journal of Systematic Theology* 12 no. 2 (April 2010): 118–43.

momentarily so. The crucial consensus existed early: The Old Testament would be read as Christian Scripture, the God of Israel its speaker and the same as the One revealed in Jesus Christ; the authoritative apostolic writings of the eventual New Testament would comprise epistles Pauline and Catholic along with four Gospels, but not their "gnostic" alternatives. Thus the Christian tradition united in reading these Scriptures as the Word of God, spending intellectual energy on doctrinal matter and not methodological prolegomena. For, in creedal language, "he has spoken through the prophets."

Henceforth Scripture has regulated, and had its interpretation regulated by, Christian faith and love. Its collected texts present a complex Christ-centered unity, with a literal sense variously defined and appropriated in light of the interplay between divine and human authorship. Beyond such basic commitments, the Christian tradition admittedly contains diverse notions of Scripture's authority, exact canonical boundaries, and interpretive approaches. The doctrine of Scripture per se did not garner significant attention between the conclusion of the Christian canon and the beginning of the Protestant Reformation. Subsequently, from modernity's onset to the present, the doctrine has frequently come under a searchlight, subject to blinding polemical heat as much as illuminating insight. Whereas a dogmatic account of Scripture should focus on authoritative church consensus regarding God's action, polemics arise because the church no longer hears the Word as one body: Parts of the church each claim to be its true heart, uniquely indwelt by the Word's Spirit. Hermeneutics cannot restore the church unity that God alone gives; yet modest hermeneutical concepts can secondarily inform dogmatics because, whatever else is involved, the church's healing depends upon hearing God speak in and through human acts of reading biblical texts.

The dogmatic framework proposed here is admittedly Protestant, albeit in grateful solidarity with Orthodox and Catholic acknowledgment of Scripture as the Word of God. While learning from the intentionally traditional and spiritual character of these alternative approaches, Protestants can contribute ecumenical insight of their own. In particular, Protestant accounts celebrate the gospel freedom that Christians enjoy when the Word of God that is binding for salvation remains clearly distinct from the human traditions that emerge from churchly wisdom.

Furthermore, the dogmatic concerns addressed here have not just Protestant but even creedally orthodox theologies as primary dialogue partners. Admittedly, liberal Protestants have made instructive contributions: from their earlier tradition, celebrating human freedom and engaging modern culture, especially scientific learning; among their present tendencies, pursuing liberation for all creatures and opposing any systemic or ideological oppression. Many conservative Protestants recognize enough shared faith with such liberal Christians that they remain in mainline denominations. Meanwhile, evangelical Christianity is hardly monolithic regarding the doctrine of Scripture, actually fostering many of its contemporary polemics.

Those qualifications notwithstanding, the most fruitful modern discussions of the doctrine of Scripture have occurred among those evangelical Protestants who are scholarly enough, and those mainline Protestants who are conservative enough, to wrestle with a broadly shared faith commitment: Scripture's authority as a form of the Word of God. Fundamentalists who have shrilly denied Scripture's need for interpretation, and liberals who have paid no more than lip service to the Bible's identity with the Word of God, have rarely offered accounts of Scripture that could sustain healthy Christian teaching over the long run.

In the background of such a bold claim lies Scripture's self-presentation: The most basic, widespread concept with which the texts identify themselves is divine speech.[2] Those who maintain the biblically-claimed, creedally-implied, and liturgically-proclaimed identity between Scripture and "the Word of the Lord" are most likely to understand the Bible's character and hear its message faithfully. In contrast with divine speech, comparatively few biblical texts focus on "revelation"—by whatever definition. The complications generated by that theological concept may be best addressed by the divine speech motif, since thereby the Bible incorporates both "personal" and "propositional" aspects in its self-presentation. God communicates the truth that fosters knowing God, while knowing God defines and then fosters hearing the truth aright. Truth makes cognitive contact with reality, while the primary reality is personal covenant faithfulness: who is our God, and who we are in relation to God.

Suppose we concede that the overwhelming majority of "logos" texts in the Bible do not directly designate written Scriptures but instead an oral, personal message. Numerous texts would still pertain to written Scriptures—minimally, Torah material in Deuteronomy; certain Psalms

---

2   Notice, e.g., how "speech" vocabulary and concepts dominate the treatment of Nigel M. de S. Cameron, "Revelation, Idea of," in *Evangelical Dictionary of Biblical Theology*, ed. Walter A. Elwell (Grand Rapids: Baker, 1996), 679–82.

and new covenant texts; some of Jesus's sayings in the Gospels; widespread appeals to "it is written"; Hebrews's appropriation of human speech as divine discourse; key Pauline passages such as Romans 15:4 and 2 Timothy 3:16–17; and Petrine mention of Pauline letters.

Of course most of these texts principally reference some portion of the Old Testament, while scholarly debate continues over the clarity and timing of its "canonical" boundaries. However, if early Christians wished to think as closely to the Bible's own idioms as possible regarding the texts' nature and authority, where else would they have gone? Hence even today's clarion calls for a minimalist, inductive, and biblical doctrine of Scripture lead to many of the traditional passages. Although Christ is God's first and final Word, biblical texts do not blush when associating themselves with God's Word. What God has joined together in the church's traditional commitment, let us not put asunder.

CONTEMPORARY TRENDS

Secondly, a dogmatic account develops in detail the church's traditional commitment. Confessional traditions and evangelical parachurch entities detail this commitment using a host of concepts such as inspiration, sufficiency, clarity, infallibility, and inerrancy. Beyond appropriating particular confessional or conceptual traditions, however, a more detailed dogmatic account must also address contemporary pastoral and intellectual contexts—which are the focus of the pan-"evangelical" framework sketched here.

A spate of important developments affecting the doctrine of Scripture surfaced following the controversies of the 1960s through the early 1980s over biblical inerrancy. Since the following developments have achieved wide influence, if not substantial consensus, in conservative Protestant circles, they ought to inform dogmatic reflection—even if I can only mention them briefly, noting one representative for each.

The first set of developments focused on the biblical texts' self-presentation, thus informing the operative principle of the present account. To begin with, Brevard Childs directed attention to the canonical shaping of biblical books for understanding biblical theology.[3] Soon Richard Hays directed fresh attention to practices of inner-biblical interpretation,

---

3   See, briefly, Brevard S. Childs, *Biblical Theology: A Proposal*, Facets (Minneapolis: Fortress, 2002); also helpful is Christopher Seitz, "Canonical Approach," in *DTIB*, ed. Kevin J. Vanhoozer (Grand Rapids: Baker Academic, 2005), 100–102.

particularly the New Testament's use of the Old, for understanding Scripture's internal unity.[4] John Goldingay then directed attention to the diversity of biblical models for understanding Scripture's authority.[5] In some respects all of these developments emphasize biblical diversity and require cautious appropriation. Yet each can positively contribute to appreciation of the biblical texts' holistic self-presentation rather than denial of any and all scriptural unity like some other "inductive" approaches.

The next set of developments reflected hermeneutical and philosophical trends, creating a measure of tension. On one hand, Nicholas Wolterstorff directed attention beyond just the mental contents of human authors or editors, and ultimately to the active force of their communication, when thinking about the object of interpretation.[6] Through this appeal to speech-act philosophy, Wolterstorff defended the possibility of divine discourse in and through Scripture as a collection of human texts. On the other hand, Stephen Fowl directed attention to the virtue(s) of the interpreter(s) as the primary aim(s) and even norm(s) of churchly exegesis.[7] Accordingly, Fowl disagreed with meta-theoretical use of speech-act philosophy, and ultimately with any normative appeal to general hermeneutics, despite apparently reflecting certain theoretical influences when emphasizing interpretive communities.

The developments chronicled so far primarily concern Scripture's interpretation, addressing only certain aspects of its authority. Perhaps that is no accident, given the involvement of biblical scholars and a philosopher, not doctrinal theologians. Their hermeneutical focus accords with David Kelsey's earlier analysis of Scripture's theological use, from which more functional accounts of biblical authority typically followed.[8] Given such developments the need became clearer for hermeneutical concreteness to impinge upon Christian teaching about Scripture.

Nevertheless, more dogmatically-oriented developments emerged at the turn of the millennium. William Abraham's "canonical theism" challenged theologians to be robustly soteriological in their accounts of

---

4   Richard B. Hays, *Echoes of Scripture in the Letters of Paul* (New Haven: Yale University Press, 1989).

5   John Goldingay, *Models for Scripture* (Grand Rapids: Eerdmans, 1994).

6   Nicholas Wolterstorff, *Divine Discourse: Philosophical Reflections on the Claim That God Speaks* (Cambridge: Cambridge University Press, 1995).

7   Stephen E. Fowl, *Engaging Scripture*, Challenges in Contemporary Theology (Oxford: Blackwell, 1998).

8   David H. Kelsey, *Proving Doctrine: The Uses of Scripture in Modern Theology* (repr., Harrisburg, PA: Trinity Press International, 1999).

Scripture—focusing on Scripture's function within a wider churchly network of means of grace.[9] John Webster challenged theologians to be robustly theological—not only focusing on divine action rather than human agency or historical contexts or hermeneutical concepts, but also coordinating divine action regarding Scripture with God's sanctification of other creaturely realities.[10] Telford Work and others challenged theologians to be robustly Trinitarian—situating Scripture's authority within a wider economy of salvation, in terms of the ministry of Word and Spirit.[11] Soon after these developments emerged, theologians began returning to scriptural commentary as a form of scholarship.[12]

Subsequent treatments of Scripture have assumed, elaborated, or occasionally contested these major trends: addressing its authority and interpretation through appeals to canonical shaping, inner-biblical inter-pretation, biblical diversity, speech acts, and/or virtues; addressing its nature and function through insistence on soteriological, theological, and thus specifically Trinitarian frameworks. Meanwhile, one of the older dogmatic frameworks for treating Scripture as both divine and human—an analogy with the Incarnation of God in Jesus Christ—came into controversy or even disfavor.[13]

These contemporary trends create a vital backdrop for engaging Scripture as God's textual medium of self-communication. They encour-age relishing the biblical texts' genuine diversity as a God-given aspect of their unity. They encourage relishing the dynamism of reading Scripture as God's saving witness to Christ in the powerful presence of the Spirit. Yet this backdrop of emerging consensus, vital as it is, does not fully detail either the nature of Scripture's authority or its resulting implications for theological interpretation. Modest hermeneutical concepts make the case of Scripture more concretely analogous—both similar to and different

---

9   William J. Abraham, *Canon and Criterion in Christian Theology* (Oxford: Clarendon, 1998).

10   John Webster, *Holy Scripture: A Dogmatic Sketch*, Current Issues in Theology (Cambridge: Cambridge University Press, 2003).

11   Telford Work, *Living and Active: Scripture in the Economy of Salvation*, Sacra Doctrina (Grand Rapids: Eerdmans, 2002).

12   E.g., the Brazos Theological Commentary on the Bible (edited by R. R. Reno) and Westminster John Knox's Belief series (now edited by Amy Plantinga Pauw).

13   Critiquing usage of the analogy for supporting historical criticism were Lewis Ayres and Stephen E. Fowl, "(Mis)Reading the Face of God: *The Interpretation of the Bible in the Church*," *TS* 60 (1999): 513–28; generating controversy for overemphasizing humanity with the analogy was Peter Enns, *Inspiration and Incarnation: Evangelicals and the Problem of the Old Testament* (Grand Rapids: Baker Academic, 2005); favoring a Trinitarian rather than Christological approach was Kevin J. Vanhoozer, "Triune Discourse: Theological Reflections on the Claim That God Speaks (Parts 1 and 2)," in *Trinitarian Theology for the Church: Scripture, Community, Worship*, ed. Daniel J. Treier and David Lauber (Downers Grove, IL: IVP Academic, 2009), 25–78.

from—other instances of human understanding, especially of texts. The operative principle here is that the modest concepts we most basically need emerge from the Scriptures themselves, so that dogmatic alliances with hermeneutics can be suitably chaste.

TEXTUAL COMMUNICATION

Thirdly, then, a contemporary dogmatic account should develop the church's teaching about Scripture in terms of the Triune God's textual self-communication: attending to the Bible's diversity and dynamism within the saving economy of the Word and Spirit. Having already suggested that the biblical texts themselves emphasize divine speech, it is now time to emphasize that biblical texts themselves wrestle with the key tension: hearing divine speech in and through these written texts. In this small space, obviously, a dogmatic account cannot provide detailed exegetical defenses of its appeals to scriptural concepts but will have to gesture at relevant texts or thematic patterns—with five claims emerging from biblical texts concerned with Scripture's writing, reading, hearing, and/or understanding.

The first, fundamental aspect of the Bible's hermeneutical self-presentation is *a twofold dynamic of theological authority, involving fixity and freedom*. Writing preserves and proclaims divine speech by, on one hand, fixing it in particular forms and, on the other hand, freely addressing new contexts through those stable and shared forms. So, for instance, fixity appears in Deuteronomy's prohibition (4:2) against adding or subtracting from its words, a prohibition reappearing at the end of the Christian canon in Revelation (22:18–19); fixity also appears in "it is written" formulas and some of Jesus's sayings such as Matthew 5:17–20. Freedom is apparent in Jesus's and others' reading practices, even those accompanying "it is written" formulas, in addition to Johannine and Pauline passages concerning the Holy Spirit; most well-known, of course, is 2 Corinthians 3. When needing a court of final appeal for adjudicating theological claims, where shall we go? "It is written." When a judgment is not so clearly written, then Protestants emphasize gospel freedom—in both Christ's Word of forgiveness and the Spirit's witness. Yet true freedom arises in the context of authority, its "objective correlate":[14] before we reach any distinct realm of "Christian liberty" in *adiaphora*, freedom is already gained from hearing

---

14   Oliver O'Donovan, *Resurrection and Moral Order: An Outline of Evangelical Ethics*, 2nd ed. (Grand Rapids: Eerdmans, 1994), especially p. 122: "Authority is the objective correlate of freedom."

the Shepherd's voice by the Spirit—with all such freedom involving God's authoritative Word via fixed scriptural texts.

Second and related in the Bible's hermeneutical self-presentation is *a twofold dynamic of human response to authoritative, written divine speech, involving remembrance and renewal.* So, for instance, remembrance appears throughout Deuteronomy, Psalms' rehearsals of God's mighty acts, Wisdom's preservation of tradition, and New Testament texts' appeals to settled Old Testament teaching about Israel's God. Renewal appears in Wisdom's interrogation of tradition, Hebrews's contemporary appropriation of Old Testament texts as present divine speaking, Pauline exhortation arising out of creative typological appropriation (see especially Rom 15:3–4; 1 Cor 9:9–10; 10:6–7), and new covenant texts' promise of inward, personal knowledge of God. Such knowledge of God transcends earlier, merely written, Torah; yet if the Torah's public hearing (e.g., Neh 8) and personal reading (e.g., Ps 119) renewed God's people, how much more the Spirit's New Testament witness to the gospel and law of Christ!

Third in the Bible's hermeneutical self-presentation, therefore, is *a twofold dynamic of divine self-communication, involving the personal agency of Jesus Christ and the Holy Spirit.* God's final, most directly personal Word has been spoken in the Incarnate Son (John 1; Col 1; Heb 1). Given the overlapping "Word" terminology, certain biblical texts cannot help but associate themselves with Jesus Christ, participating indirectly in a form of God's own Logos. When addressing the participation of the Old Testament in this Logos, we appropriate its own hints of a background in "word" or "wisdom" for the divine self-expression now clearly taking form in Christ. The Bible then participates in God's self-communication as the crucial divine act of providing an authorized written witness. Accordingly the biblical Word depends upon the Holy Spirit at every point: processes of revelation, composition, and inscripturation; the earthly overshadowing of the Incarnate personal Word, and the inspiration of the written product that bears verbal witness to him; as well as the illumination of its hearing, reading, understanding, and remembering through indwelling divine presence. The Spirit's illuminating witness has enabled not just the church's interpretation but even its initial recognition of biblical texts as Scripture, leading to their providential preservation.

In light of these three dynamics—authoritative fixity and theological freedom; human remembrance and renewal; divine self-communication by Word and Spirit—the fourth aspect of the Bible's self-presentation specifies *authorized witness* as the form of Scripture's identity with God's

Word. This category of witness—prior and subsequent to Jesus Christ—leads to another, temporal dynamic: *speaking broadly of the Old Testament as prophetic anticipation of the divine Logos, and the New Testament as apostolic attestation to the divine Logos.* The Old Testament prophetically anticipates the Logos especially by fixing the witness to God's prior mighty acts, their remembrance forming the identity of God's people. The New Testament apostolically attests to the Logos not only by bearing witness to the climactic divine act but also by freeing God's people to hear that witness through the Spirit's renewing presence. Biblical support for this dynamic, beyond that already mentioned, includes crucial texts (such as Luke 24:25–27; John 5:31–47; Eph 2:20; Heb 2:1–4; and 1 John 1:1–4) emphasizing testimony—the Old Testament's being anticipatory, the New Testament's apostolic.

Speaking of prophets and apostles does not narrow New Testament authority only to texts proving they came directly from one of the Twelve, or Old Testament authority only to texts claiming a model of prophetic inspiration. As Hebrews exemplifies, a passage can count as divine speech despite originally having its human voice(s) address God rather than a divine or oracular prophetic voice addressing the people.[15] Non-oracular Old Testament texts can be vehicles of divine address anticipating Christ despite their voice not being "prophetic" in the narrowest sense. They can anticipate Christ by addressing instead the creation, however fallen, that holds together in him.[16]

Likewise, a New Testament text can participate in apostolic witness despite coming from a wider circle proclaiming the early Christian teaching about Jesus. On one hand, oral aspects of such original processes lend a degree of communicative freedom. Exact wording and singular accounts often give way to some pastoral plenitude. On the other hand, the same oral aspects lend a degree of fixity to the resulting witness, through communal recognition shaping the record and range of authorized teaching and consistent testimony. Furthermore, the contextual limitations of oral communication eventually elicit writing. Confirmation is welcome on these points from studies of ancient writing and reading as well as ancient and contemporary orality. But the relevant phenomena—such as public,

---

15   Daniel J. Treier, "Speech Acts, Hearing Hearts, and Other Senses: The Doctrine of Scripture Practiced in Hebrews," in *The Epistle to the Hebrews and Christian Theology*, ed. Richard Bauckham et al. (Grand Rapids: Eerdmans, 2009), 337–50.

16   E.g., the approach taken to Solomon and Ecclesiastes generally in Daniel J. Treier, *Proverbs and Ecclesiastes*, Brazos Theological Commentary on the Bible (Grand Rapids: Brazos, 2011).

communal reading; amanuenses or prophetic and apostolic circles; editorial shaping; appeals to memory; stylized speeches; and so forth—these phenomena are frequently observable in the biblical texts' self-presentation, however much certain occurrences or implications remain disputed.[17]

The textual dynamic sketched here—fixity and freedom, remembrance and renewal—holds broadly across both Testaments. Yet the New Testament identifies Jesus Christ as the Logos while characterizing knowledge of God more democratically and personally in light of new covenant fulfillment by the indwelling Holy Spirit. If Christians cannot view the respective eras of the two Testaments asymmetrically—the one anticipating fulfillment in the other—then we violate the Deuteronomic prohibition, adding to the earlier divine words so as to create a new religion. But if the Old Testament anticipates the new covenant, then reading the New Testament in terms of heightened fulfillment acknowledges the divine authority of the Old.[18] This salvation-historical dynamic generates ongoing debate over reading the Old Testament as a discrete witness. At the very least, we can say that Christians must attend more carefully to Jewish exegesis, since the New Testament itself manifests ongoing Christian struggles to understand earlier revelation in light of newfound redemption—and vice versa. Those struggles comprise an aspect of the redemptive history, and its attendant revelation, in which we claim to participate.

This epistemological corollary of the salvation-historical dynamic implies a fifth element in Scripture's self-presentation: *the perennial necessity of growth in understanding on the part of God's people.* Fullness of revelation in Christ does not instantly finalize the church's epistemological recognition of its ontological realities. Biblical revelation is salvation-historical not only in its timing but even in the very form of its content. This historical character of the church's understanding appears in other ways besides the Christian canon's two-Testament structure. Put differently, if the prior concepts emerge substantially from texts focused on writing, here we must engage material focused on reading and understanding. So, for instance,

---

17   See, e.g., John H. Walton and D. Brent Sandy, *The Lost World of Scripture: Ancient Literary Culture and Biblical Authority* (Downers Grove, IL: InterVarsity Press, 2013), with a helpfully provocative theological review from D. A. Carson in *BBR* 25 no. 3 (2015): 434–37.

18   Contra, e.g., an often-helpful book by John Goldingay (*Do We Need the New Testament? Letting the Old Testament Speak for Itself* [Downers Grove, IL: IVP Academic, 2015]), the terminology of "First Testament" is true to neither the Jewish Scriptures nor the Jewish people, let alone the New Testament. What Christians believe the "Old Testament" anticipates, and the New Testament narrates, is not the second in an ongoing series but rather the climax: This climax renders certain aspects of the former covenant self-referentially obsolete, its scriptural witness now—simultaneously—foundational and secondary.

the very ambiguity or overlap in the biblical vocabulary of hearing and obedience is instructive. The salvation-historical character of churchly understanding also appears in the new covenant's promise of democratized, personalized knowledge of God—a promise that both fulfills old covenant antecedents and breaks genuinely new ground in human hearts. Apostolic prayers for the Spirit's gift of wisdom indicate that understanding is part of, not antecedent to, Christian growth in grace.

This growth is not only personal but also congregational, generational, and geographical, as the church seeks to correspond with Christ's fullness as one new humanity (Eph 4:13–16). No strictly linear model of such growth will do, for any member(s) of the church—even the cultural practice(s) of God's people depicted within the Bible itself—can only reflect incompletely Scripture's divine teaching. No cultural moment then or now could ever provide the occasion to embody completely, let alone outgrow, the "wisdom" embedded in such biblical teaching. Every cultural moment, though, will have both illuminating and blind spots, helping the church(es) to recognize some biblical wisdom more fully while hindering the ability to reflect other aspects of that wisdom. This contextual sensitivity reflects the truth involved in appeals to "trajectories" that begin with biblical patterns as a basis for going beyond their explicit forms or norms in later contexts. Yet the danger involved is that we will confuse such appeals to biblical patterns with linear or evolutionary notions of progressive development toward whatever ideals modernity celebrates. A theological appeal to biblical wisdom, with cautious appropriation of neo-pragmatic hermeneutical elements, is less likely than pervasive trajectory hermeneutics to fall into such confusion.

Hence eschatological deferral and cultural difference pertain to understanding both Testaments. Yet eschatological deferral between the verbal sense of New Testament texts and their full referents will be different in kind and lesser in degree than for the Old. So not only is God's speech fixed in writing through historical processes; the truth also liberates us for faithful hearing within the saving history of the Spirit's transforming presence. Yet that very history positions the New Testament as addressing those who inaugurally participate in the culmination of the ages.

THEOLOGICAL CHALLENGES

Two theological challenges ensue from these complexities of human involvement in the Word's history, requiring a dogmatic defense of

Scripture's identity with that Word. These ensuing challenges are inter-twined: how to construe the oral aspects preceding and succeeding written Scripture, and how to construe its moral and doctrinal authority. In today's polemical context, the oral informality of original tradents and contemporary appropriation supposedly countermands identifying writ-ten forms and norms with God's Word. Moreover, the particularity of the Bible's original contexts supposedly creates moral incoherence between texts and/or moral repugnance between modern people and ancient per-spectives or practices reflected in the texts. Given their complexity, in this short space I cannot resolve these challenges but only propose a prelimi-nary five-point response to them.

First of all, *Scripture's orality—as the background for many texts, a metaphor and eventual concept for divine appropriation of all the texts, and a dominant mode of our appropriation in response—stresses personal and contextual immediacy in a way that involves analogies of participation for subsequent textual audiences hearing the Word.* Oral immediacy makes the moral directedness of Scripture's divine self-communication highly particular: God speaks "today" to particular people in particular contexts. This very immediacy invites a text's later audiences into a drama of interpretation that depends on shared identity with the original and earlier hearers: We participate in the one people of God. This ecclesial analogy of participation is the foundational human reality corresponding to Scripture's salvation-historical divine dis-course; accordingly this analogy of participation is the proper context within which to acknowledge other aspects of historical distance.

Within such analogous participation, oral immediacy then entails the possibility of ethical difference, which may occasionally stem from evan-gelical freedom of interpretation upon hearing the text's divine voice in later contexts. Moral theology involves "deliberation" about actions that are analogically possible in any given context, not just "reflection" about past actions or abstract rules.[19] Scriptural examples acknowledge this need to address the changing ethical contexts in which we hear the command-ing divine voice. Hebrews construes hearing the Word of God in terms of a covenantal theophany such as Israel experienced at Sinai, thus broadly fol-lowing Old Testament covenantal patterns such as 2 Chronicles 34:29–33. God's people hear how they should respond "today" in faith. When God speaks on another "today" through biblical texts, their salvation-historical

---

19   Oliver O'Donovan, *Self, World, and Time*, Ethics as Theology 1: An Induction (Grand Rapids: Eerdmans, 2013), especially pp. 25–32.

setting and ethical implications may differ: For instance, an earlier oath entails a later promise while simultaneously implying another warning. Several contemporary hermeneutical models have attempted to account for such dynamics, with varying strengths and weaknesses.[20]

Second, *while orality stresses personal and contextual immediacy, the resulting drama of interpretation does not mitigate the existence of written norms but actually constitutes their nature.* Sheep must recognize their Shepherd's voice, not just generically acknowledging Scripture as God's Word and personally coming to Christian faith but also repeatedly hearing and obediently understanding particular human words of the Bible as divine self-communication in Christ. This need to recognize the Shepherd's voice arises as soon as textual critics pursue the original text forms and translators produce contemporary renderings, with both cases already and inevitably involving interpretation; this need continues to arise as pastors and teachers expound and apply, particular readers express personal or communal devotion, theologians cite, and so forth.

Modern polemics often suggest that lack of original autographs, inexact textual traditions, varying details in parallel texts, and the like preclude Scripture from serving as the written norming norm for Christian spiritual and theological life. Yet, aberrations of popular "biblicism" aside, traditional accounts actually engage the Bible's internal phenomena with considerable nuance: both qualifying Scripture's form of identity with God's Word in terms of human mediation and qualifying that human mediation in terms of Scripture's identity with God's Word. Modern literary tools and philosophical categories can help us to recover the ways in which the texts' human voices relate to God through first, second, and

---

20   Kevin Vanhoozer consistently distinguishes between illocutionary acts (being the Word of God, earlier fixed by the scriptural texts) and perlocutionary acts (Scripture becoming the Word of God, now received by another audience). Anthony Thiselton speaks of the need to "actualize" any text—including scriptural ones—in its reading ("Communicative Action and Promise in Interdisciplinary, Biblical, and Theological Hermeneutics," in *The Promise of Hermeneutics*, ed. Roger Lundin, Clarence Walhout, and Anthony C. Thiselton [Grand Rapids: Eerdmans, 1999], especially pp. 200–201). Still others appeal to relevance theory, though its application to the ontology of Scripture is not yet clear. In a PhD thesis (Southwestern Baptist Theological Seminary, 2014: "The Word of the Living God: Presentational Discourse as a Model for Contemporary Divine Address through Scripture"), Keith Quan develops a model of "presentational discourse" to acknowledge the rhetorical sense in which God presents biblical discourse afresh to later generations of God's people.

For an attempt at blending Vanhoozer's appeal to speech-act philosophy with a model of actualization suggested by Hebrews, see Treier, "Speech Acts, Hearing Hearts": The earlier illocutionary acts remain, fixed by the text, while their referential figures may expand or contract vis-à-vis salvation-historical change. New illocutionary (not just perlocutionary) acts may also arise by presupposition, implication, or entailment—or, in relevance-theoretical terms, through alterations of the shared background—in new contexts.

third person speaking modes—all modes still being appropriated as divine discourse. In the Bible earlier texts are quoted, presumably because they were copied and translated, in fluid forms—such forms being appropriated not just in surprisingly diverse ways but also for startlingly precise arguments. "It is written" generates fecundity from what was often initially oral—this fecundity confronting with oral immediacy new contexts in which God's people find themselves. Yet "it is written" generates the freedom for such fecundity precisely due to the finality of a fixed reference point to appropriate. Such is the nature of a tradition's norming norm.

A scriptural text therefore confronts God's people as God's Word at two levels. It may be read publicly or personally as direct divine address, heard rather immediately as God's Word by the aforementioned analogy of participation in God's pilgrim people. Hearing this direct divine address, seeking the Spirit's help to respond in the obedience of faith, we do not primarily study but rather submit to the God with whom we have to do. At another level, though, any particular text must eventually be encountered indirectly—within broader human understanding of Scripture's divine teaching overall. Hearing a text's divine address and encountering little or no dissonance with our previous understanding, we quickly submit. However, when encountering apparent dissonance with what we take to be the divine teaching in light of the rest of Scripture, we pause. We seek either to harmonize one or the other aspect—our previous understanding or our present hearing—or else to develop even newer understanding. We ponder not just what Scripture says but also what creation and culture seem to say—which may raise fresh questions about what Scripture does or does not actually teach.

Third, then, *in this drama of its theological interpretation Scripture incorporates and regulates moral change within its form of moral coherence.* Scripture itself contains examples of wrestling with moral coherence. In those examples, construing salvation history is consistently at issue—the rest of Scripture thereby helping to interpret the passage(s) in question. So Jesus responded to a contemporary squabble by relating Mosaic divorce legislation to God's created design, with temporary accommodations addressing fallen human hearts. Moreover, multiple voices are sometimes in play: Matthew and Mark apparently even felt free to contextualize Jesus's response somewhat differently. Similarly, in Acts 15 one text clarified salvation history in order to discern the enduring implications of other texts: When Christian experience raised the question of Gentile inclusion, Amos 9 established its legitimacy and the Torah authorized the ongoing moral framework within which to celebrate that prophetic fulfillment. Hebrews, again, insisted on a change of law corresponding to a change of the priesthood, based on a dense network of Old Testament appeals including anticipation of a new covenant. The coherence of Scripture's moral theology rests on reading salvation-historically. That the church has long recognized such a basis for Scripture's moral coherence is clear from the diverse, biblically-internal, hermeneutics with which it has construed this salvation history—whether letter and spirit, or law and gospel, or unified covenants of grace, or diverse dispensational administrations, and so forth. In that light the increasingly widespread, if imprecise, evangelical influence of "inaugurated eschatology" illustrates the ecumenical value of biblical scholarship.

Examples of Scripture's apparent internal change actually undergird, rather than weaken, the credibility of its moral norms. Scripture itself presents not only salvation-historical cases in which God's demands change but also historical needs for God's people to discern implications of earlier texts in later situations. So the Prophets recontextualize agrarian aspects of the Torah for mercantile situations. Paul asks rhetorically whether God's Torah cares about oxen, and the answer is yes but not exclusively or ultimately: The law has broader implications in subsequent contexts, especially for those "on whom the culmination of the ages has come" (1 Cor 10:11). Furthermore, we must discern when a particular aspect of a text counts as God's direct address or how instead its voice may indirectly inform a divinely-authorized moral perspective. With all due respect to St. Augustine, for instance, there is no need to allegorize David's murder of Uriah in relation to the church's mortification of sin;[21] to the contrary, in some kinds of allegory (though not all!) lies the risk of obscuring the primary message toward which the words of the literal sense are running. Indeed, plenty of textual exemplars may relate to the divine Word as photographic negatives. The same holds true for textual voices such as those of Job's friends. God's Word may communicate that "thou shalt not" adopt certain human perspectives or practices, even those associated with some of God's people. Scripture internally authorizes moral discernment regarding how later historical audiences appropriate particular aspects of particular texts, while simultaneously restraining such discernment through a guiding salvation-historical framework that emerges in its own examples.

---

21   "Reply to Faustus the Manichaean" (*Contra Faustum Manichaeum*), Book XXII, section 87, in *NPNF* 1, vol. 4, 307–8.

Fourth, however, *in this internal drama of its theological interpretation Scripture incorporates moral more than doctrinal change.* In recent literature that speaks of going "beyond the Bible" biblically, most examples are primarily moral rather than doctrinal, while most of the discussion involves biblical scholars.[22] That such discussions center on ethics rather than dogmatics is unsurprising. Aside from disciplinary factors, Scripture itself explains this focus: Its realm is practical reason, making us wise unto salvation. Scripture speaks of God in remarkably stable ways across the epochs of its overarching story: Israel's covenanting Creator is jealous, opposing all rivals, yet amazingly slow to anger and abounding in love.[23] Challenges of going "beyond the Bible" doctrinally cannot appeal to ready scriptural examples or rest substantially upon salvation-historical change; instead they primarily arise from scriptural reticence vis-à-vis reasoning about more abstract extrabiblical realities.

The exception proving this rule is God's self-revelation in Jesus Christ: The proto-Trinitarian theology emerging from the Incarnation was hard won due to the enduring stability of Jewish "monotheism." Inclusion of the Gentiles was hard won due to the Torah's enduring instruction regarding God's will. Inclusion of the Gentiles did not set aside the Old Testament as the written norm; instead, early Christians recognized prophetic ful-fillment while retaining moral norms by which the Hebrew Scriptures revealed God's unchanging character. In other words, the theology proper stayed the same while the salvation history changed: Even the exception— struggling to account for the divine identity of the Son and Spirit—was bidirectional, since that identity could only be understood in terms of the covenant history of Israel's Creator God. On that doctrinal basis, some covenantal norms apparently changed in new contexts—precisely due to the scriptural stability of God's purposes.

However much ethical complexity or moral change appears on the sur-face, then, never do such scriptural examples simply repudiate earlier texts' depiction of Israel's God or the norms of God's will for those earlier contexts. Meanwhile, internal examples rarely go "beyond the Bible" doctrinally because, apart from recognizing salvation-historical change and responding to God's Trinitarian self-revelation in Christ, Scripture need not make such moves. Scripture provides a basic vocabulary and narrative framework for

---

22   Notably, Gary T. Meadors, ed., *Four Views on Going beyond the Bible to Theology*, Counterpoints (Grand Rapids: Zondervan, 2009).

23   So, helpfully, Goldingay, *Do We Need the New Testament?*

trusting God's character, not really a theoretical doctrine of God as such. By contrast, internal examples go "beyond the Bible" ethically in particular ways because, since God does not change, God's earthly economies for the covenant people can and must change. A moral norm in a scriptural text reflects not merely the divine character but also the saving history of the divine pedagogy—God speaking to particular people in particular settings with particular possibilities, the rest of us listening in later on.

Just how far salvation-historical trajectories within Scripture alter moral norms in relation to subsequent historical change will be the crux of the difficult discernment the Bible demands. Which leads to a fifth and final assertion regarding the interplay between Scripture's oral aspects and moral authority: *God communicates for the sake of communion that evokes genuine human freedom and corresponding growth in communal wisdom.*

A decade ago I explored the association between God's Word and the Christian wisdom with which the Bible most fundamentally defines the church's theological understanding.[24] One way to understand the framework sketched here for a dogmatic account of Scripture would be to note the convergence of the Bible's oral aspects and moral authority in that earlier concept of wisdom. Biblical wisdom makes space for human experience and reflection, but ultimately the character of Christian virtue remains responsive to God's voice, hearing that voice in a dynamic of enduring tradition and ongoing inquiry. The present account of Scripture as God's textual communication, then, further details the objective corollary of the evangelical freedom that is ingredient in Christian wisdom.

As God's self-communication establishes communion, the covenant people should remain neither autonomous nor infantile; as they dwell with God they should grow into mature spiritual adulthood. On one hand, they will not seek to be autonomous: They will not misconstrue their freedom as independence from the fixity of what the biblical texts communicate. They certainly will not confuse the gospel's genuine spiritual freedom with modernity's claim to realize human maturity via moral autonomy.[25] Yet, on the other hand, they will not remain infantile: They will not misconstrue textual fixity as a basis for slavish literalism or the

---

24   Daniel J. Treier, *Virtue and the Voice of God: Toward Theology as Wisdom* (Grand Rapids: Eerdmans, 2006).

25   Here see Peter Jensen, *The Revelation of God*, Contours of Christian Theology (Downers Grove, IL: InterVarsity Press, 2002), especially pp. 255–56: Being slaves of Christ is the metaphorical corollary of gospel freedom—which is the freedom to give ourselves to others, and preeminently to God, in love, since ultimately we need not fear anything else.

wrong kind of biblicism. Recognizing that true freedom lies in the spiritual maturity that pursues the mind of Christ by Word and Spirit, they will seek to grow in their capacity for hearing God as part of their discipleship. Recognizing too that communion with God involves communion with others, they will seek to grow in their capacity for hearing from others as part of their discernment.

In the context of conservative emphases, therefore, a biblical appeal for Christian wisdom celebrates evangelical freedom. Scripture requires interpretation stemming from and seeking after Christian virtue. Such virtue responds to the Spirit's liberation of human agency, within which growing discernment is a gift of the gospel. When forms of "biblicism" need critique, the chief critique ought to be theological in this sense: focused on the mature deliberation required of the church regarding how to hear Scripture as God's Word in particular times and places. However, in the context of progressive emphases, Christian wisdom cautions against counterfeit, arrogant, worldly alternatives. Scripture evokes genuine virtue and therefore genuine freedom precisely through its fixed presentation of the voice of God. The Spirit liberates human agency by making the Word present, yet in such a way that the written governance of our hearing remains essential to growth in genuine discernment.

In other words, the relevant aspect of evangelical freedom that corresponds to the Word's textual fixity and authority is freedom of *interpretation*: freedom to hear and discern what *God* is saying. Such an account of freedom creates an asymmetry between fixity and freedom, or a certain moral conservatism in wisdom's dynamic between tradition and inquiry: Christians acknowledge the biblical texts as God's Word, and appeal to traditional interpretations of that Word, in order to promote authentically evangelical freedom rather than autonomous counterfeits. Evangelical freedom will have more generally hermeneutical analogues, but is ultimately specific to the gospel's creation of a new humanity. Because the church is simultaneously justified and still sinful, no account of growth in discernment can ever assume a simplistically modern, linear narrative of progress away from earlier traditions of interpretation.

The goal of the framework sketched above, in sum, has been to reflect the hermeneutical concreteness of Scripture's self-presentation and thereby authentically Christian wisdom—not merely abstract concepts—in discerning, developing, and defending the church's teaching. The interplay of remembering God's mighty acts and renewing God's people depends upon both the fixed authority of the divine Word and the human freedom properly involved in interpreting a collection of prophetic and apostolic writings. This scriptural Word that bears witness to Jesus Christ must be read in the Holy Spirit's empowering presence and within a saving history that includes the church's growth in understanding. In response to theological challenges regarding the Bible's oral aspects and moral authority, I have tried to show—however briefly—that the resulting drama of interpretation does not mitigate but actually upholds the authority of biblical texts as a written norm for hearing divine speech.

A dogmatic account of Scripture begins and ends with the commitment to hear in the biblical texts God himself—one Word to trust and obey. This saving Word is the same yesterday, today, and forever, speaking the Truth of the one Way to Life. This Word's Spirit frees us to hear very specifically about the next segment on our pilgrimage—precisely by hearing again, today, what God has said to and through earlier witnesses.

CHAPTER 2

"IN MANY AND VARIOUS WAYS": HEARING THE VOICE OF GOD IN THE TEXT OF SCRIPTURE

Stephen E. Fowl

INTRODUCTION

The theme of the voice of God and the text of Scripture invites a set of theological and theoretical analyses devoted to the nature of God's speaking, the nature of the text of Scripture, and how these might be related to each other. As many will recognize, my title draws on the opening verses of Hebrews. This, too, could lead one down a number of theoretical paths.

At the same time, there are a number of relatively recent exegetical studies of Hebrews that focus on images and language around God's voice or word.[1] For the most part, these studies spend much more time and space on matters around God's speaking and less time and space on matters related to human hearing or listening. Interestingly, although

---

1 There are a number of recent monographs that focus on aspects of God's speech in Hebrews. See in particular, Jonathan Griffiths, *Hebrews and Divine Speech*, LNTS (London: Bloomsbury, 2014) and Tomasz Lewicki, *Weist nich ab den Sprechenden! Wort Gottes und Paraklese in Hebräerbrief* (Paderborn: Ferdinand Schöningh, 2004). These works are primarily concerned with the speech of God and only secondarily with human hearing of divine speech. In the case of Griffiths, for example, this leads him quite rightly to pursue themes around divine speech throughout Hebrews. It does not, however, lead him to treat all of the issues around human hearing that appear, for example in Heb 3. All of this is to note that God's speaking and human hearing are not exactly the same.

themes around divine speaking appear throughout Hebrews, the more specific theme of hearing or listening to divine speech is concentrated in the first 5 chapters. This is where the various forms of ἀκούειν occur.[2] In studying these chapters, I was pleased to find that most of the issues I would have raised using a theoretical vocabulary are already anticipated to some degree in Hebrews. Thus, most of what I will do here is to move through the first 5 chapters of Hebrews, explicating issues which Hebrews already considers in its own way. I am not claiming that the author or the audience of Hebrews fully understood these matters in the ways I describe. Rather, I am unpacking implications and presumptions from the text of Hebrews in order to speak theologically in the present.

One final introductory concern: By focusing on issues around hearing and listening to the voice of God in Hebrews, it is not immediately clear how these claims about hearing the voice of God are connected to the text of Scripture.[3] This is because one may want to claim that the voice of God is not limited to speaking through Scripture. Moreover, whatever the author or first readers of Hebrews would have understood by the term Scripture, it is not precisely what subsequent Christians meant by that term. There are a number of diverse ways of understanding the relationship between the voice of God and the text of Scripture. Happily, I do not think that my purposes require me to resolve those differences. Rather, I think that diverse Christians can agree on the following: Long after the writing of Hebrews, the Christian church recognized that the texts that comprise the Old and New Testaments are definitive and sufficient records of God's speaking. This recognition, which is itself the result of a long process, provides believers with a concentrated arena within which we can think about questions regarding hearing and listening to the voice of God. Focusing on this concentrated arena does not substantially change or limit what I hope to argue here.

THE BLESSING AND CHALLENGES OF GOD'S SPEECH

Although the very first verses of Hebrews do not directly discuss matters around hearing the voice of God, one cannot get very far in thinking

---

2   See 2:1, 3; 3:7, 15, 16; 4:2, 7; 5:11. The only other occurrence is 12:19 where the use is not relevant to my purposes.

3   William Lane, *Hebrews*, WBC (Waco: Word, 1991), cxvii, notes that for the writer of Hebrews, Scripture is primarily understood as divine speaking.

about hearing the voice of God in Hebrews apart from thinking about 1:1–2. Right at its beginning Hebrews presents us with a profound dogmatic assertion and a set of challenges that accompany that assertion. The assertion in 1:1–2 is that God speaks to us. We may be so used to this idea that we miss how profound it is. Unlike the idols so often criticized in the prophets for being silent lumps of metal, stone, and wood, and unlike the silent Baal in 1 Kings 17, self-communication is part of God's triune identity. Un-coerced and unbidden God freely speaks. God does not speak out of a need but out of love.

God's desire to communicate, to speak to us, is a gracious gift. It also, however, comes with challenges. Hebrews 1:1 also touches on these. This opens up all of the important questions of interpretation. If God speaks in many and various ways then how do we understand what God is saying? How do we know that what we are hearing is the voice of God? How do we make sense out of these many and various ways in which God speaks? How do we adjudicate conflicting claims about God's speech? These are not all the questions one might ask. They should be enough, however, to show that God's speaking is an extraordinary blessing that brings substantial challenges in its wake.

These challenges are not really resolved when in the next verse we read that "in these last days God has spoken to us by the Son." There are a couple of reasons for this. First, unlike most English translations which use some sort of contrastive conjunction such as "but" between God's former speaking and God's speaking in "these last days,"[4] the Greek has no such conjunction. Moreover, although the writer of Hebrews uses a rich vocabulary and syntax for making contrasts and comparisons, none of that is on display here.[5] Instead, the parallel use of the aorist of λαλεῖν along with the preposition ἐν to describe God's speaking through both the prophets and the Son also suggests some levels of continuity. Moreover, the claim that the prophets spoke to "the fathers" without further specification or argument presumes a relationship that connects these fathers with the "us" of 1:2. All of this is to say that there is more continuity on display here than contrast.

---

4   The NRSV, NIV, and ESV are among the many English versions that do this.
5   Gene R. Smillie, "Contrast or Continuity in Hebrews 1.1–2," *NTS* 51 (2005): 550–52, gives a through accounting of this richness. Also see H. Attridge, *The Epistle to the Hebrews*, Hermeneia (Philadelphia: Fortress, 1989), 38, "While there is clear contrast between the old and the new, there is no sense that the two phrases stand in contradiction."

The prophets are instruments of God's speaking. Saying that God spoke ἐν υἱῷ could be taken to mean that the Son is primarily an instrument of God's voice in the ways that the prophets mentioned are instruments.[6] In this way, the Son is simply the most recent example of God's ongoing speech. From the way in which the subsequent verses identify this Son it is clear that the Son is not merely an instrument of the Father's speaking. Without denigrating or negating prior speaking, Hebrews presents God's speaking through the Son as definitive and authoritative. This is not because of the words God uses, but because of the nature of the Son.[7] The Son both creates and redeems. The Son fully, precisely, and without difference conveys God's words.

The claim that God spoke in the Son gives focus to what believers must listen for or to whom believers must listen if we are to hear God speak in these last days. It does not, however, resolve some of the more basic interpretive questions that accompany the blessing of God's speaking. Even if one adopts an extreme form of contrast between the many and various forms of God's speech in the prophets and God's speech in the Son, this simply pushes the interpretive questions initially located in the claim the God has spoken in many and various ways and focuses them definitively on God's speaking in the Son. Moreover, this claim adds a number of further interpretive challenges since it now becomes important to account for the relationships between God's prior speaking and God's speaking in these last days in ways that do not undermine God's integrity or righteousness. As both Romans and Galatians attest, God's invasion of the cosmos in the life, death, and resurrection of Jesus Christ merely reinforces the importance of articulating the relationships between God's former and later speaking in ways that do not result in a capricious, arbitrary God who does not keep promises. This does not mean there is only one proper way to articulate these relationships. Rather, it sets up some of the key parameters within which proper accounts of these relationships must operate.

---

6   So Smillie, "Contrast or Continuity?" 553 and Paul Ellingworth, *The Epistle to the Hebrews*, NIGTC (Grand Rapids: Eerdmans, 1993), 92 among others.

7   Though in different ways, Graham Hughes makes a similar point in *Hebrews and Hermeneutics*, SNTSMS (Cambridge: CUP, 1979), 7. See also, John Webster, "One Who Is Son: Theological Reflections on the Exordium to the Epistle to the Hebrews," in *The Epistle to the Hebrews and Christian Theology*, R. Bauckham, D. Driver, T. Hart, and N. MacDonald, eds. (Grand Rapids: Eerdmans, 2009), 69–94.

HEBREWS 2: GOD'S SPEAKING AND OUR SALVATION

The initial verses of Hebrews present readers with a number of claims about God's speaking. These claims point out both the blessing that is God's speaking and invite reflection on the challenges that come to believers in the light of God's speaking. As the letter unfolds, Hebrews 2 addresses some of these challenges. The first thing to note is that the whole of the argument in 2:1–4 depends on a fairly strong continuity between the λόγος spoken through angels and the λόγος of salvation spoken by the Lord such as one finds in 1:1–2.[8]

For my purposes I do not need to resolve the interesting issues around the claim in 2:2 that God's prior speaking is mediated to humans through angels.[9] Rather, it is sufficient to note the presumption that God's speaking in 1:1 through the prophets and the λόγος declared through angels in 2:2 are both references to God's speech prior to speaking in these last days through the Son.[10]

Hebrews 2:1–4 begins by laying out the consequences of failing to attend to God's speaking in Christ. God's speaking through the Son should be the focus of believers' attention, their listening. Such listening will keep believers from "drifting away." Paying attention "to what we have heard" is crucial to remaining closely tied or bound to God.[11] This admonition to pay attention in 2:1 leads to a comparison between the consequences of not paying attention to what has been spoken. Failure to attend appropriately to that speaking through angels brings justified punishment. If failure to attend to speech through angels brings punishment, how much more punishment will one face if one fails to attend to speaking which presents such great news of salvation?

From this we learn that God's speaking is directed to our salvation.[12] Resolving the hermeneutical issues around discerning the voice of God in Scripture or anywhere else is important. Nevertheless, these issues are

---

8   See Griffiths, *Divine Speech*, 55; Lewicki, *Weist nicht ab den Sprechenden!*, 49–50; Ellingworth, *Hebrews*, 134.

9   Griffiths, *Divine Speech*, 49–52, gives an extensive discussion and bibliography of such works.

10   "The angels in v. 4 are the counterpart to the prophets in v. 1," Lane, *Hebrews 1–8*, 17. See also, Liewicki, *Weist nich ab den Sprechenden!*, 51.

11   Ellingworth, *Hebrews*, 136, claims that the use of the present infinitive προσέχειν avoids the implication that the audience was not paying attention.

12   As Attridge, *Hebrews*, 66, notes, the soteriology of Hebrews is complex and develops over the course of the whole epistle. The key here in 2:1–4 is to note that salvation is the end towards which God's speaking is directed.

at best a penultimate concern for believers. God's speaking is designed to bring us to salvation. This reminds us that listening to and interpreting the word of God is not an end in itself. [13] The word of God is instrumental to our salvation. In the midst of demanding hermeneutical challenges, it is easy to forget that our listening to the voice of God, our engagements with God's word, are not ends in themselves. Rather, believers engage God's word, we listen to God's voice, to direct our love and our longing towards reaching our true home in God. Keeping our ultimate ends in mind is a crucial step in hearing properly the voice of God in the text of Scripture.

One should note that these are not, however, the ultimate ends of most forms of scholarly biblical criticism. Does this mean that those interested in hearing the voice of God in the text of Scripture should abandon or ignore scholarly biblical criticism? I think not. Currently a large and irreconcilably diverse number of interpretive approaches flourish in the modern academy. There is often much to learn from scholars who bring historical, sociological, literary, and other concerns to bear on the text of Scripture. Those committed to hearing the voice of God in the text of Scripture should neither ignore nor reject this work out of hand. Rather, the challenge for such believers is to make sure they properly engage, understand, and order the works of biblical scholarship in light of the larger ends for which Christians are called to engage the word of God, our salvation.

HEBREWS 2: THREE STAGED LISTENING

To return to Hebrews 2, we read that this salvific speaking was declared at first by or through the Lord (λαλεῖσθαι διὰ τοῦ κυρίου). This declaration of salvation was then confirmed[14] by those who first heard and passed it on. Finally, God's own testimony displayed in works of the Holy Spirit underwrites this message. This three staged pattern of speaking and listening touches on a host of interpretive points. First, the word of God to which believers must listen or attend in order not to drift away has its origin in speaking "through the Lord." Across the board, commentators see this as reference to Jesus, especially since in Hebrews 1:10 the writer

---

13   For relevant citations see the discussion in S. Fowl, *The Theological Interpretation of Scripture* (Eugene: Cascade, 2009), 1–12.

14   This draws on the same vocabulary used in 2:2 to refer to the λόγος attested by the angels.

has used Psalms 102:25–27 to refer to Christ as κύριος.[15] Moreover, in the light of Hebrews 5:7–9, this use of "speaking" here must be taken as more than a reference to the mere words of Jesus. It encompasses Jesus' words and deeds including the prayerful offering of his life back to God on the cross. Hence, at one level this assertion seems to be a reference to the message proclaimed by the incarnate Lord as ultimately related in the Gospels and the apostolic preaching.

A more expansive notion of ἀρχή ("at first" or "beginning"), however, ties this message of salvation to the beginning of all things, reflecting the Triune God's eternal desire to bring all things to their proper end in Christ, a desire that is already implied in all of God's prior speaking. At first glance, this may seem to be an excessively broad reading of ἀρχή or "beginning" in this verse. Nevertheless, as I just noted, Hebrews 1:10 has already related the role of the κύριος in creation. Moreover, in the light of the way the argument runs in chapter 3 I think we must keep this interpretive possibility in view. In 3:5 in particular we read that Moses bore "witness to what would be spoken by God in the future." In this light, the message of salvation spoken by the κύριος is not limited to the Gospels or the New Testament more broadly. The λόγος of God to which believers must attend if they are not to drift away, includes what we now call the Old Testament. Of course, all of that prior speaking must still be understood in the light of that definitive word spoken to us through the Son.

Secondly, the voice of God is confirmed to us "by those who heard." Again, at one level this reflects that fact that the initial recipients of this letter did not hear the message of salvation directly from the Lord. Rather, they heard from those who themselves first heard it from the Lord.[16] It is thus important to remember that even for these early generations of

---

15   So Ellingworth, *Hebrews*, 134; Lane, *Hebrews*, 39; Luke T. Johnson, *Hebrews,* NTL (Louisville: Westminster John Knox, 2006), 88; Griffiths, *Divine Speech*, 57. Liewicki, *Weist nich ab den Sprechenden!*, 53–56, devotes a significant discussion to refuting the claims of A. Bachmann, who contends that κύριος is a reference to God and not Jesus.

16   The Greek of this clause does not specify the object of τῶν ἀκουσάντων. The text simply indicates that the message of salvation was passed on by those who heard. One way of taking this is to interpret the clause as a reference to those who heard the message directly from Jesus, that is, "those who heard him." Alternatively, one could interpret the clause as reference to those who heard the message of salvation, that is, "those who heard it." Griffiths, *Divine Speech*, 59, argues that the passage's emphasis on the reliability or validity of the message of salvation requires it to be a reference to those who heard the Lord directly. This also is the way the NRSV reads it. Given the historical uncertainty of the dating of Hebrews and given the theological importance in Heb 3 that the possibility of "today" continuing well beyond the bounds of the initial audience of Hebrews, it seems better to note that both readings work and should be embraced. The claim here then argues for a continuity in transmitting the message of salvation from those who first heard Jesus down to the present.

believers, they do not hear the message of salvation immediately.[17] Rather it was mediated and confirmed through others.[18] Hebrews, however, is not really content to leave things there. By the time one reaches 3:7 it is clear that the speaking of God through the Spirit is for "today," whenever that may be. In that case, when we read in 2:3 that the message of salvation is confirmed "to us," contemporary believers are invited to find themselves in this assertion. This word of salvation is still passed on by "those who heard."

Nevertheless, there is at least one significant difference between us and them. For us, the message passed on by those who heard has received a canonical shape and form in the text of Scripture that would not have been available to those who first heard Hebrews. The canon focuses Christians' hearing the voice of God in the text of Scripture. In this way Christians already have put themselves in the hands of those who have heard and preserved this message in its particular canonical form. More significantly, Christians assert that God has providentially ordered things so that the message of salvation first spoken by the Lord has been preserved for us to hear. These convictions about God's providence must also be true of believers living before the canonical process is completed.

Although versions of historical criticism have attempted to bring us into immediate contact with the words of Jesus, by the time of Hebrews there was already a recognition that such immediacy was not essential for holding fast to such a great salvation. The audience of Hebrews and we are dependent on "those who heard." In this respect, despite being so many generations removed from the Lord, our position is different in degree but not in kind from those who first received Hebrews.

Even though the message of salvation receives an authoritative form in the text of Scripture, one cannot attend properly to the message of salvation simply by repeating the words of Scripture. This is not a new recognition. From the moment God uttered the commandments on Mt. Sinai, the people of God have had to interpret, engage, and embody those commandments in the light of the specific contexts in which they found themselves. The commandments were not self-interpreting. Simple repetition would not amount to obedience. This is because the contexts in which we and all believers find ourselves are not the same as our

---

17 Attridge, *Hebrews*, 67, notes that Hebrews is not searching for an authoritative apostolic foundation for a tradition.

18 Johnson, *Hebrews*, 65, notes that "us" includes not only those who first heard Jesus, but the author and addressees of Hebrews as well.

predecessors. Practices that constitute obedient hearing of the voice of God in one context may not do so in changed contexts. Nobody has made this case more succinctly than Nicholas Lash:

> If in thirteenth-century Italy, you wandered around in a coarse brown gown, with a cord around your middle, your "social location" was clear: your dress said that you were one of the poor. If, in twentieth-century Cambridge, you wander around in a coarse brown gown, with a cord around your middle, your social location is curious: your dress now says, not that you are one of the poor, but that you are some kind of oddity in the business of "religion." Your dress now declares, not your solidarity with the poor, but your amiable eccentricity.[19]

Lash is not seeking to denigrate the Franciscans. Instead, he is simply noting that repeating the same act in changed circumstances is not likely to convey the same message.

The work of hearing the voice of God in the text of Scripture is always ongoing because of our changing contexts. Despite this recognition believers should not neglect the fact that God's voice is also mediated and confirmed in us by the communion of saints who read, heard, and embodied those scriptural words in the various contexts in which they found themselves. Their fidelity may not be exactly the same as ours. Nevertheless, it would be odd willfully to cut ourselves off from the resources, inspiration, and guidance that they offer to us. The communion of saints past and present becomes a resource for properly hearing and obeying that message of salvation to which believers must attend if we are not to drift away.

For those who first encountered Hebrews and for us, hearing the voice of God in the text of Scripture is not an immediate experience that stands outside of the confirmation of those who have already heard. Moreover, if the voice of God is heard in the text of Scripture, Hebrews 2:4 also indicates that God is involved in the confirmation of our hearing. God's testimony is added to what was attested to us by those who heard by means of "signs, wonders and various miracles, and by gifts of the Holy Spirit" (συνεπιμαρτυροῦντος τοῦ θεοῦ σημείοις τε καὶ τέρασιν καὶ ποικίλαις δυνάμεσιν καὶ πνεύματος ἁγίου).[20]

---

19   Nicholas Lash, "What Authority Has Our Past?" in *Theology on the Way to Emmaus* (London: SCM, 1986), 54.

20   This claim closely reflects Peter's claim in Acts that Jesus was attested to by God through signs and wonders and works of power (2:22). Interestingly Peter begins by saying, "Listen to these words" (ἀκούσατε τοὺς λόγους τούτους).

The movement from Hebrews 2:3 into 2:4 indicates that there is a complex relationship between the attestation of those who have already heard and the confirming testimony of God through signs and other manifestations of the Spirit. All of the Christian confessions with which I am familiar include some statements about the necessary work of the Spirit in faithful interpretation and embodiment of Scripture. Thus, hearing the voice of God in the text of Scripture depends on the work of the Spirit. These confessions are also appropriately laconic about how the Spirit works in any particular case. Indeed, on its own a commitment to the Spirit's role in interpretation may offer little help in determining between conflicting interpretations, each of which may claim to be offered under the guidance of the Spirit. This raises the question of whether there are ways of attending to the hermeneutical significance of the Spirit so that one can better hear the voice of God.

Hebrews seems to assume that the testimony of the Spirit is often manifested through dramatic signs and powerful works. Clearly it enhances one's interpretive position if one can, in the manner of Elijah, call down fire from heaven to confirm an interpretation. Nevertheless, this is a relatively rare event. Moreover, miraculous signs are not always self-interpreting. The Corinthian correspondence makes this very clear. What one takes to be a sign and how one interprets and evaluates those signs can be very contestable matters. Appropriately reading signs of the Spirit seems already to require the work of the Spirit. This might appear to leave believers trapped in a very unhelpful circularity. This would be true if hearing the voice of God in the text of Scripture through the work of the Spirit were an activity of isolated individuals. It is not. In the same way that hearing the voice of God requires attention to the message of salvation passed on by those who have previously heard, appropriate attention to the Spirit's work cannot happen apart from the interpretive work of Spirit-directed witnesses. This seems to bind the attestation of "those who have heard" closely to the testimony of God through the Spirit.

One of the clearest examples of this is found in the narrative of Acts 10–15 which relates issues about whether and how to include Gentile believers into the predominantly Jewish body of followers of Jesus. Throughout this narrative the presence of the Spirit in the lives of Gentile believers apart from being circumcised and taking on the yoke of Torah drives the apostles towards James' judgment in Acts 15 that it seems "good to the Holy Spirit and to us to impose no further burdens on you." Strikingly, however, the manifestations of the Spirit that are so decisive in James' judgment are not manifestations that were witnessed by most of the members of this Council. Rather, the testimony of Peter, and to a lesser degree Paul and Barnabas, about the work of the Spirit in the lives of Gentile believers mediates the Spirit's work to the Council. In this way, Acts 10–15 nicely displays the interaction between attestation of those who have heard and the confirming work of the Spirit.[21] It seems quite clear that the one cannot stand without the other and that one cannot really speak of hearing the voice of God in Scripture without the presence of these two interdependent confirming voices.

For Christians seeking to hear the voice of God in Scripture today, it should also be clear that such hearing is not likely to happen simply with greater attention to the text of Scripture, though one should never discourage that. It is also not likely to happen through ever greater methodological sophistication in exegesis, though that is also to be encouraged. Instead, or in addition to attention to the text of Scripture, it becomes crucial to cultivate particular forms of common life or particular communities. These communities would depend on those more mature believers who have "heard" the message from the beginning and stand in continuity with those before them who have also heard, as well as those who are able to discern the confirming testimony of the Spirit as well as those who can imagine the appropriate way to embody such hearing in present contexts. The formation and maintenance of such communities is as significant a hermeneutical activity as any we can imagine.

HEBREWS 3: TODAY—THEN AND NOW

Returning to the text of Hebrews, there is further material related to hearing the voice of God in Hebrews 3. As with chapter 2 there is a concern with falling away, or failing to "hold fast to the confidence and boasting of hope" (3:6). Further, as in 2:1, the key lies in properly focusing believers' attention. In the case of 2:1, believers are to focus their attention on "what we have heard." In 3:1–6, believers are to consider (κατανοήσατε) both Jesus and Moses.

As with the discussion of God's speaking through angels and the Lord in chapter 2, the invocation of Jesus and Moses at the beginning of Hebrews 3 connects God's varied speaking in the past and the decisive speaking in the Son. Even so, it is tempting to focus on 3:3 and its strong

---

21   For a fuller discussion of this see S. Fowl, *Engaging Scripture* (Oxford: Blackwell, 1998), ch. 4.

assertion of the superiority of Jesus to Moses, treating this as the foundation for versions of supercession. This, however, misses the point that both Jesus and Moses are faithful (πιστός). Moses is explicitly identified as a faithful servant, testifying to what was to be spoken.

This should remind those seeking to hear the voice of God in the text of Scripture that God's diverse and varied speaking in the past is not radically distinct from the decisive speaking in Jesus. Rather, that speaking typified by Moses is connected to and in the service of God's decisive speaking in the Son.[22] Thus the point in 1:1–2; 2:1–4; and 3:1–6 is not to eliminate God's prior speaking through the prophets, angels, and Moses, but to recontextualize it in relation to God's speaking through the Son.

In this activity of recontextualizing, the first element to note is that God speaks throughout the entirety of Scripture. Any pattern of reading that presumes incommensurability between Old and New Testament threatens to undermine the claim that it is the same God speaking both then and now. As Paul understood, such a view undermines the righteousness of God.

The second point to note here is that God's speaking through Moses is in relation to and in service of God's speaking in Christ. This requires some careful unpacking. Both Judaism and Christianity read the texts Christians call the Old Testament in relation to and in conversation with other decisive texts. It is only in the context of modern biblical scholarship (and those branches of Christianity heavily influenced by such scholarship) that the importance of such claims as letting the Old Testament speak with "its own voice" carry sway.[23] There may be good reasons for such a claim. Claims to let the Old Testament speak with its own voice become particularly appealing when confronted with readers of the New Testament who impose a rigid template or predetermined pattern on what the Old Testament says. Nevertheless, Hebrews, the rest of the New Testament, and Christian theology more generally all indicate that God's speaking in Christ must decisively shape the ways in which one approaches the Old Testament and that God's speaking in the Old Testament is in service to God's speaking in Christ. Theologically speaking, Christians do not

---

22   "That it is the same Word which has come equally to Christians as to the wilderness generation, through their respective mediators, is made clear by the fact that it makes exactly the same kind of demand—namely of belief and consequently to faithful pilgrimage . . ." Hughes, *Hebrews and Hermeneutics*, 11.

23   One of the strongest proponents of this view was Brevard Childs. Although this theme appears throughout Childs' work, one can find a good example of this in his essay, "Toward Recovering Theological Exegesis," *ProEccl* 6 (1997): 16–26.

want to adopt the idea that the Old Testament has its own discrete voice, independent of God's speaking in Christ. At the same time, they should recognize, welcome, and make use of the rich scholarship produced by scholars who might hold to that view as well as Jewish scholars who study these texts in relation to Judaism.

The third point to make here is that just as God's speaking in the past was diverse and varied, Christians also should assume that the ways in which the Old Testament may be related to and serve God's decisive speaking in Christ will be many and varied. Indeed, I would argue that this is the only way to do this well.

All of this is crucial, but Hebrews also develops some further points in this regard. In Hebrews 2 the author mentions the importance of the Spirit's role in confirming our hearing of God's speaking. In this regard I have mentioned the importance of a robust common life as Christians discern the promptings of the Spirit in community. Here in chapter 3:7–19 the Spirit adds a further element, saying, "Today, if you hear his [God's] voice, do not harden your hearts." The passage goes on to mention several moments during the exodus when those Israelites who escaped from the hard-hearted Pharaoh follow Pharaoh's example and harden their own hearts.

This would indicate that to hear the voice of God in the text of Scripture one must be tenderhearted. One manifests the relevant form of tenderheartedness through obedient receptivity to God. Whether or not humans have some sort of innate natural receptivity to God is a question we can leave aside for the moment. This is because whether innate or not, this capacity is certainly damaged by sin.

Moreover, along with Hebrews, we should not assume that simply entering the body of Christ provides some sort of lifetime inoculation against a hard heart. If a tender heart is marked by an obedient receptivity to God, one might simply treat a hard heart as something that is no longer receptive. It is a self-absorbed heart, closed off to God and others, as typified by Pharaoh's approach to God.

That, of course, is one way of thinking about the ways in which we might harden our hearts. It is the case, however, that certain types of receptivity might also result in a hardened heart. In a culture filled with carnival barkers of various stripes, thousands of mediated messages each day, and distractions galore our hearts can be hardened through indiscriminate receptivity, too. A hard heart may be a heart so filled with distractions that there is no room to receive something worthwhile from

God. Tenderheartedness, then, is a discerning receptivity. As Hebrews 5 will note, tenderheartedness requires ongoing cultivation and upkeep.[24] It is not a one-time achievement. Rather it is a life's work. I assume that there are a host of everyday practices through which individual Christians cultivate and keep up tender hearts. Given the diversity of our temperaments, this is all to the good. Nevertheless, despite this individual variation, prayer, both corporate and individual, worship, and generous hospitality are practices that would seem to be relevant to all believers eager to cultivate tender hearts capable of hearing the voice of God.

Further, as 3:12–15 develops the quotation from Psalm 95 it is clear that both the Hebrews and we are living in "today." That is, the words spoken by the Spirit in Psalm 95 are words to believers in this and all "todays" for as long as "today" will last.[25] This point reminds us that the writer of Hebrews believes that God's speaking in many and various ways in former times is still audible even after God speaks in the Son. Further, the claim that we, like our forebears in the faith, reside in "today" is a point of hope. There is still time to cultivate a tender heart.

HEBREWS 4: UNITED IN FAITH WITH THOSE WHO HAVE HEARD

On this basis chapter 4 begins with an urgent admonition, "Therefore, while the promise of entering his rest is still open, let us take care that none of you should seem to have failed to reach it" (4:1). Then in 4:2 we learn that the situation of contemporary believers is just like those who first received the good news about entering into God's rest. For those who did not enter into God's rest, the problem did not lie with God's speaking but with their hearing. We are told that they were not "united" in faith with those who heard appropriately (ἐκείνους μὴ συγκεκερασμένους τῇ πίστει τοῖς ἀκούσασιν).[26]

---

24   See Daniel J. Treier, "Speech Acts, Hearing Hearts, and Other Senses," in *The Epistle to the Hebrews and Christian Theology*, R. Bauckham, D. Driver, T. Hart, and N. MacDonald, eds. (Grand Rapids: Eerdmans, 2009), 345.

25   "'Today' is no longer the today of the past, surveyed by the psalmist in his situation, but the today of the present which continues to be conditioned by the voice of God that speaks day after day through the Scriptures and the gospel tradition. Moreover, its perspective extends from the present to the approaching Parousia and judgment" (Lane, *Hebrews*, 87).

26   There are some textual variants regarding συγκεκερασμένους. Ellingworth, *Hebrews*, 242–43, makes case for the reading of NA[28] cited here (also Attridge, *Hebrews*, 122 n.2). It has the best textual witnesses and yields the translation that "they" [the wilderness generation] were "not united in faith with those who heard." The difficulty here is that it takes "those who heard" to have heard appropriately. This stands in contrast with the unprofitable "word of hearing" in 2:2 and 3:16

This reminds us of a point to which I have already spoken. Hearing the voice of God is not simply an act performed more or less well by individuals. Rather, it requires a body of believers manifesting a particular type of common life in the Spirit. Hebrews 4:1–2 develops this point further. These verses suggest that one may discern the quality and effectiveness of one's hearing of the voice of God by whether or not it draws one into closer communion with those who have already faithfully heard. This is not surprising. If the ultimate end of hearing the voice of God in the text of Scripture is to draw us to salvation, into ever deeper communion with the God who has spoken decisively in the Son, then it would be very odd if such hearing did not also draw us closer to our brothers and sisters in Christ, both past and present, who are also engaged in that same journey.

Recognizing that appropriate hearing of the voice of God is manifested in being united in faith with those who have already heard should also disturb those of us whose "today" encompasses that time when Christ's body is so divided. Under such circumstances, what sense can one make of being "united in faith with those who heard"? One must at least grant that church division, such as has marked us for the past 500 years, must frustrate and inhibit our capacities to hear the voice of God in the text of Scripture.[27] Although I do not fully subscribe to Ephraim Radner's account of the effects of church division in the west, I think we must reckon with the possibility that division has completely deafened us. I am not sure we can confidently rule out the prospect that our divisions actually put us on the side of those described in 4:2 whose hearing was of no benefit to them. Our division may be a particularly contemporary form of that disqualifying disobedience discussed in 4:3–11. If that is true, there is not much point in continuing this paper. In order to proceed at all, we should assume that although our divisions may have rendered us hard of hearing, we are not completely deaf.

In the light of the way chapter 4 continues, we may expect that the

---

which seems to indicate that no one in the wilderness generation did hear appropriately. The only response to this is to also note that Moses is already identified as "faithful." Moreover, Joshua (and Caleb) are implicitly in view as faithful in Heb 11:29–30. Hence, some of that wilderness generation did hear appropriately. Thus, 3:16 must be taken to be hyperbole. Attridge's interpretation that the wilderness generation was not united to "us," the author and audience of Hebrews, is, as he says, "a bold conceit." He does not really offer reasons for this interpretation (see *Hebrews*, 126).

27   See Ephraim Radner, *The End of the Church: A Pneumatology of Christian Division in the West* (Grand Rapids: Eerdmans, 1998) and Bruce Marshall, "The Disunity of the Church and the Credibility of the Gospel," *ThTo* (April, 1993): 78–89.

λόγος of God may play a role in revealing the extent to which our divisions debilitate our hearing of God's voice. In 4:12 we read that the λόγος of God is a two-edged sword, an instrument that God may use to display the deepest truths about us and subject those truths to judgment. This λόγος may be the word of God in Scripture and/or a reference to the Son as the Word of God. In either case, 4:12 seems to grant this λόγος the function of discerning judge.

In that case, we may find some hope in the obscure end of 4:13. If one reads it as leading into the discussion of Christ's priesthood in 4:14ff., then there is a case to be made for following Rebekah Eklund's translation of this clause, "'concerning which, to us, is the Word'—both the word spoken 'Today!' and the Word that intercedes for us in heaven."[28] That is, this λόγος that will reveal our deafness and subject it to judgment is also a λόγος that can intercede on our behalf.

HEBREWS 5: FORMATION

This paves the way for the more detailed discussion of Christ's priesthood in 4:14–5:10. Here Christ's priestly role as the word of God that intercedes on our behalf is explicated in terms of Melchizedek's priesthood. Before this discussion gets too far, the author informs his readers that this is a complicated discussion and the readers are not yet ready to engage it because they have become "sluggish in their hearing" (νωθροὶ γεγόνατε ταῖς ἀκοαῖς). Their facility in hearing the voice of God is not what it ought to be.[29] Although this deficiency in hearing may extend beyond hearing the voice of God, it certainly includes that.

For the purposes of thinking about hearing the voice of God in the text of Scripture, this passage raises some interesting issues. First, the metaphors of growth from infants drinking milk to mature believers capable of digesting solid food indicates that hearing the word is a skill where success should build upon and lead to further success. Indeed the accusation of sluggishness with regard to hearing displays the expectation that one will advance in this process, gaining greater skill and capacities for discernment over time. Growth is expected, not optional. Hence, no matter how

---

28 Rebekah Eklund, "'To Us, the Word': The Double-λόγος of Hebrews 4:12–13," *JTI* 9:1 (2015): 114.

29 Johnson, *Hebrews*, 155, develops the point that "hearing" in this verse also entails obedience and leads to maturity. Moreover, Heb 5:8–9 has already made the point that Christ became mature [τελειωθείς] through obedience.

believers characterize the voice of God in the text of Scripture, hearing that voice well is a cumulative process of disciplined cultivation of skills, habits, and dispositions. Over time this should result in increased capacities to hear the voice of God in new and deeper ways.

All of that leads me to my final observation. Enhancing our capacities to hear the voice of God in the text of Scripture requires intentional formation, particularly the formation of young hearers into mature hearers, to use Hebrews' way of putting it. The formation of wise and discerning hearers or interpreters is both a crucial and a neglected task within most churches. In contrast to most churches, the academy as a whole does a remarkably good job of forming young scholars to be technically accomplished interpreters of Scripture. Those of us who have passed through this formative process understand that it requires the disciplined cultivation of specific skills, habits, and dispositions; it takes time. All of this formation may contingently be useful for hearing the voice of God in the text of Scripture, but it is not necessary. Other types of formation are necessary to hear the voice of God in the text of Scripture.

Over the past years I've tried to account for and describe many of these skills, habits, and dispositions believers must cultivate to enhance their prospects of hearing the voice of God in the text of Scripture in mature ways.[30] I am less interested in repeating that here. Instead, I want to take a step back and note that such formation also requires institutions. That is, if hearing the voice of God in the text of Scripture wisely is the result of the systematic formation of believers to read in "mature" ways, it also requires institutions that will support such formation. In my experience, churches do not and in some cases cannot devote resources to this. Clergy are rarely formed this way when it comes to dealing with Scripture. Hence, it is rare for them to have the requisite skills, habits, and dispositions to impart to their congregations. Moreover, there are precious few places where the scholars who would form these clergy can themselves be formed.

Nevertheless, it is clear that such formation does happen. If my own example is anything to go by, such formation has largely been the result of contingent non-repeatable circumstances. Perhaps God will continue providentially to order the circumstances of sufficient people so that they, too, will cultivate such skills, habits, and dispositions in their lives. This strikes me as more of a hope than a strategy. For those interested in the

---

30   Most comprehensively in *Engaging Scripture* and *The Theological Interpretation of Scripture* where I discuss such matters as interpretive charity, humility, and patience.

continuing growth of theological interpretation of Scripture, there would seem to be no more important task than the development and maintenance of institutions devoted to the formation of future generations of theological interpreters.[31]

31   I am grateful to Rebekah Eklund and Rob Wall for their comments on earlier drafts of this paper.

CHAPTER 3

HEARING GOD SPEAK FROM THE FIRST TESTAMENT

JOHN GOLDINGAY

IF HANS FREI IS RIGHT, the fall took place in Biblical Studies in the eighteenth century.[1] In theory, at least, until that time biblical scholars made two assumptions that then ceased to be taken for granted; two questions that they had not asked now came to be asked. One assumption was that the story the biblical text told, and the actual history of Israel, of Jesus, and of the beginnings of the church, were the same thing. The unasked question was thus whether there might be a difference between the two. The other assumption was that theology or faith or interpretation involves setting our story in the context of the biblical story and evaluating or reformulating our story in light of the biblical story. The second unasked question was thus whether our story might ask testing questions of the biblical story, whether we might question the convictions expressed in the biblical story in light of the convictions that emerge from our story.

The fall, then, involved asking about the difference between the story and the history, and recognizing that they were indeed different. That recognition implied a choice about whether greater significance attached to the story or to the history. In the short term the answer was inevitable; it's

---

1   See Hans Frei, *The Eclipse of Biblical Narrative* (New Haven: Yale University Press, 1974).

the history not the story that counts. As John Reumann put it, "History is God nowadays."[2]

The fall naturally led to a departure from the garden of Eden and to a period of wandering in the country of Nod, which refers allegorically to biblical study's focus for two centuries on uncovering the actual history of Israel, of Jesus, and of the infant church. The new unquestioned assumption was that this actual history is the locus of revelation.

But the attempt to trace the actual history turned out to be a period of fruitless wandering. There are two pieces of evidence for the conclusion that the journey led nowhere. One is that it generated no theology and no insight on the Scriptures' significance for the thinking and life of the world and the church. It generated nothing that would preach. The uselessness for theologians and preachers of nearly all scholarly biblical commentaries written over these two centuries witnesses to the point. The commentaries were useless whether written by more liberal or more conservative scholars, because everyone shared the starting point that a story needed to be factual in order to have significance, to have authority, to be revelatory, and the starting point that interpretation consisted in investigating its having-happened-ness. Both liberals and conservatives worshiped the god history and their scholarship served this god. When people of either theological persuasion sought to do theology or to preach, their message came from somewhere other than the Scriptures as interpreted in the scholarly world.

The other evidence that the journey was one of fruitless wandering is the fact that the quest for historical actuality proved futile. No actuality was gained. Two centuries of work by great minds has hardly given birth even to a mouse. The wise assumption is that such study is never going to escape the country of Nod. As far as the Old Testament is concerned, there will never be a critically-justifiable consensus on key questions about the story of Israel's ancestors, about the exodus, about how Israel became Israel in Canaan, and maybe about David and Solomon and much of the later history. It's actually easy enough to see why it is so. The material in the Old Testament with which historical criticism has to work is not such as can answer the question that historical criticism asks.

The meetings and publications of the Society of Biblical Literature (SBL) continue to pay much attention to historical investigation on the

---

2   J. Reumann, "*Oikonomia*-terms in Paul in comparison with Lucan *Heilsgeschichte*," *NTS* 13 (1966–67): 147–67 (147).

assumption that progress is possible, without considering the evidence that it's not possible. One reason we continue is that scholars have to keep propounding new theories in order to get jobs and achieve tenure and promotion. But my hunch is that more broadly scholars are a bit like addicts, who continue to take their drug without asking why they do so.

If history is God, but progress in historical study of the Old Testament is a will-o'-the-wisp, we are screwed. Fortunately, the assumption that history is God was simply a culture-relative presupposition made by liberals and conservatives for a couple of centuries. It is not one we are bound to.

Now, we stand on the shoulders of giants. When we put ourselves into the position of our theological great-grandfathers and imagine we are working in the context of the parameters of nineteenth-century debate and are confronted by the challenge of historical criticism, we could hardly have responded otherwise than they did. But the literary turn which came to affect scholarship half a century ago has made it possible to contemplate jumping the opposite way from the direction that was previously inevitable. It has made it possible to read Karl Barth, whose protests in the prefaces to his Romans commentary[3] had previously been unreadable.

Let us now assume that for theological purposes the story counts for at least as much as the history. The basic historicity of the story indeed matters. If Christ is not raised, then our faith is vain, and I think it probably also matters that Yahweh did make some promises to Israel's ancestors and did bring some Israelites out of Egypt. But the story about those events, the scriptural text, is what counts for theology and preaching.

My first assumption about how we might expect to hear the voice of God coming to us in the Scriptures is thus that it happens textually. I will go on to talk about how it happens historically, spiritually, homiletically, and submissively.

BEING TEXTUAL

But first, it happens textually. There is a paradoxical aspect to historical-critical study. Its aim was to discover the text's own meaning, not least over against the meaning that traditions of interpretation had given it, but it relocated the meaning of the text out from the text itself into the

---

3   See *The Epistle to the Romans* (repr. Oxford; New York: Oxford University Press, 1963); cf. Richard Burnett, *Karl Barth's Theological Exegesis* (Tübingen: Mohr, 2001).

historical events to which it refers. It was the literary turn that made it possible to perceive this point and to consider alternatives.

It might seem self-evident that at least one aspect of the interpretation of a text would be to tease out the text's own meaning, to consider the significance of the text in its own right. But historical criticism did not do so, and for that matter most biblical interpretation continues not to do so. As I have hinted, a look at the list of papers read at an SBL meeting provides evidence for the point, but so does one's reading of student papers. In both cases, interest lies not in the text but either in what lies behind the text (the events to which it refers) or in what lies in front of the text (its relevance to questions that interest us). Both foci are troubling, and they have more in common with each other than is implied by contrast between the language of "behind the text" and "in front of the text," because both foci take their agenda from what seems important to us. The interest in what lies behind the text, the events to which the text relates, is an interest that has its background in front of the text.

There is a further scandal to the focus on matters behind the text and on contemporary significance. An old story tells of a young assistant pastor arriving at a church and asking a senior church member what to preach about. The reply is, "Preach about God, and preach about twenty minutes." The first half of the exhortation, at least, corresponds to the focus of the Scriptures themselves, but God is not much of a focus in biblical interpretation. Our agenda lies elsewhere.

Maybe it is not so surprising, therefore, that hearing the voice of God in the Scriptures will mean hearing God talk about himself. The Scriptures are the story of God working out his purpose to bring a world into being.

A look at the sermon topics advertised by churches suggests that God is not a major preoccupation in preaching. We are more interested in what we can be and in what we can do. The ethical turn at a philosophical level, which followed the literary turn, is accompanied by an ethical turn in priorities at an everyday level. You will get nowhere with millennials, I have heard it said, unless you talk about justice. The generation before the millennials, toward the end of the twentieth century, thought that God might be bringing renewal to the church, but the millennial generation spotted that God has left us, and it has inferred that we ourselves need to bring renewal to the church. It also spotted that the world is in a mess and that God isn't doing much about it. God isn't bringing in the reign of righteousness and justice, so we had better do so.

But the voice of God in the text of the Scriptures speaks of God working out a purpose, and of human beings not making much of a contribution. The Scriptures aren't as interested in ethics as we are. Sure, they presuppose some ethics, but they don't agonize over tricky ethical issues or about how to get the world to be more ethical. Their stance suggests that the appropriate response to God's withdrawal is not to try to make up for the absence but to petition God to return.

We need to reflect on the way developments in biblical interpretation are inclined to mirror developments in the study of English literature and the wider critical environment. The literary turn, post-structuralism, post-colonial study, reception history, and so on, did not start as developments within biblical interpretation. They were brought into biblical interpretation from the cultural context. That fact doesn't in itself make them wrong, and those approaches to interpretation make fruitful contributions to our hearing the voice of God in the Scriptures, but the dynamic of the process raises questions about the ease with which we sell our souls to the latest hermeneutical idea. This consideration might suggest another angle on the importance of the question, how do we hear the voice of God from the Scriptures. While the hearing may happen in part because approaches that emerge from our context are ones that speak to us, it will also happen because we are not confined to such approaches but are open to ones that correspond to the nature of our text.

At this point, biblical scholarship may be inclined to invoke the word *canonical*, as suggesting an approach to interpretation that does not emerge from the developments in the critical environment, but I do not invoke the word, for several reasons. One is that it is a boo word for some and a hurrah word for others. Another is that it has such a variety of implications, not least for the scholar who especially advocated its use. Another is that on average I don't find that people who use the word *canonical* are actually more illuminating on what God may be saying to us out of the Scriptures than people who have no great use for that word.

But the most important reason is that canonical interpretation simply means interpreting the scriptural text that we actually have, in light of its own nature, and there is nothing especially theological about the idea that one should interpret a story or any other kind of text in light of its own nature. To treat Shakespeare's plays as a source for information about the periods of English history to which they refer, or about things that were going on in the playwright's own day, is quite legitimate, but it surely doesn't count as interpreting Shakespeare's plays.

I do like Brevard Childs's observation in his Isaiah commentary that the book of Isaiah is not merely a repository of expressions of the faith of Israel but a repository of material about God.[4] And reading Isaiah as a repository of material about God is not so complicated. Interpreting the Scriptures needs to be textual in the sense that it asks that simple question, what is this text about? And quite often the answer is, "God."

I could have given the impression that being canonical or textual implies an antithesis over against being historical. I do not imply such an antithesis, and I come now to affirm that we should expect the word of God to come to us through reading the Scriptures historically.

BEING HISTORICAL

The Scriptures result from God's speaking and acting in relationship to people in a way that is linked with their historical contexts and circumstances, as is the case with God's speaking and acting with us, and their accounts of God's speaking and acting also related to the historical contexts and circumstances of these accounts. My assumption is that the works we have in the Scriptures are ones that the people of God received at different times because they recognized that they were expressions of remarkable smartness, and my further assumption is that they are ones that the people of God then held onto when others fell away because they perceived them to possess a smartness that spoke beyond that immediate context. I am prepared to believe that Childs is right that in some cases the very form of the work (for instance, the Torah-like structure of the book of Psalms) indicates this assumption or claim.

The meaning of the Scriptures is then time-related and history-related, and in this sense it is not timeless. The Scriptures are timeless in the sense of transcending time and speaking to times other than their own. But one reason why they are time-transcending in significance is that they were timely. And one appreciates their meaning by understanding them in their historical context. Seeing how they were timely can aid an appreciation of how they are time-transcendent and can be timely for us.

A contemporary way to make the point is to note that they are speech acts. Although we ourselves have them as written works and we may mostly get to know them by reading them silently, they began life as expressions of communication that would mostly get home to people through being

---

4   See e.g., his comments on 1:2–31 and on 40:12–31 (*Isaiah* [Louisville: Westminster John Knox, 2001], 17, 307).

read aloud and as expressions of communication whereby one party sought to do something to another party. Another way of formulating the process whereby they became the Scriptures would be to infer that their aim of seeking to do something to people was effective in relation to some of their hearers, and that this fact led to their being preserved. So the aim of the books of Kings was to get people in Judah to own the books' account of their history and therefore to turn from their rebellion against Yahweh, and the presence of the books in the Scriptures indicates that some people did so turn. The speech act worked, for them. The aim of the psalms was to get people to worship God, pray to God, trust God, and give thanks to God in certain ways (as well as to live faithful lives and to hope in God's promises), and the presence of the book of Psalms in the Scriptures indicates that some people accepted that challenge. The book of Isaiah is a prophetic vision concerning Judah and Jerusalem (Isa 1:1), and this description marks it as designed to get people in the Judahite community much later than Isaiah's own day to live in hope and commitment; the presence of the book of Isaiah in the Scriptures indicates that some people responded to it with hope and commitment. An implication of the fact that the Scriptures started off as speech acts is that we come to appreciate them through discovering our way into the historical speech-act.

The implicit invitation to future generations of the people of God is then, "In the context of our lives we heard God and we heard our brothers and sisters speaking to us in these writings, and we urge you to do so."

Preserving those works had two contrasting implications. It both liberated them from their historical context and bound them to their historical context. A parable of its liberating effect is the omission on the part of most of the works to provide us with information on their precise historical context. Yet there is no doubt about the general fact that the First Testament Scriptures come from the life of Israel between (say) 800 and 150 BC. Their preservation also binds them to their context, because they come with an implicit label saying, "God spoke to us through these writings in the particular context of our lives."

One way whereby we may hope to hear God speak through them, then, is to put ourselves into the position of the Israelites who were on the receiving end of these speech acts in order to see what they do to us. We may then find that the gap between centuries and cultures dissolves because God is the same God for us as for the people whom these Scriptures first addressed, and that we are the same human beings relating to that same God.

In a meeting of the Society of Biblical Literature that was discussing the sense in which we may find Jesus in the Old Testament, I allowed myself the opinion that the rule of the faith is a disaster for interpretation of the Old Testament. A gasp ran round the room. I didn't realize how directly I was challenging a conviction held by many people present. Many people who are committed to theological interpretation of the Scriptures hold the view that such interpretation does or can involve bringing to the Scriptures the rule of the faith (embodied, for instance, in the Nicene Creed), and associated convictions such as the doctrine of the Trinity, and interpreting the Scriptures in their light.

If this assumption means that the rule of the faith and the doctrine of the Trinity can be a lens that enables us to see some things that are actually there in the Scriptures, I have no objection, though I don't know of many examples of their having that effect. Even if it means we build some extra meaning on the scriptural text, I might have no objection. But neither of these processes should count as constituting theological interpretation of Scripture, period. The Scriptures themselves are theological texts affirming truths about God as these truths were preached in historical contexts, and we would be foolish to miss what emerges from focusing resolutely and expectantly on the way the writings functioned in those contexts.

In this connection, our danger with regard to hearing the voice of God from the Scriptures is as follows. The voice of God and truth about God are there in the Scriptures. But I have noted how a century of historical interpretation of the Scriptures ignored that voice. I don't imply that the interpreters didn't believe that the voice was there; many certainly did so believe. But they got stuck in that narrower set of historical questions. The last quarter-century has seen a reaction on the part of people who know that there is something about God in the Scriptures and who want to articulate it. The problem is that it is a reaction that has understandably inferred, from the way historical study has been conducted, that historical study cannot make it possible to hear that voice. So it brings those convictions about God that emerged in the church's tradition and uses them as the basis for articulating the statements about God that are present in the text. But it is thereby involved in reading into the text as much as reading out of it.

What we require is not a move from a non-theological historical reading of the Scriptures to a non-historical theological reading of the Scriptures. What we require is a move from a non-theological historical reading to a theological historical reading, which will be a fuller historical reading because it articulates the text's own theology. Our theological interpretation needs to avoid anachronism. It requires us to be seriously canonical, or rather seriously textual, and therefore to be seriously historical. It requires it because that is the way we can hear how God was actually speaking then, rather than being confined in our listening to things that the people of God have articulated since.[5]

Yet I have hinted that I don't necessarily object in principle to our building things on the scriptural text that aren't there. And I guess my major reason for restraining that objection is that God sometimes builds things onto the scriptural text that aren't there. I will discuss it in terms of being spiritual, because it involves the activity of the Holy Spirit.

BEING SPIRITUAL

Fifty years ago, as a seminary student in England, I went through a religious crisis that didn't involve wondering whether the Christian faith was true but involved wondering whether I belonged to the elect. During this crisis I went to the regular seminary chapel service one morning, and the Old Testament lesson came from Deuteronomy 17, where Moses recalls Israel's having come from Egypt and says to the people's potential king, "You shall not return that way again" (Deut 17:16). This declaration came to me as a promise that God had taken hold of me and would not let me go. That morning I had gone to chapel unsure of my position; I left chapel sure of it. The significance of this experience in our present context is that Moses' words to the king are not a promise but a challenge; "You *are not* to return that way again." God used the Scripture to minister to me by ascribing to it a significance that was not its own meaning.

Eighteen years ago I had given in my notice from my job at another seminary in England and I was contemplating an invitation to come to Fuller. My first wife was wheelchair-bound, and there were various ways in which such a move might therefore be hazardous. During this period, in the regular chapel service at that seminary, one morning God told a student, "Tell John 'Judges 18:6.'" The passage reads, "Go in peace. Your journey has the LORD's approval"; or in another translation, "Go in peace. The mission you are on is under the eye of the LORD." There is no real analogy between my position and that of the person who is given that

---

5   I have argued these points further in "Theological Interpretation: Don't Be Christ-Centered, Don't Be Trinitarian, Don't Be Constrained by the Rule of Faith," in *Do We Need the New Testament?* (Downers Grove, IL: InterVarsity, 2015), 157–76.

message in Judges. Once again, God used a Scripture to minister to me by giving it a significance that was unrelated to its meaning.

Many Christians have experiences of this kind. They are analogous to a feature of the way the New Testament refers to the Scriptures. The opening chapter of Acts records such an appeal to verses from Psalms 69 and 109. These psalms are protests and prayers appealing to God for deliverance from attackers and for the punishment of the attackers; amusingly, they are the kind of psalms that embarrass modern Christians. In Acts, Peter appeals to them to support his conviction that the believers need to appoint someone to take Judas's place in the Twelve. His use of the psalms is unrelated to their own meaning. The same judgment applies to subsequent appeals in Acts to psalms and other texts, and more generally to many New Testament appeals to the Scriptures. Some New Testament appeals to the Scriptures do work with the texts' inherent meaning, but here I focus on ones that provide an analogy for that later Christian experience to which I have referred.

There are a number of Christian approaches to this aspect of the New Testament's use of the Scriptures. It is possible to argue that typology implicitly underlies much New Testament interpretation. Whether typology actually does underlie it or not, it can be used to provide some justification for it. Raymond Brown included this consideration in arguing that texts may have a fuller sense not intended by the human author but intended by the divine author of the Scriptures, and Paul Ricoeur argued more generally that texts may have a surplus meaning, partly because once texts escape their (human) author, their meaning is no longer limited to what that author envisaged.[6] I have had that notion in mind in my comments about texts gaining liberation from their historical context.

But I am not clear that these approaches help a great deal our understanding of those experiences of mine to which I have referred, or our understanding of what Acts does with the texts it quotes. These experiences and interpretations didn't involve typology except in the thinnest of senses. And they didn't involve appeal to a fuller sense in the text. The nearest thing one could say along those lines is that they possibly appealed to something that was in the back of the Holy Spirit's mind in inspiring those texts. But in any case I think it's worthwhile to continue to preserve the difference between the meaning of texts and the significance of texts,

---

6   See e.g., Raymond E. Brown, *The Sensus Plenior of Sacred Scripture* (Baltimore: St. Mary's University, 1955); Paul Ricoeur, *Interpretation Theory* (Fort Worth: Texas Christian University, 1976).

which I associate especially with E. D. Hirsch.[7] Texts have an inherent *meaning* as an act of communication between some parties but they can also gain limitless further *significance* in new contexts.

It then seems to me helpful simply to recognize that the Holy Spirit sometimes takes up lines from the Scriptures in order to provide answers to questions we have, in light of which they gain new significance that's not necessarily related to their inherent meaning.[8] It's a theologically interesting question why the Holy Spirit should use the Scriptures in the way he does. God could easily enough have spoken to me in those two tricky contexts with a message through a prophet, and God could have done the same in Acts. And God does speak via prophets. In between those two experiences, at the service when I was installed as Principal of the seminary in England, and when my wife was well on the way to her disabled state with all the pressure that was bringing to me, through one of my colleagues God gave me the promise, "I will make the north wind your warmth, the snow your purity, the frost your brightness, and the night sky of winter your illumination." It has meant as much to me as those reapplied scriptural verses.

In Acts 1, Peter himself describes the verses from the two psalms as ones that the Holy Spirit spoke, and such formulations appear elsewhere in the New Testament. Their idea seems to be that the extraordinary significance that a passage turns out to have in a context quite other than that in which it arose (and a significance that seems to have nothing much to do with its intrinsic meaning) is explained by the fact that the Holy Spirit was involved in its original coming into being. The Letter to the Hebrews makes a related point when it declares that the Holy Spirit *says* (present tense) a certain thing, and goes on to quote a Scripture. The Holy Spirit is speaking those scriptural words now. The fact that the Holy Spirit was involved with the people of God then and is also involved now makes it not hard to believe that words from back then can speak now. God's reuse of scriptural verses perhaps also affirms for God and for us that we live in the context of the Scriptures and in the context of the relationship between God and us that they describe.

---

7   E. D. Hirsch, *Validity in Interpretation* (New Haven: Yale University Press, 1967); *The Aims of Interpretation* (Chicago: University of Chicago Press, 1976).

8   J. Gordon McConville notes that my interpreting Matthew's use of Isa 7:14 in this way "simply cuts the connection between the literal meaning of Isa. 7:14 and its ('inspired') re-application in Matthew" ("Figures in Isaiah 7:14," in McConville and Lloyd K. Pietersen, eds., *Conception, Reception, and the Spirit* [A. T. Lincoln Festschrift; Eugene, OR: Wipf & Stock, 2015], 3–18 [16]): which I accept, with the comment that this seems to be what God does.

Whatever the Holy Spirit's reasons for using the Scriptures in this way, the implications for thinking about hearing "The Voice of God in the Text of Scripture" are at least twofold. On one hand, we cannot control the process whereby we come to be addressed by God through the Scriptures. God controls whether and when and how his own voice comes to us in the text of the Scriptures. Thus one aspect of the answer to that question about the voice of God and the text of Scripture is that the voice comes on God's initiative by God's sovereignty in accordance with God's timing and in a way that God controls. What is true about prophecy also applies to this speaking. We can long for God to speak or ask God to speak and we can listen, but we cannot make speaking happen. God's speaking in the way I have described suggests that point.

The second implication is that, when it happens, it's not amenable to being tested in any finally conclusive way. It's a speaking that raises the same tricky questions as the evaluation of prophecy, over which Jeremiah agonizes in Jeremiah 23. Jeremiah is perhaps well aware that he is vulnerable to one test of the authenticity of prophecy, that prophecies that don't come true are shown not to have come from God. Jeremiah's prophecies keep not coming true, so he has to sidestep that test. He rather affirms there that there are also moral and theological tests whereby one may prove that a prophecy is not from God, and these tests are all that he needs in order to demonstrate that Hananiah's prophecies came from elsewhere. But the moral and theological tests do not quite prove that Jeremiah's own words come from God, and at another level, Jeremiah is reduced to the simple declaration that he knows he has listened in on a meeting of Yahweh's cabinet and that other prophets haven't. For me, with hindsight I can declare that the way Deuteronomy spoke to me passes the theological test. The way Judges spoke to me I had to accept on the basis that it came from God's cabinet. Some pretty big coincidences would otherwise have been required to make this particular speaking happen. But I was reduced to trusting God over the matter; I made the comment that God himself was going to look silly if our move didn't work out, and of course it did work out, and the student's word passed the "Does it come true" test.

The kind of interpretation that I am calling spiritual involves starting from a question that we have and finding God speaking to that question through a Scripture in a way that has nothing much to do with its own meaning. But there is also a kind of interpretation that starts from a question we have and has God speaking to that question through a Scripture in a way that does work with its own meaning.

BEING HOMILETICAL

The Sunday before I write, the Episcopal lectionary presented me with Proverbs 31, Psalm 1, James 2, and Mark 10. More often than not I talk for five minutes after each of the set Scriptures rather than for fifteen or twenty minutes after the Gospel, and I don't feel obliged to link the passages, but the collocation sometimes stimulates thought and awareness.

In this case, wondering how God spoke to Israel through Proverbs 31, I realized that the dynamic of that speaking might not be so different than it is for modern Westerners. The Old Testament as a whole begins by declaring that women as much as men are made in God's image and it portrays a series of active, enterprising, and confident women who embody something that anticipates the portrait of the resourceful woman of Proverbs 31, people such as Sarah, Miriam, Aksah, Deborah, Ruth, and Abigail. At the same time the Old Testament is realistic about the fact that such women's menfolk can stop them being assertive, active, and enterprising. Proverbs 31 could then have functioned to remind men and women of the scriptural vision of womanhood and to urge them not to give up on it. And maybe it does the same in our context, because we too both assume women's equality and also know about glass ceilings and about women doing the same work as men but not getting the same pay.

There was something else about that vision that closes Proverbs. At the other end of the book, the opening paragraph of Proverbs describes the book's aim. It exists to help its readers be smart people. But this opening description of smartness includes on one hand a commitment to what is right, to what is faithful, and to what is fair, and on the other hand a commendation of living in awe of Yahweh, in submission to Yahweh. Indeed, it says, such submission to Yahweh is the first principle of being smart.

So the first paragraph of Proverbs. Smartness involves ethics and spirituality. Lo and behold, the vision of the resourceful, smart woman with which the book closes incorporates the same two notes. On one hand, this woman opens her arms to the poor and extends her hands to the needy: in other words, she's concerned for what is right and faithful and fair. And on the other hand, she's someone who lives in awe of Yahweh, in submission to Yahweh, in obedience to Yahweh. To put it another way, she is also an embodiment of Psalm 1, which followed this Proverbs reading in our service.

Out of the James passage I focused on my favorite scary verse from the Scriptures, "You have not because you ask not." I noted how that verse contradicts the popular Christian teaching that prayer is the way we conform our will to God's will. On the contrary, prayer is the way we relate to God as our father, and we ask our father for what we want, though like smart children we may recognize that there are often good reasons why our father doesn't give it. But we don't let that fact stop us asking. In the sermon I spoke about some things I'm hesitant to ask God to do because they seem so big, like bring harmony to the Middle East or unify the church or enable a particular person I care about to see the glory of God in the face of Jesus Christ.

In the Mark passage, I focused on the disciples' desire to be the greatest, and I noted the pressure that has come to the disciples through their already being appointed to be the twelve people who will rule the twelve Israelite clans. It tempts them to want to be the number one among these twelve. I noted that the story suggested a focus for our prayers for a new Bishop of Los Angeles and for the incoming Presiding Bishop of the Episcopal Church and for a new President of the United States. The question raised by the Gospel thus linked with the scary verse in James in that it points us to a vital and/or outrageous prayer for such leaders. And further, it linked with that feature of Proverbs that sees concern for the needy and awe for God as aspects of being a smart woman.

What happened to me through preparing to preach was that I heard God speak through the Scriptures in old and new ways through the collocation of the four passages with each other, with questions arising from our present context, with concerns of my own, and with the week's events and news.

Now it's possible to be critical of the lectionary, mostly because it's not very balanced.[9] But we might see the glass as half-full. The lectionary presented me with a collocation of passages that I didn't choose and it thus opened up new possibilities of God's speaking through the Scriptures. Further, the voice of God comes to us in the text of the Scriptures through our letting there be an interweaving between the way they speak in their context and the way our context relates to the questions they raise. A preacher is someone who lives in two worlds, the world of the Scriptures and our contemporary world.[10] I express the point as a descriptive statement, but of course it's really prescriptive, and it presupposes that it's easy for a preacher to live in neither world.

---

9   See John Goldingay, "Canon and Lection," in *To Glorify God: Essays on Modern Reformed Liturgy*, ed. B. D. Spinks and I. R. Torrance (Edinburgh: T&T Clark, 1999), 85–97.
10   Cf. James D. Smart, *The Strange Silence of the Bible in the Church* (London: SCM, 1970), 163; cf. John Goldingay, *Models for Interpretation of Scripture* (Grand Rapids: Eerdmans/Carlisle, UK: Paternoster, 1995), 278.

BEING SUBMISSIVE

I began by noting two long-unquestioned ideas to which Hans Frei drew attention. The first was the identity between the scriptural story and the events to which the story refers. The second was the assumption that we interpret our story by setting it in the context of the scriptural story. The reversal that took place in the eighteenth century generated not only that interest in events rather than text, but also a new assumption about the relationship of the scriptural story and our story, that we evaluate the Scriptures in light of our convictions. In other words, biblical study became critical.

Admittedly, the word *critical* is used in confusing ways. Arguably, modern biblical study first became critical by insisting that interpretation of the Scriptures was critical of any received tradition of interpretation, and thus of what the church said the Scriptures meant. Critical biblical study means letting the Scriptures determine their meaning by the usual procedures for ascertaining the meaning of anything. One's aim is "to read Scripture like any other book,"[11] though the fact that they are not one book means a wide variety of approaches.[12] I have noted that being critical means not letting the rule of faith determine the Scriptures' meaning.

In general, however, critical interpretation of something means criticizing it as well as criticizing traditional interpretations of it, and this meaning is the one that more commonly attaches to the expression "biblical criticism." Such criticism then takes its basis for criticism from somewhere other than the Scriptures themselves, though rare are the interpreters who make explicit where this basis lies.

Among interesting and illuminating current hermeneutics are postcolonial interpretation, disability interpretation, and ecological interpretation. They manifest an ambivalence in their relationship with the Scriptures, an ambivalence that they share with earlier hermeneutics such as feminist interpretation. On one hand, the perspective from which they start enables them to draw attention to features of the Scriptures that had often been missed. So postcolonial interpretation enables us to recognize that the Scriptures do not come from communities that are in power,

---

11   Cf. Benjamin Jowett, "On the Interpretation of Scripture," in Frederick Temple and others, *Essays and Reviews* (London: Parker, 1860), 330–433 (338); cf. James Barr, "Jowett and the 'Original Meaning' of Scripture," RelS 18 (1982): 433–37; "Jowett and the Reading of the Bible 'Like Any Other Book,'" *Horizons in Biblical Theology* 4.2/5.1 (1982–83): 1–44.

12   Cf. R. W. L. Moberly, "'Interpret the Bible like Any Other Book'?" *JTI* 4 (2010): 91–110 (101–3).

the kind of communities from which scholarly interpreters usually come. They come from communities that are more like colonies than like superpowers. This awareness opens up the possibility of a sharper reading of (say) Isaiah in its own right, not to say Nahum in its own right, and also of such texts' significance for people in our world who belong either to colonial communities or to superpower communities.[13]

So a postcolonial hermeneutic opens up the possibility of hearing the text more clearly and more sharply as it functioned for its original hearers, and thus of discovering its significance in our world. But such a hermeneutic also becomes a basis for critique of the biblical text, on the grounds that the text itself is affected by quasi-colonial or imperial assumptions.

There is then a paradoxical aspect to this critique. The nature of a superpower's relationship with its colonies is that it exercises power not only in economics or politics but in ways of thought and values. Postcolonial thinking seeks to subvert and destabilize the power relationship between the superpower and its colonies and to enable subaltern writers to speak with their own voice and within the parameters of their own ways of thinking. And postcolonial biblical study seeks to destabilize that power relationship. The paradox is that postcolonial biblical study commonly takes an imperial stance in relation to the Scriptures. That is, the Scriptures are mostly permitted to relate to postcolonial thinking in one of two ways. Either the postcolonial perspective allows one to see ways in which the Scriptures themselves validate postcolonial attitudes rather than the imperial attitudes that they had been assumed to support. Or the postcolonial perspective allows one to see that the Scriptures themselves embody imperial attitudes.[14]

The Scriptures are thus the victims of postcolonial study in the same way that colonies are the victims of the imperial power. The imperial power claims to be bringing positive benefits to the colonies, and indeed it does so, but the presupposition of its approach is that the superpower knows best and that its framework of thinking needs to govern the colonies' thinking. Postcolonial study treats the Scriptures in the way a superpower treats its colonies. They become resources that the superpower can appropriate where it approves of them or where it deems them useful, but that it can dismiss where it does not approve of them or does not deem them

---

13   See e.g., Andrew T. Abernethy and others (eds.), *Isaiah and Imperial Context* (Eugene, OR: Pickwick, 2013); W. J. Wessels, "Nahum," *OTE* 11 (1998): 615–28.

14   Mark G. Brett's *Decolonizing God* (Sheffield: Sheffield Phoenix, 2008) helped me articulate this point.

useful. And there is no way in which "the empire can write back."[15] Like the colonies of an empire, the Scriptures are the victims of postcolonial study's imperialism. The empire continues to maintain control but by different means. It continues to impose its value system.

Admittedly I oversimplify, because I fail to allow for hybridity. An imperial culture such as Britain's set itself over against a colonial culture such as India's and presupposed its superiority, yet its doing so was both unrealistic and unwise. Where would Britain be without Indian tea, Indian curry, and pajamas? In practice, cultures influence one another; they are regularly hybrid. This fact deconstructs the claim that the imperial culture is inherently superior.

Postcolonial biblical study is likewise hybrid, as is all critical biblical study. It lives in the world of the West, of the Enlightenment, of modernity and postmodernity. It also lives in the world of the Scriptures. Its practitioners are commonly people who began their academic lives with a traditional adherence to the Scriptures, though they likely "grew out of it." So postcolonialism, like most biblical criticism, has an uneasy relationship with the Scriptures. Indeed, postcolonial cultures commonly have an uneasy relationship with their former overlords, like that of teenagers to their parents. The point is illustrated by the ambiguous attitude that the United States takes to Europe.

The result of the stance that postcolonialism takes to the Scriptures is that such study can never have God's voice come to it except to confirm what it thinks already. Unless by some miracle the study already assumes a scriptural viewpoint without recognizing that it is so, it will follow that by being partly scriptural, it is bound to be unscriptural.

Ironically, then, postcolonial study deconstructs because it operates on an imperialist basis. Something similar without irony and perhaps without self-contradiction is true of other hermeneutics such as feminist interpretation or disability interpretation or ecological interpretation.

Yet there is a further irony in the fact that people who abjure a critical or liberal stance towards the Scriptures are affected by the same aftermath of that fall which is analyzed by Hans Frei. That is, more conservative Christians are also inclined to be concerned with how relevant are the Scriptures to us, rather than how relevant are we to the Scriptures. Christian faith is about me and my personal relationship with God, they

---

15 See Bill Ashcroft and others, *The Empire Writes Back*, 2nd ed. (London; New York: Routledge, 2002).

may assume, or about me and my making my life work out. More recently, I have noted, it is about justice. We evaluate the Scriptures on the basis of how far they speak to our agenda, or we covertly pass judgment on them by deciding to pay attention to some parts and not to others. To be fair, I guess it has always been so.

It has been argued that biblical study is necessarily critical in the sense that it will accept some perspectives from the Scriptures, and ignore others, because the Scriptures themselves express a variety of viewpoints on the issues they cover. When James E. Brenneman so argues in *Canons in Conflict*,[16] his subtitle is *Negotiating Texts in True and False Prophecy*. Brenneman is especially interested in the texts that speak on one hand of beating swords into plowshares and on the other of beating plowshares into swords, and his basis for deciding which text has authority is the stance of the interpretive community.[17] But the implication is that the voice we hear is the voice of the current community rather than the voice of the Scriptures.

I have recently been involved in a project to facilitate the study of the Scriptures across the Anglican Communion. You could say that we were asking the question, how do we as Anglicans hear the voice of God in the Scriptures? Part of the background is that for us as for other denominations, reading the Scriptures has become contested because of the fracas over same-sex relationships, and the Scriptures are read differently in this connection according to whether you come from Africa or from North America, with England maybe somewhere in between.

As part of our work we looked at Jonah, and we then thought that we should consider the different stance to Nineveh taken in Nahum compared with that taken in Jonah. It is a similar difference to the one Brenneman considers. But a principle we tacitly accepted is that seeking to hear the voice of God in the Scriptures means listening to Nahum as well as Jonah. Enlightened Western people prefer Isaiah and Jonah to Joel and Nahum, but living by that preference again means that we have decided what we will hear simply on the basis of our presuppositions. To put it in late twentieth-century terms, our preunderstanding has ceased to be a preliminary understanding that opens up a conversation. Our preunderstanding has hardened into a final understanding. But the function of the Scriptures is more than merely to fill out what we know already. As is

16   James E. Brenneman, *Canons in Conflict* (New York: Oxford University Press, 1997).
17   *Canons in Conflict*, 140.

the case with prophecy, the point about the Scriptures is to confront what we think already, not merely to confirm it.

Interpreting the Scriptures like any other book does not mean giving them the same status as any other book.[18] It does mean that the process of understanding is similar to that for any other book. But their status is different. The Scriptures being the Scriptures means we yield to what they say when we don't like it. And discerning the voice of God in the Scriptures likely depends in part on our advance willingness to do so. If someone's will is to do God's will, Jesus says, he will know whether or not Jesus' teaching comes from God (John 7:17). You don't first discover what the teaching is, then decide whether to do what it says. You write God a blank check, and then you discover how God will cash it.

I ponder the mystery of how communities and individuals come to change their minds, especially about things that matter. It's my way of articulating the election-freewill question. I love the way Psalm 119 walks round this question at great length. It keeps promising God commitment but it also keeps asking God to teach us his expectations of us. It doesn't mean we don't know what the expectations are, that we don't know what the Torah says. It means we recognize that our knowledge of the content of the Torah has not reached and changed our inner being. To use Jeremiah's expression, it's not written on our hearts. How do we hear God's voice through the Scriptures? By being people who are already committed to obeying God's voice there.

---

18 See the discussion in Moberly, "'Interpret the Bible like Any Other Book'?"

CHAPTER 4

THE VOICE OF GOD IN ISRAEL'S WISDOM LITERATURE

Amy Plantinga Pauw

IN SCRIPTURE, GOD IS DEPICTED as having hands, feet, a back, nostrils, eyes, ears, arms, fingers, lungs, bowels, a womb. God is depicted as using human body parts to—among other things—walk, breathe, hear, see, smite, carry, taste, hold, feel compassion, sit on a throne, rise up, and give birth. As G. B. Caird notes, "All, or almost all, of the language used by the Bible to refer to God is metaphor."[1] Not surprisingly, most God-language is anthropomorphic, drawn from our experience of having a human body and being social creatures. So when the prophet Isaiah says to God, "You have put all my sins behind your back" (Isa 38:17), the prophet expresses his confidence in God's forgiveness in a metaphor drawn from the human experience of being creatures with eyes in the front of our heads.[2]

Many human body parts are metaphorically ascribed to God in Scripture, but it is God's mouth and vocal cords that have had a preeminent hold on Christian theology, especially in its Protestant versions. The metaphor cluster of God's voice, God's speech, and God's words has had

---

1   G. B. Caird, *The Language and Imagery of the Bible* (Philadelphia: Westminster, 1980), 18. For the metaphorical quality of human language in general, see Janet Martin Soskice, *Metaphor and Religious Language* (Oxford: Clarendon, 1987).
2   Caird, *The Language and Imagery of the Bible*, 18.

an outsize influence on how we think about God's relating to humanity, and indeed to all that God has made. Verbal divine communication has been our central theological paradigm for how we know God and for how God relates to us. On the one hand, this is not surprising, given the centrality of Scripture for Christian life and the importance of words and speech to human life in general. On the other hand, this *is* a bit surprising, given how little of the Bible is actually said, in context, to be utterances of God. As John Barton notes, "the prophetic 'thus says the Lord' is the exception rather than the rule in Scripture."[3] However Protestant theologians especially have tended to make this kind of oracular model the rule, rather than the exception, in their understanding of Scripture and of how God relates to us through Scripture. As the Princeton Seminary theologian Benjamin Warfield put it, Scripture is to be thought of "as the living voice of God speaking in all its parts directly to the reader."[4] According to Warfield, God is the sole originator of all of Scripture— whether it be narratives, psalms of praise and lament, prayers, or letters. In Warfield's reading, Scriptures "affirm, indeed, with the greatest possible emphasis that the Divine word delivered through men is the pure word of God, diluted with no human admixture whatever."[5] The delivery of these words happens by God's direct inspiration of human beings, so that there is in all of Scripture a double author of speech, God's voice behind a human voice. This authorial-discourse interpretation of Scripture is the centerpiece of a larger theological paradigm that sees all God's relating to creatures as belonging to an economy of communication.

In this essay I call into question the dominant oracular model by taking Proverbs and Ecclesiastes as my starting point for thinking about the voice of God in the text of Scripture.[6] Attention to these wisdom books also challenges the unduly narrow paradigm of God's economy of communication by showing it to be a subset of the larger economy of God's relations to creation. More broadly, attention to Israel's wisdom traditions helps avert what Karl Barth called "the constant danger that the Bible

---

3   John Barton, *People of the Book? The Authority of the Bible in Christianity* (Louisville: Westminster John Knox, 1988), 45.

4   Fred G. Zaspel, *The Theology of B. B. Warfield: A Systematic Summary* (Wheaton, IL: Crossway, 2010), 3.

5   Benjamin Warfield, *Inspiration and Authority of the Bible*, 2nd ed. (Phillipsburg, NJ: P&R Publishing, 1980), 86.

6   For a fuller theological treatment of these books, see Amy Plantinga Pauw, *Proverbs and Ecclesiastes*, Belief: A Theological Commentary on the Bible (Louisville: Westminster John Knox, 2015).

will be taken prisoner by the Church."[7] The church's concern to provide a consistent account of Scripture's character and function as a whole must not eclipse honest attention to its parts. Systematic theological reflection on Scripture must begin with acknowledging the irreducible diversity of the biblical witness.

WISDOM'S DISTINCTIVE VOICE

Proverbs and Ecclesiastes are biblical wisdom books. Israel's wisdom traditions look at the world through a wide-angle lens. They are concerned with the God-given meaning and purpose of creaturely life in general, not with the story of a particular nation or tribe. Israel's sages probed everyday human experiences of the world and reflected on God's presence in them. As Gerhard von Rad put it, "The experiences of the world were for Israel always divine experiences as well, and the experiences of God were for Israel experiences of the world."[8] This is because the created world, in all its intricacy and beauty, is a reflection of God's wisdom. Wisdom is woven into the fabric of the universe, and God invites creatures to become wise by paying attention to the patterns of creation. The goal of human wisdom is creaturely flourishing, which requires living according to the grain of God's universe. Once we start attending to the particular voice of biblical wisdom, we notice that its influence reaches far beyond the books usually designated as wisdom literature. Wisdom's witness extends from the Psalms and prophets all the way to the teachings of Jesus. In fact, John Barton claims that "the Bible is . . . mostly more like what biblical scholars call wisdom literature than oracular divine utterances."[9]

Proverbs sounds the dominant themes of Israel's wisdom tradition and provides what can be taken as "a majority report." Proverbs radiates confidence that God's wisdom, grandly personified in Proverbs' opening chapters as Woman Wisdom, can be found by those who seek her. Human flourishing and faithfulness depend on acquiring wisdom. Acquiring wisdom is not a human self-help project, but a creaturely response to the fearsome, gracious, and wise presence of God. God's gift to us as creatures is the space and time to become wise, that is, the opportunity to learn to

---

7   Barth's concern is that the Bible's "own life will be absorbed into the life of the church, that its free power will be transformed into the authority of the church, in short, that it will lose its character as a norm magisterially confronting the church." Karl Barth, *Church Dogmatics* I/1, eds. G. W. Bromiley and T. F. Torrance, 2nd ed. (Edinburgh: T&T Clark, 1975), 106.

8   Gerhard von Rad, *Wisdom in Israel* (Nashville: Abingdon, 1972), 62.

9   Barton, *People of the Book?*, 45.

live in the presence of the just and holy God so as to reflect in our modest creaturely ways God's own wisdom. Ecclesiastes, by contrast, supplies "a minority report," casting a critical eye over Israel's mainstream wisdom. Qohelet, the narrator of Ecclesiastes, also searches for Woman Wisdom, but finds her much more elusive. "I said, 'I will be wise,' but it was far from me. That which is, is far off, and deep, very deep; who can find it out?" (Eccl 7:23–24 NRSV). Ecclesiastes sounds the theological themes of the transcendent mystery of God, and therefore of the opaqueness of divine revelation. Ecclesiastes urges us to trust God, even when God's voice seems faint and far off. In their different ways, both books reflect Israel's struggle to find its footing in a time of cultural crisis, when the monarchy and the priesthood were no longer sources of authority and stability. Seeking wisdom is a distinctive and integral part of Israel's faith in God, neither contradicting nor derivative of its other emphases on law, cult, and sacred history.

However, until rather recently, Proverbs and Ecclesiastes were viewed by many Christian biblical scholars as stepchildren of the canon, awkward presences whose concerns were largely alien to the center of Israel's faith. As John Bright put it, "some parts of the Old Testament are far less clearly expressive of Israel's distinctive understanding of reality than others; some parts (and one thinks of such a book as Proverbs) seem to be only periph-erally related to it, while others (for example Ecclesiastes) even question its essential features."[10] After all, the big events in Israel's history—the covenant with Abraham, the exodus from Egypt, the giving of the law, the stories of the kings of Israel, the exile and return—are all missing from Proverbs and Ecclesiastes. As Paul Ricoeur notes, "Wisdom overflows the framework of the Covenant, which is also the framework of the election of Israel and the promise made to Israel."[11] Wisdom's reflection on God's presence and agency is not overtly connected to the covenant history of Israel, thus subverting a common Christian strategy for construing the unity of the whole biblical canon as a record of God's saving words and deeds.[12] Proverbs and Ecclesiastes are loose cannons within the canon.

It is fair to say that Christian theologians have generally *not* had Proverbs and Ecclesiastes in mind when constructing their theologies of

---

10   John Bright, *The Authority of the Old Testament* (Nashville: Abingdon, 1967), 136.
11   Paul Ricoeur, "Toward a Hermeneutic of the Idea of Revelation" *HTR* 70 (January–April 1977): 11.
12   Proverbs' repeated use of the Tetragrammaton in referring to God provides an implicit link to Israel's covenant history, but even this verbal link is missing in Ecclesiastes.

biblical revelation. Discussions of revelation tend to occur rather piecemeal in Christian theologies before the modern period. Full-fledged doctrines of revelation accompany modern theology's pervasive concern with the problem of knowing God. These modern doctrines of revelation have generally searched for some one underlying concept of revelation, or one underlying logic of the use of the expression *to reveal*, by which all the genres of Scripture can be systematized. Prophetic discourse has often been taken as paradigmatic: the word of the LORD comes to a particular person in a particular time and place, who is then deputized to speak in God's name. This theological drive toward a coherent, unified understanding of Scripture has had the unfortunate effect of homogenizing the biblical witness, and in particular of muting the distinctive voice of canonical wisdom.

Proverbs and Ecclesiastes may seem like a strange biblical model for theological reflection on the voice of God in Scripture, because on a straightforward reading these books do not present God as saying anything. They contain no claims for special visions or directives from God, no "Thus says the LORD." Proverbs and Ecclesiastes model and commend the discernment of God's presence in the world without appeal to verbal messages from God to a particular individual or people. In the prophetic paradigm, the voice of God is heard through the voice of the prophet. In the wisdom paradigm, God "speaks" through creation. God's "speech" is steady, it is heard, but it is not verbal. Al Wolters draws on the wisdom paradigm in his reflections on farming:

> The Lord teaches the farmer his business. There is a right way to plow, to sow, and to thresh, depending on the kind of grain he is growing. Dill, cumin, wheat and spelt must all be treated differently. A good farmer knows that, and this knowledge too is from the Lord, for the Lord teaches him. This is not a teaching through the revelation of Moses and the Prophets, but a teaching through the revelation of creation— the soil, the seeds, and the tools of his daily experience. It is by listening to the voice of God in the work of his hands that the farmer finds the way of agricultural wisdom.[13]

Like the faithful farmer, the sages of Proverbs and Ecclesiastes acknowledge humanity's radical dependence on God in the search for wisdom and commend a lifelong attention to the voice of God in the experiences of everyday life.

---

13 Al Wolters, *Creation Regained: A Transforming View of the World* (Grand Rapids: Eerdmans, 1985), 28.

While there are no words explicitly ascribed to God in Proverbs, perhaps nowhere else in the Bible is there so much focus on the importance and function of human words. The book of Proverbs testifies to the power of words again and again. It says that a word fitly spoken is like apples of gold in a setting of silver (Prov 25:11). It says that even a soft word is strong enough to break bones (Prov 25:15b). Words can pierce like a sword and sting like vinegar in a wound (Prov 25:18, 20). Words can refresh the exhausted and persuade the powerful—they have enormous capacity to delight, to rebuke, to instruct, and encourage. Words also have the capacity to do great harm.[14] Proverbs and Ecclesiastes share a worldview permeated by faith in God's active and mysterious presence in the world, and draw on the power of human words to reflect on this divine presence and shape an appropriate human response to it. These biblical books offer human words of witness to God; they do not claim to be a record of God's words to humans. If John Barton is right and the Bible is mostly like this, human words of witness to God's ongoing nonverbal presence and activity, then our theological reflection on the metaphor of God's voice needs to take place in this larger scriptural context. Faithfulness to God's voice in Scripture requires attention to Scripture's various textures, not attempts to conform that voice to a particular theological model.

To think about this larger scriptural context, it is instructive to compare two biblical texts. The first is Psalms 19:1–4:

> The heavens are telling the glory of God;
> *and the firmament proclaims his handiwork.*
> Day to day pours forth speech,
> *and night to night declares knowledge.*
> There is no speech, nor are there words;
> *their voice is not heard;*
> yet their voice goes out through all the earth,
> *and their words to the end of the world. (NRSV)*

In this psalm, the voice of the whole creation praises God's glorious work. Nature also voices God's manifestations to creatures in the Psalms. In Psalms 29:3–9, for example, thunder is repeatedly referred to as "the voice of the LORD." It makes no sense in either case to ask whether the voice that shakes the wilderness is soprano or baritone, whether the words that go to the end of the world are in Hebrew or Hungarian. In

---

14   The New Testament wisdom book, James, contains a similar acknowledgment of the power of the human tongue (Jas 3:2–12).

the biblical wisdom paradigm, the voice of God is like the voice of the heavens in Psalm 19, or the voice that shakes the wilderness in Psalm 29.

The second text to consider is 2 Peter 1:16–18:

> For we did not follow cleverly devised myths when we made known to you the power and coming of our Lord Jesus Christ, but we had been eyewitnesses of his majesty. For he received honor and glory from God the Father when that voice was conveyed to him by the Majestic Glory, saying, "This is my Son, my Beloved, with whom I am well pleased." We ourselves heard this voice come from heaven, while we were with him on the holy mountain. (NRSV)

Here it does make sense to ask whether the voice conveyed to the author from heaven is soprano or baritone, whether the words spoken are in Hebrew or Hungarian. The author of 2 Peter is fending off skepticism about the validity of his community's eschatological teachings. He defends himself by claiming to be an eyewitness of Christ's transfiguration. But his apologetic reaches its rhetorical height in his claim to have been an "ear witness." Unlike the synoptic accounts of the transfiguration, in which Peter is sleepy (Luke 9:32), overcome with fear (Matt 17:6–8), or terrified and confused (Mark 9:5–6), the author of 2 Peter presents himself as "a conscious and intelligent recipient of a sacred communication; the nonidentification of James and John heightens [his] unique position as witness."[15] The author claims to have personally heard the voice of God speaking an explicit, verbal message. Therefore his teaching is certainly not conjecture or myth, as his opponents charge. It would be even better if biblical scholars would rise up with one voice and assure us that the author of 2 Peter was actually Peter the apostle.

This second text illustrates the lure of an audible, verbal message direct from God. It satisfies our perennial human hunger for certainty and clarity in our faith, seemingly leaving little room for confusion and disagreement. To paraphrase Warfield, there is something deeply reassuring about thinking of the whole Bible as the result of the living voice of God speaking audibly in all its parts directly to the biblical writers. On this model, *all* the biblical writers can say, "we ourselves heard this voice," whether whispered in their ears or proclaimed from the heavens.

This desire for a sacred text that is uniformly oracular in origin and

---

15 Jerome Neyrey, "The Apologetic Use of the Transfiguration in 2 Peter 1:16–21," *CBQ* 42 (1980): 509.

function is understandable for reasons of both piety and theological consistency, and has encouraged the production of texts like the book of *Jubilees*, a second-century BCE text that presents itself as the divine revelation which God communicated to Moses through an angel on Mt. Sinai. Part of what scholars call "the Rewritten Bible," *Jubilees* takes the variegated biblical material and fixes discrepancies, solves puzzles, and streamlines it into a single oracle. God's voice in the book of *Jubilees* is clear and consistent, so unlike the voices of the irreducibly distinct texts we find in Scripture, which steadfastly resist wholesale assimilation to the model of divine communication to humanity. For the most part, the texts of Scripture do not claim to be a record of God's verbal communication; instead they present human words of witness to God, the fruit of a living encounter with the Holy One. It does violence to Scripture to view its narratives, laws, hymns, proverbs, and letters as merely "a rhetorical façade which it would be possible to pull down in order to reveal some thought content that is indifferent to its literary vehicle."[16] Our attempts to hear God's voice in Scripture must reckon with the texts as they actually come to us. As Eberhard Busch notes, "The witness of Scripture is there for us only in the fullness of the various witnesses, which resists our manipulating grasp. These witnesses need to be seen, each in its own particular color."[17] To change the metaphor, the various biblical witnesses need to be heard, each in its own particular voice.

GOD'S LARGER ECONOMY

As the text from 2 Peter illustrates, the "voice of God" metaphor is most at home in theologies that center around God's historical action. God's voice accompanies God's mighty acts in history. This modern Christian preoccupation with history has governed theological interpretation of God's economic dealings with the world. Within this theological framework, communication is God's paradigmatic means of relating to human creatures and human redemption is God's paradigmatic act. Emil Brunner can even say that "The cosmic element in the Bible is never anything more than the scenery in which the history of mankind takes place."[18] This

---

16   Ricoeur, "Toward a Hermeneutic of the Idea of Revelation," 15.
17   Eberhard Busch, "Reformed Strength in Its Denominational Weakness," in *Reformed Theology: Identity and Ecumenicity*, ed. Wallace Alston and Michael Welker (Grand Rapids: Eerdmans, 2003), 24.
18   Emil Brunner, *Revelation and Reason* (Philadelphia: Westminster, 1946), 33n.

preoccupation with God's words and deeds in history has truncated theological understanding of the scope of God's economy and flattened biblical interpretation. It has obscured the fact that God's special purposes for Israel and the church are always penultimate to God's larger purposes for the life and well-being of all creatures. God's work of redemption is for the sake of God's creation, not the other way around. God's economy of communication with humanity falls within the larger frame of God's economy of creating, sustaining, and embracing the entire cosmic order.

Attention to Israel's wisdom traditions helps restore this fuller picture of God's economic dealings, because the theological horizon of Israel's wisdom books is creation, not redemption. In these books, the main emphasis is not on "originating creation,"[19] but on God's ongoing work of creation, in which God continues to relate to and sustain all God has made. Creation is best understood theologically as "original grace"[20] or the "grace of radical dependence."[21] Along with God's grace of reconciliation and consummation, this grace is also a constant for the life and identity of humanity, and our faith in God is impoverished when God's creative grace is neglected or denied. Our creaturely existence is not to be conflated with the reality of human sinfulness, and so viewed as something to be overcome. Nor should it be viewed as a theologically neutral "given" awaiting the advent of grace. Our creaturely identity is an ongoing divine gift, neither erased nor rendered superfluous by God's work of redemption. Israel's search for wisdom is the search for creaturely faithfulness before God. The knowledge of God cultivated in accordance with the teachings of the sages is aimed at earthly life lived according to the Creator's gracious purposes.

God's creative concern and engagement do not stop at the cultural and ethnic boundaries of Israel, nor does the human search for wisdom. Carole Fontaine finds in Israel's wisdom traditions an "intellectual ecumenism," a willingness to share intellectual resources across boundaries of culture and religion.[22] Egypt and Mesopotamia were the motherlands

---

19 Terence E. Fretheim, *God and World in the Old Testament: A Relational Theology of Creation* (Nashville: Abingdon, 2005), 5. Fretheim distinguishes three modes of God's creative work: originating, continuing, and completing.

20 David B. Burrell, "Creation as Original Grace," in Philip J. Rossi, ed., *God, Grace, and Creation*, The Annual Publication of the College Theology Society, vol. 55 (Maryknoll: Orbis Books, 2010), 97–106.

21 Philip J. Rossi, "Creation as Grace of Radical Dependence," in Rossi, *God, Grace, and Creation*, ix–xviii.

22 Carole R. Fontaine, *Smooth Words: Women, Proverbs and Performance in Biblical Wisdom*, JSOT Supplement 356 (Sheffield: Sheffield Academic, 2002), 19.

of wisdom in the ancient Near East, and there is general scholarly agreement that Israel's wisdom is internationally inspired. Fontaine notes that the sages of Israel "were wise precisely because they honed their thought on the words of the sages and the experience of the cultures that preceded and surrounded them."[23] In the "Words to the Wise" section of Proverbs (Prov 22:17–24:34), for example, scholars have discovered direct literary dependence on the Egyptian wisdom text known as Instruction of Amenemope, written late in the second millennium BCE.[24] It is not clear exactly how this literary contact between Egypt and Israel was made, but it is likely that the royal courts in both countries played a role. Israel's piety was capacious enough to include theological reflection that was not tied to Israel's self-understanding as a special covenant people of God. God is the God of all people and of all creation, and so Israel confidently expected God's voice to sound beyond the borders of its national experience. As Leo Perdue insists, "Divine activity and providence cannot be limited to Israel's election and history."[25]

While this transcultural feature of Israel's wisdom literature has sometimes led Christian theologians to caricature it "as a pagan religious understanding that crept uninvited into the dwelling places of sacred Scripture,"[26] this feature should instead prompt a rethinking of how God speaks to us, both through Scripture and through human experience. In Proverbs' "Words to the Wise," Israel is overhearing what God said to the Egyptians. This direct literary dependence on Egyptian wisdom in the book of Proverbs plays havoc with the traditional theological distinction between general and special revelation. According to this distinction, God is made known in a general way through nature and conscience, in a special way through words and deeds recorded in Scripture, and unsurpassably in Jesus Christ. So should we see "Words to the Wise" as general revelation, since they arise from the human experience of the Egyptians, or as special revelation, because they are in the Bible?

A better theological strategy is to soften this hard-and-fast distinction, because it is not reflective of the biblical witness. What the Bible shows us is that the metaphor of God's Word is much broader than what

---

23   Fontaine, *Smooth Words*, 19–20.

24   See James B. Pritchard, ed., *The Ancient Near East: An Anthology of Texts and Pictures* (Princeton: Princeton University Press, 1958), 237–43.

25   Leo G. Perdue, *Wisdom Literature: A Theological History* (Louisville: Westminster John Knox, 2007), 343.

26   Perdue, *Wisdom Literature*, 347.

God is said to have declared or revealed verbally: it includes what God's people have borrowed from their neighbors and the results of their own reflections. For example, many of Israel's laws have parallels in ancient Near Eastern law codes and reflect "self-evident standards of morality, a shared perception of that which is right, a basic sense for the created order of things."[27] As Terence Fretheim observes, "human constructs for the ordering of community may be revealing of the divine intention quite apart from the reception of a specific divine directive to that effect."[28] The distinction between revealed law and so-called "natural law" should not be overdrawn. God's voice goes out through all the earth, and is heard in many and various ways.

Assimilating all of Scripture to the model of special revelation has broader theological problems. The special revelation model is linked to certain theological assumptions about Israel's relation to the other nations of the world. Being the beneficiary of God's special revelation privileges Israel and sets her apart from her neighbors. The dire warnings in the Torah and the prophets against adopting the beliefs and practices of other peoples reinforce this theological perspective and then are extended to serve as a theological model for how Christians are to live in the world as the guardians of biblical revelation.

Proverbs' and Ecclesiastes' approach to knowing God through God's universal operation in creation suggests a different theological model of Israel's relations to other peoples. Instead of calling Israel to separate itself from and reject the ways of its neighbors, these books model a critical acceptance of the insights and teachings of other nations. What God intends Israel to learn about creaturely life binds them to people from other cultures and religious traditions, making Israel their debtor in her search for wisdom. As John Collins observes, "This international character is a very important aspect of proverbial wisdom. The fact that the sages could speak of their God in such an international idiom was a confident affirmation that their God was not the God of Israel alone, but of all humanity, and was in principle accessible to all."[29]

The people of God, whether in ancient Israel or today, have never existed in political, religious, or intellectual isolation from their neighbors. Proverbs' appropriation of Egyptian wisdom reflects better than the

---

27 Fretheim, God and World, 141.
28 Ibid., 137.
29 John J. Collins, Proverbs, Ecclesiastes (Atlanta: John Knox, 1980), 7.

rhetoric of passages like Deuteronomy 7:1–6 what scholars suspect is the real history of ancient Israel's relations with its neighbors—not a total and violent separation, but a complex mix of cultural assimilation and differentiation. Faithfulness requires discernment about when cultural adhesion is appropriate and when cultural resistance and separation are needed. The search for wisdom is a constant in human life, and the wisdom found within any particular religious tradition can never claim to be fully "homegrown." It is always, to a degree that is impossible to measure precisely, imported from or at least genetically modified by the traditions and teachings of other communities. Israel's wisdom traditions remind us that there is in fact a wide range of biblical approaches towards the practices and texts of religious others. Christians concerned to privilege the category of special revelation have tended to adopt the oppositional tone of some parts of Scripture, while ignoring the rest.

WISDOM AS NATURAL THEOLOGY?

We have seen how one strategy for establishing the validity of Christian knowledge of God is to insist that the Bible enshrines God's special revelation, even God's very own words, and thus can be regarded as a deposit of true information about God and God's purposes. Aside from courting the theological danger of a deism that renders Scripture a self-standing revelatory agent, this account does not do justice to God's presence in Scripture. As John Barton notes, "the biblical writers often argue not from what God has declared or revealed, but from what is apparent on the basis of the nature of human life in society."[30] That is, the biblical writers pursue a kind of natural theology.

This pursuit is especially evident in the wisdom traditions. Israel's sages listen for God's voice by observing the patterns in the created order and reflecting on human experience. In their teaching, they drew on a fund of social and ethical perception that was common across peoples of different cultural and religious backgrounds. Israel's sages claim no awareness of God, or capacity to know God, that is theirs just by using their natural faculties. However and wherever human wisdom is found, abroad or at home, in royal courts, in scribal academies, or in the household, the pursuit of it is not to be dissociated from trust in God's wise

---

30   John Barton, *Ethics and the Old Testament* (Harrisburg: Trinity Press International, 1998), 61.

and active presence in the created world. Another way to say it is that in Israel's wisdom traditions all human searching for wisdom occurs inside a relation already established by God, who is the source of all wisdom, and indeed of the very lives of those who search for it. "God is in heaven and you are on earth," Ecclesiastes 5:2 insists. God is known on God's terms, not on ours. Since knowledge of God is God-given, the pursuit of wisdom in Proverbs and Ecclesiastes is fraught with moral peril: "You see one who is wise in his own eyes? There is more hope for a fool than for him" (Prov 26:12). For the sages, all searching for wisdom in ordering human life takes place within the framework of faith in God's wise ordering of creation.

This is quite different from forms of natural theology in the modern period that embrace a foundationalist fantasy of a universal grounding for beliefs about God and the world in the deliverances of an autonomous human reason.[31] On this model, Christian theology must demonstrate its intellectual respectability by appeal to generically acceptable evidence, whether within the natural world or within human consciousness or history, as a justification for its efforts. This project reflects an Enlightenment quest in Christian theology to be rid of the "scandal of particularity" by establishing a supposedly universal rational and moral order accessible to all persons. This epistemic foundation can then serve as a propaedeutic for further special claims Christian theologians might want to make.

According to the natural theology of Israel's sages, the work of God the creator is not less hidden from human beings than any other dimension of God's work. Here too the knowledge of God is dependent on God's initiative. The sages listen for the voice of God as God speaks in and through the created order. The sages' discovery of the moral regularities of human life, though always hedged in by ambiguities and an awareness of their human limitations, is understood in terms of God's active commitment to human well-being. Thus the natural theology in play in Israel's search for wisdom has a deeply self-involving, existential character. Israel's wisdom instruction is an intellectual activity, requiring analysis and the clarification of concepts. But what is analyzed and clarified are not the abstract principles of the universe but human attitudes and forms of life.[32] The goal is *phronesis*, practical know-how, not *theoria*. In Michael Foster's words, it

---

31   See the critique of this approach in David B. Burrell, *Faith and Freedom: A Interfaith Perspective* (Chichester: Wiley-Blackwell, 2004), 200.

32   David H. Kelsey, *Eccentric Existence: A Theological Anthropology* (Louisville: Westminster John Knox, 2009), 77.

is inquiry that involves "something like a repentance in the sphere of the intellect."[33] Biblical wisdom is oriented towards a practical understanding of how to relate oneself and the world to the fuller, truer order of God's creative presence.

Karl Barth, the arch foe of natural theology, might have let his appreciation for Israel's wisdom traditions complicate his blanket condemnations of the natural theology enterprise. "Divine wisdom," he asserts, "is obviously the meaning and ground of creation and therefore of the sphere in which man can live. The whole art of living and understanding life consists in heeding and accepting divine wisdom and in this way becoming wise."[34] The divine wisdom that grounds and gives meaning to creation speaks in a distinctive register, in that its purpose is not to announce God's reconciliation of sinners or God's promised consummation of the world; it is instead aimed at the flourishing of creaturely life. In Israel's wisdom traditions, natural theology receives biblical endorsement. Scripture directs us outside of itself to heed God's voice speaking to us in creation.

Barth and others in Reformation traditions have worried that the pursuit of natural theology can lead to arrogant, demonic claims about our place in God's purposes. But surely the neglect of the knowledge of God given in the natural order has also led to unfaithfulness, including a pervasive anthropocentrism in our theological constructions. As Ellen Davis points out,

> In this century, powerful technological knowledge has proliferated, yet it is not sufficiently tempered and disciplined by a discerning understanding of how God has ordered the world. If technology is to be helpful and not destructive, then we—not only as scientists and technicians but also as ordinary consumers of technology—must learn to *contemplate* the world and ask what is God's intention for it, and how that sets limits on our own tinkering with the world.[35]

Following the lead of Proverbs and Ecclesiastes and cultivating a broader understanding of how God speaks, one more attuned to the voice of God in creaturely reality, might be a start.

---

33 Quoted in Kelsey, *Eccentric Existence*, 77.
34 Karl Barth, *Church Dogmatics* II/1, eds. G. W. Bromiley and T. F. Torrance (Edinburgh: T&T Clark, 1957), 430.
35 Ellen F. Davis, *Proverbs, Ecclesiastes, and the Song of Songs*, Westminster Bible Companion (Louisville: Westminster John Knox, 2000), 5.

A VOICE THAT GOES OUT
THROUGH ALL THE EARTH

There is a beautiful icon of the fourth-century exegete John Chrysostom interpreting the letters of the apostle Paul. The iconographer depicts Chrysostom with the biblical text on a stand in front of him, holding a scroll on which he is writing. But the text of Paul's letters is evidently not enough, because behind Chrysostom stands the apostle Paul, whispering in his ear. This is our situation too. We have the text, but we need illumination to interpret Scripture aright. God's voice is heard in many and various ways in the text of Scripture, and supremely in Jesus Christ, who is the power and wisdom of God, God's "word fitly spoken." But just as we need to pay honest attention to God's voice in the parts of Scripture that do not fit our systematic constructs, so we need to acknowledge our capacity to mishear and drown out God's voice as God continues to speak to us through Scripture. We need the Spirit's guidance to hear God's voice because, as John Calvin put it, "without the illumination of the Holy Spirit, the Word can do nothing."[36]

Mark Noll has written a sobering new book called *In the Beginning Was the Word*, a fascinating account of the role of the Bible in American public life from the beginnings of European colonial presence through the eighteenth century. It is sobering because Noll shows in convincing detail the disastrous consequences of "biblicism, the attempt to believe and act on the basis of 'the Bible alone' that always attended the Protestant exaltation of scriptural authority."[37] Revering Scripture as "a God-given fulcrum outside of space and time"[38] ironically made it all too easy to take Scripture prisoner. Confident that they heard God's voice, American Christians repeatedly raided the storehouse of Scripture in service of Whig political ideals, imperialist adventures, and the defense of chattel slavery. What Noll finds sorely missing among these devout and sincere Christians is the capacity for self-criticism in their use of Scripture.[39] Self-criticism in our approach to Scripture is a virtue for us to cultivate as well. Acknowledging the interests and cultural borrowings of the biblical writers prompts us to lay bare our own.

---

36   John Calvin, *Institutes of the Christian Religion*, ed. John T. McNeill, trans. Ford Lewis Battles, LCC (Philadelphia: Westminster, 1960), 3.2.33, p. 580.

37   Mark A. Noll, *In the Beginning Was the Word: The Bible in American Public Life, 1492–1783* (Oxford: Oxford University Press, 2016), 324.

38   Noll, *In the Beginning*, 326.

39   Ibid., 331.

And when we are tempted to say with the author of 2 Peter that "we ourselves have heard this voice come from heaven," the bracing skepticism of Ecclesiastes about the human ability to clearly hear God's voice may be just what we need.

CHAPTER 5

THAT WAS THEN, THIS IS NOW: READING HEBREWS RETROACTIVELY

MYK HABETS

INTRODUCTION

I have long had a fascination with the book of Hebrews; its emphasis upon the high priestly ministry of Jesus Christ, and its talk of such subjects as angels (1; 13) and Melchizedek (7), for instance, have made it a favorite of mine.[1] More recently I have come to appreciate it for another reason, namely the way in which the author of Hebrews is able to hear the voice of the triune God through the words of Holy Scripture. As a seminary professor, an elder in my local Baptist church, and a friend to many fellow-believers, I have to admit to being a little less than optimistic about the ability of congregants in the church today to hear the voice of God in the Word of God, as the author of Hebrews holds out. As Kenda Creasy Dean, a youth specialist, has written in regard to today's youth (but I think it holds true for adults too, and not just in America), many congregants appear to have been victims of what she calls "theological malpractice." Her comment is worth hearing in context:

---

1   There are many other elements unique to Hebrews, of course; see Jon C. Laansma, "Hebrews, Book of," in *DTIB*, ed. Kevin J. Vanhoozer (Grand Rapids: Baker Academic, 2005), 279.

What if the blasé religiosity of most American teenagers is not the result of poor communication but the result of excellent communication of a watered-down gospel so devoid of God's self-giving love in Jesus Christ, so immune to the sending love of the Holy Spirit that it might not be Christianity at all? What if the church models a way of life that asks, not passionate surrender but ho-hum assent? What if we are preaching moral affirmation, a feel-better faith, and a hands-off God instead of the decisively involved, impossibly loving, radically sending God of Abraham and Mary, who desired us enough to enter creation in Jesus Christ and whose Spirit is active in the church and in the world today? If this is the case—if theological malpractice explains teenagers' half-hearted religious identities—then perhaps most young people practice Moralistic Therapeutic Deism not because they reject Christianity, but because this is the only "Christianity" they know.[2]

The audience to which Hebrews was addressed, we are told, were Christians, perhaps in Rome, who were being tempted away from the gospel with immoral behavior (13:4), strange teachings (13:9), and outright apostasy (3:12), to name but a few behaviors.[3] Not quite Moralistic Therapeutic Deism, but nonetheless serious. In response, the author of Hebrews gives them a "word of exhortation" (13:22), and he does so, primarily, by recalling the words of Scripture but—and this is the significant thing—literally *hearing* such Scripture as the present living Word of the triune God.

Starting where the writer of Hebrews starts, at the beginning, with the opening words of the letter or sermon or book (take your pick), we read:[4]

God, after he spoke long ago to the fathers in the prophets in many portions and in many ways, in these last days has spoken to us in his Son, whom he appointed heir of all things, through whom also he made the world (Heb 1:1–2).[5]

---

2   Kenda Creasy Dean, *Almost Christian: What the Faith of Our Teenagers Is Telling the American Church* (Oxford: Oxford University Press, 2010), 12.

3   Paul Ellingworth, *The Epistle to the Hebrews: A Commentary on the Greek Text* (Grand Rapids: Eerdmans, 1993), 78–79, neatly classifies the dangers threatening the recipients of Hebrews into three groups: (1) passive dangers, (2) active dangers, and (3) external and outward pressures.

4   It is debated in scholarship whether or not Hebrews was originally a letter. For instance, F. F. Bruce, *The Epistle to the Hebrews*, rev., NICNT (Grand Rapids: Eerdmans, 1990), 3, 25, sees it as a sermon, as does William L. Lane, *Hebrews 1–8*, WBC 47a (Dallas: Word, 1991), lxxv. Peter T. O'Brien, *The Letter to the Hebrews,* The Pillar New Testament Commentary (Grand Rapids: Eerdmans, 2010), 20–22, has one of the better summaries of the issues. A resolution to this debate does not affect the argument of this essay and so I will leave it to the experts to battle it out. The same goes for the authorship of Hebrews and its *Sitz im Leben*.

5   All Scripture quotations taken from the NASB (The Lockman Foundation, 1997), unless otherwise stated.

Here God the Father (and I think we are right to infer this is God *the Father* speaking, given it is speech about his Son), spoke: past tense.[6] The Father spoke through prophets: human instruments; created media. Second Peter 1:21 of course is the clearest testament to this, "men moved by the Holy Spirit spoke from God." The Father speaks the Word by means of the Holy Spirit. This is a familiar formula that theologians have come to make much of, and rightly so. We see this in the creation account in Genesis 1–2 and echoed in many texts thereafter. From such texts theologians develop doctrines of inspiration—the Father's speaking of the Word by means of the Holy Spirit which is then revealed to men and women in personal and propositional form such that God's self-revelation is made to creation, summarized by 2 Timothy 3:16, "All Scripture is inspired (θεόπνευστος) by God." The result is that Hebrews affirms in 1:1–2 that through prophets and in many and diverse ways, it is God who is speaking and it is God who is revealing himself. The first thing to note, then, is that God reveals himself in all acts of genuine revelation.

Hebrews makes good on this premise of God's self-revelation by going on to assert that the living God who has spoken in the past continues to speak in the present as Father, Son, and Holy Spirit. As such, communities of the faithful can hear his voice and obey. Hebrews 4:12 beautifully summarizes this when it rewrites Isaiah 55:11:

> For the word of God is living and active and sharper than any two-edged sword, and piercing as far as the division of soul and spirit, of both joints and marrow, and able to judge the thoughts and intentions of the heart.

The suggestion is not that the author of Hebrews consciously sought to re-write Isaiah 55:11,[7] but, rather, steeped in the Hebrew Scriptures, the dynamic, powerful, and divine nature of God's word continues to manifest its presence in the event of revelation. The word is living because God is living: "His Word is 'living and active' (4:12) like God himself (3:12; 9:14; 10:31; 12:22), and by it he speaks to his people now."[8]

A key feature of Hebrews then is the emphasis on God's present word.

---

6   Hebrews 1:5 and 12:9 are the only passages in which the term "Father" is applied to God.

7   "So will My word be which goes forth from My mouth; It will not return to Me empty, Without accomplishing what I desire, And without succeeding in the matter for which I sent it" (Isa 55:11).

8   Peter T. O'Brien, "God as the Speaking God: 'Theology' in the Letter to the Hebrews," in *Understanding the Times: New Testament Studies in the 21st Century; Essays in Honor of D. A. Carson*, eds. Andreas J. Köstenberger and Robert W. Yarbrough (Wheaton: Crossway, 2011), 198.

Hebrews treats biblical quotations not as the Word written but as the spoken Word of the tripersonal God. Where other New Testament writers such as Paul introduce biblical quotations with such formulas as "it is written" (i.e., Rom 9:13, 33; 11:8), "the Scripture says" (i.e., Gal 4:30), or "Moses says," (i.e., Rom 10:19), the author of Hebrews puts such texts directly into the mouth of God (the Father) or God the Son, or God the Holy Spirit. While not alone in this regard, Hebrews offers a comprehensive example in the canon of experiencing a *prior* word of God as the hearing of a *present* word.

To make sense of such phenomena this paper will utilize and explain a "retroactive hermeneutic of triune discourse." This hermeneutic is also available to the faith community today such that when reading Holy Scripture we too can hear the Word of God in the present tense and experience the event of God's self-revelation. In what follows I set myself a modest task. First, I simply want to identify and name what Hebrews is doing with Old Testament texts. Second, I want to identify what biblical commentators have made of such features. And finally, I wish to show that what I term a retroactive reading of Scripture holds out the promise for readers today to hear the Word written as a present and real Word of God spoken to them today.

HEBREWS AND HEARING THE VOICE OF GOD

The Letter to the Hebrews is one of the most unique and difficult books in Holy Scripture. As William Lane expressed it, "Hebrews is a delight for the person who enjoys puzzles. Its form is unusual, its setting in life is uncertain, and its argument is unfamiliar."[9] Its use of Scripture, we may add, is also distinctive. The use of the Old Testament in Hebrews is a topic of much interest and much debate. It is not my brief to trace a history of interpretation at this point; I leave that to more qualified biblical scholars and even textual critics. It is worth mentioning, however, that Hebrews is steeped in Old Testament citations and allusions, almost always from the Septuagint (or what Jon Laansma calls "a Greek *Vorlage*"[10]), and the author to the Hebrews takes liberty with texts, at numerous points, in order to make his theological and pastoral points. Every chapter of this book is marked with explicit or implicit references to the Old Testament. As

---

9   Lane, *Hebrews 1–8*, xlvii.
10   Laansma, "Hebrews," 276.

many have pointed out before me, the author of Hebrews expresses a high view of the continuity of old and new covenant revelation, he presupposes an essential unity and also a progressive development between the old and new economies of redemption, and his detailed knowledge of the Old Testament is impressive and was obviously used deliberately to convince his readers/listeners of the truth of his exhortation. Hebrews contains so many allusions, references, and quotations that it is near impossible to accurately count them. Merely as an example and indication of the scope of the use of the Old Testament, Lane proposes that there are:

> thirty-one explicit quotations and four more implicit quotations, a minimum of thirty-seven allusions, nineteen instances where OT material is summarized, and thirteen more where a biblical name or topic is cited without reference to a specific context.[11]

Unlike Paul who typically introduces Old Testament texts with "as it has been written" (καθὼς γέγραπται), the writer to the Hebrews never uses the term "to write" (γράφειν), instead using the verb "to say" (λέγει), especially in the present tense, "saying" (λέγων). By making this simple but profound move, Hebrews *hears* the Old Testament as God speaking in the present tense and in the active voice, thus dynamically, and not as a past event and thus statically. As Lane highlights, "Although the representation of a biblical quotation as the word that God is speaking to the audience *at that moment* can be documented from other Jewish-hellenistic [sic] homilies . . . this manner of presenting the OT text is without parallel elsewhere in the NT."[12] By using this strategy Hebrews cuts behind the human speaker or author of a text, to God, the real speaker. And surely that is what Scripture (its words and canon) actually is, a created media through which God's voice might be clearly heard.

More specifically,

> In twenty of the thirty-five quotations in Hebrews, God is the grammatical subject in the context (1:5*a*, 5*b*, 6, 7, 8–9, 10–12, 13; 4:4, 5:5, 6; 6:14; 7:17, 21; 8:5, 8–12; 10:30*a*, 30*b*, 37–38; 12:26; 13:5). Four quotations are assigned to the Son (2:12, 13*a*, 13*b*; 10:5–7), and five others are attributed to the Holy Spirit (3:7*b*–11; presumably 4:3, 5, 7; 10:16–17).[13]

---

11   Lane, *Hebrews 1–8*, cxvi.

12   Ibid., cxvii.

13   Ibid. Exact numbers depend upon the texts used and the definitions adopted. See Richard Longenecker, *Biblical Exegesis in the Apostolic Period*, 2nd ed. (Grand Rapids: Eerdmans, 1999), 147, and Pamela Eisenbaum, *The Jewish Heroes of Christian History: Hebrews 11 in Literary Context*, SBLDS 156 (Atlanta: Scholars Press, 1997), 92.

Lane notes the ways in which the author of Hebrews exhibits the rabbinic reading practices of his contemporaries in schools and synagogues throughout the diaspora. None of this is exceptional; the use of reinforcement, middot, typology, and homiletical midrash, for example, are all clearly attested in contemporary use. In reference to Hebrews 2:12, Leon Morris can simply state that, in light of Christ's use of Psalm 22 on the cross in the cry of dereliction (Ps 22:18 / Mark 15:34), "It was thus the most natural thing in the world for the writer of Hebrews to see Jesus as the speaker in this psalm."[14] I wonder how many contemporary readers could easily share that sentiment. Such evidence leads Lane to conclude,

> The determining factor for the distinctiveness of his interpretation of Scripture is not the methodology he employed in appropriating the OT text but his Christian theology of the interrelationships among history, eschatology, and revelation.[15]

It is important to note that the way Hebrews conforms to the Judaic tradition of homiletical midrash presupposes a shared understanding between the author and his audience over the ways in which God has revealed himself. Hebrews clearly exhibits "C. H. Dodd's thesis that the principal Old Testament quotations of the New Testament are not isolated proof texts, but carry their contexts with them by implication."[16] It also presupposes "certain shared assumptions about how the voice of God is recovered."[17] One cannot help but reflect upon the relative absence of such shared presuppositions amongst congregants in churches today, and to what extent this causes a breakdown in communication between the preacher and congregants, and more importantly, between the congregants and the hearing of the Word of God. My earlier reference to the work of Creasy Dean sought to make the point that unlike previous generations of Bible readers, we have forgotten the old ways and neglected to follow the rules or guiding principles for reading Holy Scripture.

Twice in Hebrews an Old Testament text is appropriated and put into the mouth of Christ; Hebrews 2:12 cites Psalm 22:22 and ascribes it to Jesus Christ speaking in the Old Testament, and Hebrews 10:5–10 does the same thing with Psalms 40:6–8. The same thing occurs with reference

---

14 Leon Morris, "Hebrews," in *The Expositor's Bible Commentary*, ed. Frank E. Gaebelein (Grand Rapids: Zondervan, 1981), 12:28.

15 Lane, *Hebrews 1–8*, cxxiv.

16 Bruce, *Hebrews*, 82, in reference to C. H. Dodd, *According to the Scriptures: The Sub-Structure of New Testament Theology* (London: Nisbet and Co., 1952), 20.

17 Lane, *Hebrews 1–8*, cxxvii.

to the Holy Spirit. Hebrews 3:7–11 cites Psalm 95 and says this is not ultimately David speaking then but the Holy Spirit speaking now. By way of explanation, and commenting on Hebrews 3:7–11, Calvin notes, "*As the Holy Ghost Saith*. It is far more effective in touching the heart than to quote the name of David. It is useful to accustom oneself to this form of speaking, so that we remember that it is the words of God and not of men which are found in the books of the prophets."[18] We see the same thing in Hebrews 9:8 and 10:15. The writer to the Hebrews is not denying the human subjects through whom the Word of God came; for instance, in Hebrews 4:7 he clearly recognizes David as the human author of Scripture, but he[19] is wanting to get beyond the human authors of Scripture, or behind them, to the real source of the words—the triune God. And the author of Hebrews wishes to do that so that the community of faith might hear God's Word again, as a present reality and a personal address.

The author of Hebrews states that as good as God's revelation of himself was in the old dispensation, it is fully and finally made manifest in the person of Jesus Christ, the beloved Son. In a helpful summary Laansma reminds us:

> The common thread [in Heb 1:4–4:13] is the need properly to receive the revelation (word) of God in the Son. Thus, statements of the preexistent and exalted Son's superiority to the prophets, angelic mediators of the old covenant (2:2), and the lawgiver Moses are capped by an extended appeal to receive God's word of promise in obedient faith (3:7–4:11), and finally by a most emphatic affirmation of the ineluctability of God's judging word (4:12–13). All of this summons the readers sharply to attentiveness before the fresh teaching of 5:1 and following.[20]

As Calvin put it more succinctly, "It was not a part of the Word that Christ brought, but the last closing Word."[21] Christ, in fact, does not simply come to speak the words of God; if so he would remain simply a prophet, and prophets, we have already been told in Hebrew 1:1, are good

---

18   John Calvin, *The Epistle of Paul the Apostle to the Hebrews and The First and Second Epistles of St Peter*, Calvin's Commentaries, eds. David W. Torrance and Thomas F. Torrance, trans. William B. Johnston (Grand Rapids: Eerdmans, 1963), 38.

19   While Priscilla has been suggested as the author of Hebrews, it is almost certain the author was a man, given the self-reference at Heb 11:32 with a masculine, singular participle. We do well to follow the conclusion of Origen when he said, "who wrote the Epistle, God only knows the truth" (Eusebius, *Ecclesiastical History*, 6.25.14).

20   Laansma, "Hebrews," 277.

21   Calvin, *Hebrews*, 6.

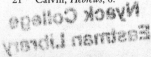

but not great. Christ, by contrast, is *the* Word of God who as the Word speaks the Word. Furthermore, Christ the Word has been resurrected and has ascended to the right hand of God the Father (Heb 1:3) from where he governs the universe (Heb 1:2). The ascended Christ is thus alive and well, and as the living Word he continues to speak, to reveal, and to reconcile. As the Logos, the Word who is with God, toward God, and is God, as we know from John 1:1, he is the depth dimension behind all the words of God.

Hebrews, in fact, has a sophisticated and complex notion of triune speech. The Father-Son dialogue in scriptural idiom is overheard by God's people and is the basis of the exhortation to them by the Spirit.[22] There are two conversations going on in the book, that between the Father and the Son and that between God and his many sons.[23] By the Spirit the people of God participate in the Father-Son dialogue both by overhearing it and the exhortations that address them as "sons." And both the intratrinitarian and economic conversations are in Scripture and through Scripture—that is, they converse with the words of Scripture (Heb 1–2). In the words of Harold Attridge:

> Hebrews, that is, operates with the conceit that readers and hearers of scripture can listen in to God speaking, first to the Son, and ultimately to all God's children. In this conceit, the character of God and the character of his scriptural speech provide the raw material for both reflection and parenesis. The technique thus models a response to the divine address and invites its hearers to share that response.[24]

The writer of Hebrews works from the theological principle that God continues to speak, that all God's words are made manifest in Christ, and that by the Spirit of Christ, believers are reconciled by the Word to the Father and are able, in faith, to hear his voice and obey. Martin Emmrich emphasizes the Spirit's role in the direct address to the audience.

---

22 "God's conversation with his Son provides the context for his ongoing conversation with his people. The Old Testament words that God spoke to the Messiah long ago he now speaks to the Son. Moreover, the Son answers with the voice of faithful people from the Old Testament. The Father's speech installs the eternal Son as the all-sufficient Savior at his right hand. The Son's answers affirm the incarnate obedience by which he has obtained this exalted place of ultimate authority." Gareth Cockerill, "The Truthfulness and Perennial Relevance of God's Word in the Letter to the Hebrews," *BSac* 168 (2015): 194.

23 See the discussion in Gareth L. Cockerill, *The Epistle to the Hebrews*, NICNT (Grand Rapids: Eerdmans, 2012), 193–95.

24 Harold Attridge, "God in Hebrews," in *The Epistle to the Hebrews and Christian Theology*, eds. Richard Bauckham, et al. (Grand Rapids: Eerdmans, 2009), 103–4.

Oftentimes oracles are cited to invite the reader to "listen in on a dialogue between God and the Son" (cf. 1:5–13; 2:12–13; 5:5–6; 10:5–7). On the other hand, direct divine address (i.e., first person) to the community is notably attenuated in the author's use of the LXX. It is here where he prefers to bring the Spirit into focus.[25]

The two main threads of Hebrews essentially track these two conversations. Hebrews' Christology—focused on the appointment, installation, and enthronement of the Son—is expressed through the God-Son dialogue in scriptural idiom. And the exhortation—much of which is developed through the Sinai-Zion contrast—is centered on heeding God's voice.[26]

In discussing the way the author of Hebrews uses Scripture, Jon Laansma concludes that while "there is no question that the Scriptures came to this writer as already interpreted," still,

He gives every indication of conducting an independent, fresh reading of the OT, which is finally to be measured by the implicit claims that this is *truth*. It is true both in terms of what the Scriptures were/are saying (from his own perspective, he is simply articulating the meaning that is in fact *there*, in the text) and in terms of how things are with God and the world, "yesterday and today and forever" (13:8).[27]

What most interests me, but is seldom if ever picked up in the commentaries or even here in theological treatments of the book of Hebrews, is how the Word of God written continues to be heard afresh as a present Word today, in faith communities gathered around Scripture, full of the Spirit, acknowledging Christ in their midst. Laansma acknowledges this aspect of Hebrews, even if he does not go on to develop the insight, when he writes, "As certainly as Hebrews contemporizes the OT Scriptures in the mouth of the Holy Spirit, so also in it the Spirit speaks, as the church has acknowledged."[28]

William Lane helpfully reminds us that,

The majestic opening statement of Hebrews is programmatic for the entire discourse: God spoke! As the argument unfolds, it is alternatively God, the Son, the Holy Spirit who speaks. The several strands of

25 Martin Emmrich, "Pneuma in Hebrews: Prophet and Interpreter," *WTJ* 63 (2002): 61.
26 Felix H. Cortez, "'See that you do not refuse the one who is speaking': Hearing God Preach and Obedience in the Letter to the Hebrews," *Journal of the Adventist Theological Society* 19/1–2 (2008): 98–108.
27 Laansma, "Hebrews," 280.
28 Ibid.

the development are then taken up and reaffirmed in a final climactic warning: 'Be careful that you do not disregard the one who is speaking' (12:25).[29]

What I find so confronting is the unfamiliar nature of this experience of Scripture as the spoken Word of God for many congregations today. As Barnabas Lindars once understated, "The way in which Hebrews handles Scripture also seems alien to many modern readers."[30]

READING RETROSPECTIVELY

Biblical scholars have taken note of this feature of Hebrews, and have sought to account for it in various ways, almost all usefully. One might allocate the state of biblical scholarship on this issue to what I term "reading retrospectively," or, as Richard Hays provocatively puts it, "reading backwards." Hays' work is especially useful in this regard.

We see in New Testament texts "a retrospective hermeneutical transformation of Israel's sacred texts,"[31] writes Hays. Hays is the most proficient exegete to read the New Testament figurally, a hermeneutic which reads the New Testament in light of the Old Testament in order to re-read the Old Testament in light of the New Testament, and specifically in light of the incarnation.[32] The discernment of a figural correspondence is necessarily retrospective rather than prospective—that is, there is no claim that the Old Testament authors were conscious of or technically predicting or anticipating Christ. "The act of retrospective recognition is the *intellectus spiritualis* ('spiritual understanding')." What Hays offers is a deeply theological reading of Holy Scripture and one that recognizes the unity of the canon in meaningful ways. While the focus of his latest book is upon the Gospels, it is my contention that the book of Hebrews also

---

29 Lane, *Hebrews 1–8*, l.

30 Barnabas Lindars, *The Theology of the Letter to the Hebrews*, New Testament Theology (Cambridge: Cambridge University Press, 1991), 130. The reasons for this alienation are legion, but to my mind, uppermost is surely the contemporary preoccupation with the study of the text of Scripture dislocated from the world of the reader. Here, the text has been co-opted by a study of history, as the exegete seeks to describe God and his works in an objective way. This is in contradistinction to pre-critical readings of Scripture whereby God is the living and active speaker to contemporary readers who hear God's voice through the living Word of Holy Scripture. The literature on these issues is immense but as an indication, see Paul B. Decock, "On the Value of Pre-Modern Interpretation of Scripture for Contemporary Biblical Studies," *Neot* 39/1 (2005): 57–74.

31 Richard B. Hays, *Reading Backwards: Figural Christology and the Fourfold Gospel Witness* (Waco: Baylor University Press, 2014), xv.

32 Ibid., 2, 4.

exemplifies these impulses, even if I would want to argue for a predictive and eschatological element to the Old Testament in a way Hays may not.[33]

In his brief exposition of the account of Jesus' confrontation with the two disciples on the road to Emmaus in Luke 24:13–35, Hays notes,

> For those who participate in the practices of sharing modelled by Jesus, an "opening" occurs. It is not by accident that Luke uses this word twice in quick succession. When Jesus broke the bread and gave it to them, their eyes were *opened* (. . . v.31) to recognize him; and as they recall his teaching, they say, "Weren't our hearts burning within us as he was speaking to us on the road, as he *opened* . . . to us the Scriptures?" (v.32). The disciples' faculties of perception are opened by God in such a way that they now not only recognize Jesus but also recognize the Scriptures to have been opened by Jesus' readings. The same word appears once more in the following account of Jesus' teaching of the disciples in Jerusalem: "then he opened . . . their minds to understand the scriptures" (v.45). Reading the OT anew in light of the story of Jesus' death and resurrection opens both the text and reader to new, previously unimagined, possibilities.[34]

And it is just such an account which happens today when believers read Scripture. Not only does Scripture have retrospective elements to it, it also has a retroactive element as well. It is this which I believe Hebrews exemplifies for us.

Richard Hays concludes his richly textured and provocative work *Reading Backwards* with these delightful words:

> The one Lord confessed in Israel's *Shema* is the same God actively at work in the death and resurrection of Jesus Christ. Apart from the truth of that claim, any talk of the unity of the OT and the NT is simply nonsense. There is only one reason why Christological interpretation of the OT is not a matter of stealing or twisting Israel's sacred texts: the God to whom the Gospels bear witness, the God incarnate in Jesus, is the same as the God of Abraham, Isaac, and Jacob. Either that is true, or it is not. If it is not, the Gospels are a delusional and pernicious distortion of Israel's story. If it is true, then the figural literary unity of Scripture,

---

33   For arguments in favor of a predictive and eschatological element in the Old Testament see Donald A. Carson, "Mystery and Fulfillment: Toward a More Comprehensive Paradigm of Paul's Understanding of the Old and the New," in *The Paradoxes of Paul*, ed. D. A. Carson, P. T. O'Brien, and M. A. Seifrid (Tübingen: Mohr-Siebeck, 2004), 2:298–412. Whether or not Old Testament authors were conscious of Christ see Greg K. Beale, "The Cognitive Peripheral Vision of Biblical Authors," *WTJ* 76 (2014): 263–93.

34   Hays, *Reading Backwards*, 15.

OT and NT together, is nothing other than the climactic fruition of that one God's self-revelation.[35]

Hays shows how a figural reading of Scripture works, and it is compelling to say the least. And he is not alone in this, of course. I want to build upon his suggestions and move even further beyond the retrospective hermeneutic of Hays to the retroactive hermeneutic (of Hebrews).

From the perspective of the risen Christ and the subsequent Trinitarian theology this revealed, the New Testament authors tell, re-tell, and re-work God's *logoi* for the faith community. As they do, they are guided by the risen Christ, by the Holy Spirit, and by the Father in recalling previous words of God, sharing new words, and importantly, interpreting, by divine inspiration, the ways of God in the world. One might more technically say that each New Testament author is providing an interpretation of the Christ event from the perspective of a narrative of salvation history. As Ken Schenck has argued in an essay on the nature of Scripture in Hebrews, "although the author constructed his sense of the overarching story and overarching word from materials *in* the biblical texts, he comes to see the speaking of God as the broader category of which the biblical texts themselves are only a subset of speaking."[36] The biblical texts thus act as "windows" on history, a history of which the interpreter is a part: "In a sense, the text disappears as the interpreter *outside* the text becomes a part of the world *within* the text and the world within the text is seen as part [sic] of the world outside the text."[37] Windows then turn into "witnesses" to what God is saying today; "Text as *window* on past words and events becomes text as *witness* to truths arguably of the Holy Spirit."[38]

But can we go beyond Schenck, and argue that what was possible for the biblical authors is also possible for all Christian readers, ancient or modern, for this is the nature of Holy Scripture, this is the *revelatory* action of the Holy Spirit, the *reconciliatory* action of the Son, and the *redemptive* action of the Father? Having hinted at this possibility throughout this paper, it is now time to make some direct comments on what a retroactive hermeneutic of triune discourse might entail.

---

35 Ibid., 109.
36 Ken Schenck, "God Has Spoken: Hebrews' Theology of the Scriptures," in *The Epistle to the Hebrews and Christian Theology* (Grand Rapids: Eerdmans, 2009), 323.
37 Ibid.
38 Ibid., 324.

READING RETROACTIVELY

Taking the text of Hebrews seriously and paying particular attention to the ways in which we have noted the author interprets the Old Testament by means of the Christ event, and then uses the Old Testament to in turn reveal more of the New Testament, I want to offer a theological explanation for what is happening, and along with that, a recommendation for how we might read Holy Scripture and hear the voice of God in our contemporary contexts by means of a retroactive hermeneutic.

A retroactive hermeneutic recognizes that the experienced presence of Christ in the Spirit, post-Easter, brought to mind the life of Jesus thereby reawakening remembrances of his life, words, and deeds.[39] In this sense, the present and the past correspond such that the present does not contradict the past, nor vice versa. This same retroactive process is available for the exegete today. We have seen this retroactive hermeneutic clearly illustrated throughout Hebrews. Hebrews brings the dialectic between the historical words of Christ and the present experience of the Spirit into sharp focus, along with the dialectic between prior words of the prophets and so forth and the present Word of the triune Lord. Consequently, Hebrews *hears* Old Testament texts as the voice of God, presenting both inspiration in the present and an interpretation of the past, and both are bound up in the framework of illumination.[40] What this interpretive work of the Spirit meant for the author of Hebrews is that he would undoubtedly regard his own "word of exhortation" as the product of this inspiring Spirit.[41]

What is true of Hebrews is true of the other books of Holy Scripture as well. To take just one example, in Revelation we read, "let anyone who has an ear listen to what the Spirit is saying (λέγει, present tense) to the churches" (Rev 2:7). The canonical authors are consciously writing

---

39   Advocating a similar idea as presented here see Ray S. Anderson who labels his a Christological hermeneutic, *Ministry on the Fire Line: A Practical Theology for an Empowered Church* (Downers Grove: InterVarsity Press, 1993), 111; *An Emergent Theology for Emerging Churches* (Downers Grove: InterVarsity Press, 2006), 134–35; and *Dancing with Wolves While Feeding the Sheep: The Musings of a Maverick Theologian* (Eugene, OR: Wipf & Stock, 2001), chapter 3, where it is described as a hermeneutic of "eschatological preference." Another close example is the "christotelic" hermeneutic developed by Peter Enns, *Inspiration and Incarnation* (Grand Rapids: Baker Academic, 2005). This merely highlights the reciprocity between Christ and Spirit.

40   See the same conclusions in Stephen E. Fowl, *Engaging Scripture: A Model for Theological Interpretation* (Oxford: Blackwell, 1998), 99–100.

41   For a comparable proposal to my retroactive hermeneutic that adopts more tradition terminology such as inspiration and illumination, and magisterial and ministerial authority, see Keith A. Quan, "The Word of the Living God: Presentational Discourse as a Model for Contemporary Divine Address through Scripture" (PhD diss., Southwestern Baptist Theological Seminary, 2014).

to and for Spirit-inspired readers.[42] This last point has been recognized by Markus Bockmuehl who writes, "The implied reader is drawn into an act of reading that involves playing an active role on stage rather than the discreet spectator on the upper balcony."[43] This is similar to the approach advocated by Thomas Torrance, who borrows an idea from William Manson in which we must indwell the New Testament as a whole in such a way as to look through the various books and passages of Scripture and allow the message to be interiorized in the depths of our mind. For this reason his approach is called "depth exegesis."[44]

We might, then, conclude that: It is the Spirit of Light who illuminates the significance of the Christ event through Scripture (*retro*); it is the presence of the Spirit of Life that moves the church on (*active*); and it is the Spirit of Truth who brings the word of God into new situations (*retroactive*).[45]

Being a theologian, it is natural to turn to the category of dogmatics for explanatory help at this point. We find an ally for a retroactive hermeneutic in the concept of revelation itself and in what the early church terms the *depositum fidei*; something I will touch on shortly. As Alister McGrath notes,

> Revelation as divine action gives rise to what the New Testament articulates in terms of categories such as 'tradition (παράδοσις)' and 'deposit (παραθήκη)'—concepts which convey the general idea of holding something in trust as a treasured possession. A series of past revelatory acts gives rise to a present revelation, both of which the church is required to affirm and safeguard.[46]

Later he writes, "The term 'revelation' thus bears an extended meaning, which embraces the original revelational acts and the witness to those acts in Scripture and in the proclamation of the church."[47] The very

---

42   I have developed this hermeneutic in dialogue with the Johannine writings in Myk Habets, "Developing a Retroactive Hermeneutic: Johannine Theology and Doctrinal Development," *American Theological Inquiry* 1/2 (2008): 77–89.

43   Markus Bockmuehl, "'To Be or Not To Be'": The Possible Futures of New Testament Scholarship," *SJT* 51 no. 3 (1998): 300.

44   Thomas F. Torrance, *The Christian Doctrine of God, One Being–Three Persons* (Edinburgh: T&T Clark, 1996), 37. He also draws heavily from the work of Michael Polanyi; see *Belief in Science and in Christian Life: The Relevance of Michael Polanyi's Thought for Christian Faith and Life*, ed. T. F. Torrance (Edinburgh: Handsel, 1980).

45   This terminology has been used by Philip J. Rosato, "Spirit Christology: Ambiguity and Promise," *TS* 38/3 (1977): 444. Anderson, *Ministry on the Fire Line*, 35, speaks of theology as being both historical (backward or retro) and contemporary (future or active) due to Christ and the Spirit.

46   Alister E. McGrath, *Theory* (Grand Rapids: Eerdmans, 2003), 3:144.

47   Ibid., 145.

concept of revelation thus has a dynamic, even a Trinitarian, quality to it that matches the sort of retroactive readings of Scripture I see Hebrews and other biblical books advocate.

This retroactive motif parallels to some degree the so-called neo-orthodox and existentialist schools who realize that the moment of understanding is at once the moment of response. The words of Scripture in this sense do become the Word of God. In the words of Barth, "revelation is reconciliation." According to Barth "Revelation takes place in and with reconciliation; indeed, the latter is also revelation. As God acts in it he also speaks. . . . Yet the relationship is indissoluble from the other side as well. Revelation takes place as the revelation of reconciliation."[48]

THE EXEGETE AND THE SPIRIT

Having established a retroactive hermeneutic that accounts for the mission of the Holy Spirit, we are left with the task of briefly pointing out some of the implications of a pneumatological hermeneutic for the biblical exegete. There are generally two approaches to the role of the Holy Spirit in interpretation. One focuses on what the Spirit does with the *text,* the other on what the Spirit does with the *exegete.* The first approach, while becoming a popular option in contemporary hermeneutics, is rejected by a retroactive reading of Scripture.[49] Proponents of the first approach aver that the Spirit enables the text to be read in a way which would not have been obvious to the first recipients (a "Spiritual" reading) and so in this way renders Scripture of continuing relevance to the church. On this view the Spirit is the creative power behind the fusion of the text's and the reader's horizons, with the second horizon exerting a clear dominance over the first. The second approach, the one adopted here, appeals to the Spirit as the minister of the Word, the one who leads the community into a correct interpretation of the text. The locus of the Spirit's re-creative work is not the letter of the text; this is fixed and hence forms our *retro.* Rather the Spirit's re-creative work centers on the life of the interpreter, who, as sinner, is inclined to distort the text insofar as its

---

48　Karl Barth, *The Doctrine of Reconciliation,* IV/3.1 in *Church Dogmatics* (London: Continuum, 1961), 8. Following Barth the other major presentation of this theology has been by Thomas F. Torrance, especially in his work *The Mediation of Christ,* 2nd ed. (Edinburgh: T&T Clark, 1992); also see *Divine Meaning. Studies in Patristic Hermeneutics* (Edinburgh: T&T Clark, 1995), 8, for a clear example.

49　For a brief survey see Kevin J. Vanhoozer, *Is There a Meaning in This Text?* (Leicester: Apollos, 1998), 415.

message is perceived as threatening the *status quo*.[50] Given this distortion, the Spirit guides and leads the interpreter to the truth of the text and its correct application into new situations and hence forms our *active*.[51]

After developing a three-tier taxonomy of positions on the relationship between the discipline of theology and biblical interpretation, Darren Sarisky concludes, "Theological interpretation of Scripture should take its cue from a specifically theological ontology of both text and reader."[52] In terms of an ontology of the reader of Scripture, we would do well to remember the words of John Webster, which I quote in full.

> First, the reader is to be envisaged as within the hermeneutical situation as we have been attempting to portray it, not as transcending it or making it merely an object of will. The reader is an actor within a larger web of event and activities, supreme among which is God's act in which God speaks God's Word through the text of the Bible to the people of God, as he instructs them and teaches them in the way they should go. As a participant in this historical process, the reader is *spoken to* in the text. This speaking, and the hearing which it promotes, occurs as part of the drama which encloses human life in its totality, including human acts of reading and understanding: the drama of sin and its overcoming. Reading the Bible is an event in this history. It is therefore moral and spiritual and not merely cognitive or representational activity. Readers *read*, of course: figure things out as best they can, construe the text and its genre, try to discern its intentions whether professed or implied, place it historically and culturally—all this is what happens when the Bible is read also. But as this happens, there also happens the history of salvation; each reading act is also bound up within the dynamic of idolatry, repentance and resolute turning from sin which takes place when God's Word addresses humanity. And it is this dynamic which is definitive of the Christian reader of the Bible.[53]

The work of the Spirit is, thus, a work *in* community and *for* community and so an examination of the communal nature of the Spirit's role in interpretation is required.

---

50 Ibid.

51 For Vanhoozer, the formula is not retro + active but "biblical relevance = revelatory meaning + relative significance." Ibid., 423.

52 Darren Sarisky, "A Prolegomenon to an Account of Theological Interpretation of Scripture," in *Theological Theology: Essays in Honour of John Webster*, eds. R. David Nelson, Darren Sarisky, and Justin Stratis (London: Bloomsbury T&T Clark, 2015), 256.

53 John Webster, "Hermeneutics in Modern Theology: Some Doctrinal Reflections," *SJT* 51/3 (1998): 336.

THE COMMUNITY AND THE SPIRIT

Of special importance is the communal aspect of the reading and inter-preting of Scripture. On the basis of Acts 2, James McClendon argues that Scripture is addressed directly to readers *today*: Peter declares "this" (the event of Pentecost) is "that" (the meaning of the prophecy of Joel).[54] Such an interpretation is not merely Peter's human projection but a product of the Spirit's guidance. Only his sharing in the life of the believing commu-nity allowed Peter to see "this" as "that." Whether it be the Gospels, Acts, Hebrews, or the prophets of the Old Testament, in fact, the entire canon of Scripture is witness to the ongoing revelatory voice of God. Here is no dead letter, no tired book, but a text which speaks directly to people's hearts and minds because the triune God speaks through it.

While a communal reception of the text under the guidance of the Holy Spirit is acknowledged, when this approach is taken to an extreme it reveals a problem, notably: How can the church know what God is saying through Scripture if what God is saying fails to coincide with the verbal meaning of the text? Hauerwas appeals to the leading of the Spirit.[55] But is this sufficient? The solution has problems. First, the Spirit's leading is often difficult to discern or to distinguish from merely human consensus. Second, it relocates the Word of God and divine authority from the text to the tradition of its interpretation.[56] When individualized, there is the constituent problem of subjectivity. However, when this is done in the context of ecclesial community it is perhaps similar to the early church and their use of the "deposit of faith" (*depositum fidei*). For Tertullian and Irenaeus, Scripture is rightly understood only in the context of the living tradition handed down through apostolic succession; tradition being both the content and context. Ultimately the criterion for right interpretation is the consensus of the catholic church, best represented by the earliest creeds. On this view, the arbiter of right interpretation is Christ as he speaks to the church, of which the church enjoys not canonical but "*char-ismatic* authority, grounded in the assistance of the Spirit: *for it seemed good to the Holy Spirit and to us.*"[57] The function of the *depositum fidei* is thus not

---

54 James W. McClendon, *Ethics: Systematic Theology* (Nashville: Abingdon, 1986), 31–33. Following McClendon's position would be Richard B. Hays, *Echoes of Scripture in the Letters of Paul* (New Haven: Yale University Press, 1989), and Stanley Hauerwas, *Unleashing Scripture: Freeing the Bible from Captivity to America* (Nashville: Abingdon, 1993).

55 See for instance Stanley Hauerwas, "The Moral Authority of Scripture: The Politics and Ethics of Remembering," *Int* 34/4 (1980): 356–70.

56 All criticisms made by Vanhoozer, *Is There a Meaning in This Text?* 411.

57 Cited by Vanhoozer, *Is There a Meaning in This Text?* 411.

overturned but placed within its proper context: the community which "stands under" the text of Scripture and the Spirit of Truth.[58]

These issues are only a problem when a pneumatological hermeneutic is not at the same time a retroactive one. A retroactive hermeneutic seeks to hold together the plain sense of Scripture ("what it meant") with its use by the Spirit in the community ("its significance today").

How do we foster this ecclesial context in which a Spirit-inspired hermeneutic or reading of Scripture takes place? By returning to, and developing our own, theologically attuned strategies for reading, praying, living, and worshipping in community, such that our own ideas, agendas, and ideologies are laid bare before the Word of the living God. In this process our ears and not our eyes will need to be our primary sense.

CONCLUSION

In conclusion, a retroactive hermeneutic is one in which the text of Scripture, the life of Christ, and the ongoing illumination of the Holy Spirit are equal participants in the church's ongoing task of understanding and articulating the Word of God for today.

God has spoken; we know this to be true. But all too often this blinds us to the fact that God still speaks. The authors of Holy Scripture understood and lived in this reality, as have others throughout church history. As the Holy Spirit inspired Scripture, so the Holy Spirit continues to speak to the church today, by means of those same Scriptures, and as such they are "living and active" words. As the Spirit continues to inspire the text in our hearing through the event of revelation, then it is incumbent upon believers—faithful exegetes—to listen, to indwell, and to live out of this retroactive movement of triune discourse.

As the Lord God speaks a "Word of exhortation" (Heb 13:22) I, along with countless numbers of Christians, can confidently affirm he succeeded. Amen![59]

---

58   For a comprehensive evaluation of the Deposit of Faith see Thomas F. Torrance, "The Deposit of Faith," *SJT* 36/1 (1983): 1–28.

59   I am grateful to Keith Quan for his expert comments on an earlier draft. I would like to thank Fred Sanders, Oliver Crisp, Katya Covrett, and those who attended my presentation at the LATC16 conference for their helpful critical questions.

CHAPTER 6

PATHS BEYOND TRACING OUT: THE HERMENEUTICS OF METAPHOR AND THEOLOGICAL METHOD

Erin M. Heim

INTRODUCTION

As a biblical scholar writing for an audience of theologians, I am keenly aware of two things: (1) that Alan Torrance is right about how quickly and imperceptibly biblical scholars tend to move from second-order talk about God (the "god-talk talk" of historical inquiry) to first-order talk about God (the "God-talk" of theology),[1] and (2) that I am a biblical scholar by training, and thus have probably been guilty of this. In fact, maybe this paper should have been titled "Paths beyond Tracing Out: A Biblical Scholar's Circuitous Journey toward the Distant Land of Systematic Theology." So, I do not presume to approach the question of metaphor and theological method as the biblical scholar "in-the-know" on a crusade to make those

---

1   Alan J. Torrance, "Can the Truth Be Learned?: Redressing the 'Theologistic Fallacy' in Modern Biblical Scholarship," in *Scripture's Doctrine and Theology's Bible: How the New Testament Shapes Christian Dogmatics*, eds. Markus Bockmuehl and Alan J. Torrance (Grand Rapids: Baker Academic, 2008), 144.

theologians pay attention to the historical minutiae of Scripture's metaphors. On the contrary, my hope is to offer some humble observations on the relationship between the historical particularity of Scripture's metaphors, situated as they are within texts with particular audiences, authors, and historical contexts, and theology's "God-talk" of the first order.

According to Alan Torrance, Murray Rae, Samuel Adams, and others,[2] biblical scholars often go about the interpretation of Scripture, and by extension Scripture's metaphors, precisely backward, bracketing the question of God out of the historian's task, beginning instead with an "objective" account of the historical data,[3] and then imperceptibly adding God-talk of the first order (rather than god-talk talk) back into their conclusions. To honor and learn from their valid objections, I will approach the question of the historical particularity of Scripture's metaphors and the correlated question of theological method by attempting to wear the hat of a theologian. In other words, I will operate from the assumption that theologians like Torrance, Rae, and Adams are essentially right about the relationship between history, Scripture, and theology,[4] and I see my job as to situate within this framework an account of how God speaks through Scripture's metaphors. In short, following Torrance, my point is that a responsible account of Scripture's metaphors must be rooted in the assumption that Scripture is God's self-revelation and requires the *phronema tou pneumatos* (mind of the Spirit) to be read aright. Within this framework, I will argue below that we must understand God as the Maker of Scripture's metaphors,[5] which were revealed within particular historical and cultural contexts, but through the Spirit continue to speak to the church as God's people in every age. As a Metaphor-Maker (a term I will unpack below), God invites the audience of Scripture to enter into a "sameness of vision" and to share in the divine perspective presented in the text.

---

2   See Torrance, "Can the Truth Be Learned?," 143–63; Murray Rae, *History and Hermeneutics* (London: T&T Clark, 2005); Samuel V. Adams, *The Reality of God and Historical Method: Apocalyptic Theology in Conversation with N. T. Wright* (Downers Grove: IVP Academic, 2015).

3   See, e.g., Alan Torrance's critique of James Dunn ("Can the Truth Be Learned?," 146), and Samuel Adams' extended engagement with the methodology in N. T. Wright's Christian origins series (*The Reality of God*, 20–64).

4   I say "essentially" because as a biblical scholar, I have some minor qualms about how certain biblical texts are handled in each of their works, particularly in regard to the implications some formulations have for our understanding of texts of the Hebrew Bible (e.g., Adams' argument on the significance of the incarnation seems to dismiss the possibility for genuine theological knowledge prior to the advent of Christ [*The Reality of God*, 81]).

5   Within scholarship on metaphor, a "metaphor-maker" is a technical term used to discuss the unique relationship forged between makers and understanders of metaphor. Here, I will use the term "Metaphor-Maker" of God to meld together theological categories and current research on metaphor.

To build a bridge between Scripture's metaphors and theological method, I must first lay a foundation that defines and defends the presence of metaphor in the texts of Scripture. In order to elucidate the relationship between Scripture's metaphors and constructive theology, we must understand what metaphors are and how they work to create meaning for their readers/hearers. This is the task of the first section of the paper. Having laid this foundation, the next section will give an account of God as Metaphor-Maker and Scripture's metaphors as lenses through which to view God and his acts in history. The final section will suggest a possible trajectory that moves from Scripture's metaphors (revelations) to an account of metaphor and revelation, which is held together by the grace of God the Metaphor-Maker, who, in and through the Spirit, is present and active in the church.

IN PRAISE AND DEFENSE OF METAPHOR
PRELIMINARY DEFINITIONS

Although most responsible biblical scholars and theologians would agree that Scripture is full of metaphor, much of the interpretation of these metaphors is guided by the Enlightenment's legacy to view metaphor as "a sort of happy extra trick with words."[6] Indeed, John Locke pointedly claimed, metaphors only "insinuate wrong *ideas*, move the passions, and thereby mislead the judgment."[7] As such "in all discourses that pretend to inform or instruct, [metaphors are] wholly to be avoided and, where truth and knowledge are concerned, cannot but be thought a great fault either of the language or person that makes use of them."[8] Standing as a testament to the enduring influence of the Enlightenment's view, the goal of interpretation for a contemporary biblical scholar is often to "nail down" a metaphor's meaning in a suitable "literal" paraphrase,[9] usually

---

6   I. A. Richards, *The Philosophy of Rhetoric* (New York: Oxford University Press, 1965), 90. N.b., Richards himself does not subscribe to such a sentiment.

7   John Locke, *An Essay Concerning Human Understanding*, bk. III, ch. 10 (emphasis in original).

8   Locke, *Essay*, bk. III, ch. 10; see also Thomas Hobbes, *Leviathan*, pt. 1. ch. 4 "On Speech"; Bertrand Russell, *Logic and Knowledge: Essays 1901–1950*, ed. Charles Marsh (London: Allen & Unwin, 1956), 178–89; Ludwig Wittgenstein, *The Wittgenstein Reader*, ed. Anthony Kenny (Oxford: Blackwell, 2006), 70–83; for an overview of metaphor in the philosophy of the Enlightenment see Oliver R. Scholz, "Wit und Regeln: Metaphern und ihre Auslegung in der Philosophie der Aufklärung," in *Metapher und Innovation: Die Rolle der Metapher im Wandel von Sprach und Wissenschaft*, eds. Henri Lauener, Andreas Graeser, and Gerhard Seel (Bern: Haupt, 1995), 39–52.

9   See Kevin Vanhoozer's discussion of the exegesis of metaphor in *Is There a Meaning in This Text?: The Bible, The Reader, and the Morality of Literary Knowledge* (Grand Rapids: Zondervan, 1998), 98–147.

focusing on the historical context of the metaphor to flesh out "what it really means." For scholars influenced by this view, metaphors are decorative ornaments of the text, and they detract from its "plain sense" meaning. This under-appreciation of metaphor, especially metaphors in Scripture, seems to stem from the well-intentioned desire to affirm that Scripture speaks truthfully (i.e., not metaphorically) about God. Jesus "truly," not "metaphorically," is the sacrificial Lamb (John 1:29). Yahweh "truly," not "metaphorically," is the Father of Israel (Isa 63:16), and so forth. However, to insert a false dichotomy between metaphor and truth is to misunderstand the nature of metaphorical language, and to privilege literal language as "more accurate" or "true" than metaphorical utterances. As I will show below, this is simply not the case.

Research in cognitive and sociolinguistics has shown that metaphors are, in fact, not decorative add-ons at all, but rather they are indispensable cognitive instruments of communication that enable readers/hearers to gain knowledge or insight that is often only available through a particular metaphorical lens.[10] Moreover, their meanings are not wholly determinate, nor paraphrasable into literal speech.[11] So, if a metaphor is not an extraneous adornment, nor a placeholder for literal speech, what shall we say that a metaphor *is*? As a starting point, I find Janet Martin Soskice's definition of metaphor to be helpful: *"A metaphor is that figure of speech whereby we speak about one thing in terms which are seen to be suggestive of another."*[12] In Scripture then, we have metaphors such as God is a rock (Ps 18:2), or God is a shepherd (Ps 23; Ezek 34) or God is a mother bear (Hos 13:8) which, in Soskice's view, are figures of speech whereby we speak about God in terms which are suggestive of rocks, shepherds, and bears. Key to Soskice's point is that *words* are not metaphorical in and of themselves. Thus we cannot have both literal and metaphorical definitions of "shepherd," but rather we have instances where the word "shepherd" is used in a non-metaphorical utterance, and instances where "shepherd" is used in a metaphorical utterance. The individual word "shepherd" retains the same range of meaning regardless of whether it is used in a literal

---

10   See e.g., Zoltán Kövecses, *Metaphor: A Practical Introduction* (Oxford: Oxford University Press, 2002); Mark Turner, *Death Is the Mother of Beauty: Mind, Metaphor, Criticism* (Christchurch, NZ: Cybereditions, 2000), 32–33; Marx Wartofsky, *Models: Representation and the Scientific Understanding*, Boston Studies in the Philosophy of Science 48 (London: Reidel, 1979), 38–39.
11   See Vanhoozer, *Is There a Meaning?*, 126–29; Paul Ricoeur, *The Rule of Metaphor* (London: Routledge, 1986), 109.
12   Janet Martin Soskice, *Metaphor and Religious Language* (Oxford: Clarendon, 1985), 15 (emphasis in original).

or metaphorical utterance.[13] In order to speak about one thing in terms which are suggestive of another, metaphors like "God is a shepherd" or "God is a rock" rely on the underlying "models," which are defined as consistent imaginative constructs or patterns of thought that connect to a "real world" object (e.g., a rock or a shepherd).[14] It is here where the question of historical particularity emerges.

The models that underlie Scripture's metaphors are bound by culture and chronology, and to understand Scripture's metaphors we need to grasp and flesh out the underlying model or models. For example, if we do not have a clear understanding of Greco-Roman adoption as a model underlying the adoption metaphors in Romans 8:15 and 8:23, we will miss the clear cultural cues surrounding adoption and inheritance in that text. Likewise if we do not have a clear understanding of the Passover (Exod 12:1–14), we miss or misunderstand the significance of Jesus' metaphorical statement "I am the Bread of Life" (John 6:35). However, a metaphor is not reducible to its underlying model, and not all parts of an underlying model necessarily refer in a given metaphor. For example, in the metaphor "I am the Bread of Life," it is unlikely that Jesus' audience would have inferred that Jesus was baked over a fire, despite this being part of the underlying model "bread." Rather, the audience of a metaphor draws intuitively upon knowledge of the underlying model, and then creates a new vision of the metaphor's subject by thinking of it in terms suggestive of the underlying model (or models). Thus in the case of a metaphor like "God is a breastfeeding mother" (see Hos 11:3–4) the audience is able to think about God in terms suggestive of a breastfeeding woman without becoming confused that God might be anatomically female.[15]

Moreover, the meaning of a metaphor, Scriptural or otherwise, lies at the level of a complete utterance, and is formed in the midst of the intricate dance between the metaphor and the model. One particularly salient implication for this view of metaphor is that in Scripture we have, for instance, a collection of shepherd metaphors, not the "same metaphor" in

---

13   For the importance of individual words or lexemes retaining their conventional (i.e., "literal") meaning in metaphorical utterances see Donald Davidson, "What Metaphors Mean," in *The Philosophy of Language*, 5th ed., ed. A. P. Martinich (Oxford: Oxford University Press, 2008), 473–84.

14   For an overview of metaphors and models see Gregory W. Dawes, *The Body in Question: Metaphor and Meaning in the Interpretation of Ephesians 5:21–33*, BibInt 30 (Leiden: Brill, 1998).

15   Perhaps it should go without saying that the same is true for the metaphor "God is Father," but a survey of scholarship shows this to be a much more contentious claim. See especially Aída Besançon Spencer for an overview and critique of the relevant literature ("Father-Ruler: The Meaning of the Metaphor 'Father' for God in the Bible," *JETS* 39.3 [1996]: 433–42).

various iterations. The meaning of a shepherd metaphor in one place is not identical to the meaning of a shepherd metaphor in another. Iterations of the "same metaphor" are not transferrable between contexts. For example, Yahweh as the shepherd of Israel in Ezekiel 34 illuminates Yahweh's eschatological actions of gathering and restoring the scattered nation of Israel, along with judgment upon Israel's wicked shepherds, whereas Yahweh as David's shepherd in Psalm 23 illuminates his tender care and protection of David in the midst of his enemies. The shared underlying model produces overlap, to be sure, but these metaphors function in different ways in their respective contexts, and their meanings are not wholly transferrable between contexts.[16] This claim has some substantial implications for constructive theology, and I will revisit it in the final section of the paper.

METAPHOR AND EPISTEMIC ACCESS

Having briefly discussed what metaphors *are*, I want to give a short account of a couple of things metaphors *do*. Perhaps the most interesting feature of metaphors is that they are not neutral conduits of information. Instead, through a metaphor, a metaphor-maker extends an invitation to his or her audience that beckons them to consider its subject through a particular lens. Thus metaphors create intimate bonds between their makers and understanders by enacting a shared perspective of a particular subject. This shared perspective is, in many ways, non-paraphrasable, and indeed, in the case of the shared vision created by Scripture's metaphors, ineffable.[17] To take a mundane example, if I were to say after a particularly trying day of Christmas shopping, "The mall was a zoo!" this not only conveys cognitive information about the mall (e.g., that it was busy), but it invites you into my experience of the mall (e.g., that it was wild and filled with animalistic shoppers). As the hearer of this metaphor, you then have the (perhaps unconscious) choice to imagine my shopping experience in terms suggestive of a zoo.[18] If you accept my invitation to see

---

16   See the discussion in chapters 2–3 in my doctoral thesis ("Light through a Prism: New Avenues of Inquiry for the Pauline *Huothesia* Metaphors" (PhD diss., University of Otago, 2014).

17   See Herbert H. Clark, *Using Language* (Cambridge: Cambridge University Press, 1996), 29–58; Albert N. Katz, "Preface," in *Figurative Language Comprehension: Social and Cultural Influences*, eds. Herbert L. Colston and Albert N. Katz (Mahwah, NJ: Lawrence Erlbaum Associates, 2005), ix; Ted Cohen, "Some Philosophy: 1," *Raritan* 10.2 (1990): 30; William Horton, "Metaphor and Readers' Attributions of Intimacy," *Memory & Cognition* 35.1 (2007): 87–94.

18   N.b., in order to understand this metaphor a hearer must possess the necessary common ground (e.g., a knowledge of malls, the culture of Christmas shopping in the United States, and zoos). For a discussion of common ground see Raymond Gibbs, *The Poetics of Mind: Figurative Thought, Language, and Understanding* (Cambridge: Cambridge University Press, 1994), 134.

the mall as a zoo, this metaphor creates a bond of shared understanding between us; however fleetingly, we become a community of "shopping commiserates." This simple example shows that metaphors, unlike literal language, provide "thick" and multifaceted epistemic access into the metaphor-maker's view of the world. Moreover, the "shared vision" that metaphors create must be thought of holistically, encompassing cognitive and affective/emotive attributes. As Ted Cohen remarks,

> When your metaphor is "X is Y", you are hoping that I will see X as you do, namely as Y, and, most likely, although your proximate aim is to get me to see X in this way, your ultimate wish is that I will feel about X as you do.[19]

However, I acknowledge that the "sameness of vision" created by a metaphor does not necessarily translate to genuine knowledge of a subject, and so here we must also briefly examine a metaphor's capacity to communicate truth. Although Locke and Hobbes viewed metaphor as something between self-deception and outright lying,[20] a quick survey of current philosophical inquiry regarding metaphor shows that the invisible barrier between "literal" truth and "metaphorical" truth erected by the Enlightenment is slowly eroding, and contemporary philosophers of language overwhelmingly affirm that metaphor-makers aim at truth.[21] Indicative of this paradigm shift, Max Black remarks, "An emphatic, indispensable metaphor does not belong to the realm of fiction, and is not merely being used, as some writers allege, for some mysterious aesthetic effect, but really does say something."[22] Moreover, the knowledge

---

19 Ted Cohen, *Thinking of Others: On the Talent for Metaphor* (Princeton: Princeton University Press, 2008), 23.

20 Locke, *Essay*, bk. III, ch. 10; Thomas Hobbes, *Leviathan*, pt. 1. ch. 4 "On Speech"; Bertrand Russell, *Logic and Knowledge: Essays 1901–1950*, ed. Charles Marsh (London: Allen & Unwin, 1956), 178–89; Wittgenstein, *The Wittgenstein Reader*, 70–83; for an overview of metaphor in the philosophy of the Enlightenment see Oliver R. Scholz, "Wit und Regeln: Metaphern und ihre Auslegung in der Philosophie der Aufklärung," in *Metapher und Innovation: Die Rolle der Metapher im Wandel von Sprach und Wissenschaft*, eds. Henri Lauener, Andreas Graeser, and Gerhard Seel (Bern: Haupt, 1995), 39–52.

21 Of course it is also possible for a speaker to use metaphor to mislead a hearer or reader, either intentionally or accidentally. The capacity for misinformation goes part and parcel with a metaphor's ability to highlight certain features of a subject while camouflaging others (see esp. Gerald O'Brien, "Metaphors and the Pejorative Framing of Marginalized Groups: Implications for Social Work Education," *Journal of Social Work Education* 45.1 [2009]: 31; George Lakoff and Mark Turner, *More Than Cool Reason: A Field Guide to Poetic Metaphor* [Chicago: University of Chicago Press, 1989], 39). Of course, misleading an audience can also be accomplished perfectly well with literal language that is either intentionally or accidentally false.

22 Max Black, "More about Metaphors," in *Metaphor and Thought*, ed. Andrew Ortony (Cambridge: Cambridge University Press, 1979), 39.

accessible through metaphorical utterances is not inferior or "less real" than propositions communicated in "literal" speech. In my example above, "The mall was a zoo," the one who understands my metaphor possesses genuine knowledge not only of the busyness of the mall on the day I went shopping, but also possesses genuine knowledge of my feelings and experience of this busyness.[23] In other words, we need not literalize or paraphrase my metaphor in order to make it say something "true;" it is already true.[24] It is also worth noting that if we were to change the metaphor from "the mall was a zoo" to "the mall was a madhouse," we do not end up with precisely the same knowledge of the mall. Although both metaphors convey busyness, the second metaphor has a darker connotation and hints at a more negative experience. Thus the knowledge accessible through the first metaphor is unique to that metaphor, and substituting another metaphor would yield a different set of implications.

Furthermore, within some areas (theology, philosophy, and many sciences included) without metaphor it is very difficult, if not impossible, to make meaningful, truthful statements about an object (or subject, as is the case in theology).[25] The authors of Scripture employ metaphors, and expect the audiences of the biblical texts to respond to metaphors, not because they are attempting to persuade their audiences through elegant or sophisticated modes of expression, but because these metaphors are God's self-revealed way of depicting transcendent states and relations.[26] Conversely, to assert the incapacity or inadequacy of metaphor to communicate genuine knowledge or truth is also, albeit tacitly, to assume the incapacity and inadequacy of God's chosen means of self-revelation, which we surely want to avoid. By connecting transcendent reality to a familiar model, a metaphor-maker is able to communicate knowledge (both objective and subjective knowledge) *via* a metaphor that can only be accessed as such.

---

23   I am not necessarily arguing that metaphors completely eradicate the distance between author and audience as distinct persons with distinct experiences, but rather I am affirming that an understander of a metaphor, if pressed, would be able to articulate *my* experience of the mall based on the knowledge the metaphor conveyed.

24   This assumes that the metaphor-maker has not spoken falsely or otherwise deceived the audience. As such, I argue that the truth and trustworthiness of metaphorical statements is wrapped up in the trustworthiness of the metaphor-maker. In the case of human metaphor-makers, metaphorical statements can be evaluated using the same criteria as literal statements under a correspondence view of truth. In the case of God as Metaphor-Maker, we can affirm that God's metaphors are true because God's word is true and trustworthy.

25   I do not mean to imply here that Scripture's metaphors are primarily statements that we make about God, but rather they are examples of God's self-revelation and condescension to the realm of human language and experience.

26   Soskice, *Metaphor and Religious Language*, 112.

Scripture's Metaphors and the Metaphor-Maker

Having laid at least a foundational case for the capacity of metaphor to communicate genuine knowledge, I turn now to the question of *how* metaphors function in this capacity within the larger framework of revelation. Rae rightfully argues that the knowledge of God depends on the hospitality and generosity of his own self-disclosure.[27] The knowledge that comes to us in Scripture is always *revealed* knowledge that results from a gracious encounter with the word of God illuminated by the Spirit, rather than knowledge of human discovery or inquiry. As Adams observes, "Theological knowledge begins with an already existing relation between the knower and the one known," and therefore any investigation of the relationship between God and the human subject is necessarily an *a posteriori* investigation.[28] As many have rightly affirmed, to begin with a positive view of humanity's ability to come to real theological knowledge through our own capacity to reason, or through our own methodological prowess, is to create an epistemological idol.[29] Instead, beginning with an affirmation of God's self-disclosure in Scripture, Rae helpfully explains that our responsibility as readers of Scripture is not "domination" but "attentiveness."[30]

When this epistemological launching point is put into conversation with how scriptural metaphors work to convey meaning, it necessarily raises the question of what it means to "attend to" and "understand" the metaphors in Scripture. I contend that the knowledge accessible through metaphors is inherently relational knowledge. To draw briefly here upon Kierkegaard's framework, I am arguing that Scripture's metaphors cannot be viewed at an objective distance, but instead passionately involve their readers/hearers not only in the "what" of objective knowledge, but in the "how" of our subjectivity, where God as the Metaphor-Maker has revealed himself as the object.[31] Understanding metaphor in Scripture is therefore also an *a posteriori* investigation of God's self-revelation through which we come to know him.

---

27 Murray Rae, "Incline Your Ear So That You May Live: Principles of Biblical Epistemology" in *The Bible and Epistemology*, (Milton Keynes: Paternoster, 2007), 162.
28 Adams, *The Reality of God*, 77.
29 See Torrance, "Can the Truth Be Learned?," 150–53; Rae, "Incline Your Ear," 163–66.
30 Rae, "Incline Your Ear," 161–62.
31 Søren Kierkegaard, *Concluding Unscientific Postscript* to Philosophical Fragments, vol. 12.1 in *Kierkegaard's Writings*, ed. and trans. Howard V. Hong and Edna Hong (Princeton: Princeton University Press, 1992), 326.

Furthermore, as Scripture itself testifies (e.g., Rom 8:1–13; 12:1–2; 2 Cor 5:16–17), this revelation can only be grasped by the *phronema tou pneumatos* (mind of the Spirit), without which the reader cannot truly understand and participate in the "shared perspective" created by Scripture's metaphors. As Torrance puts it, this renewed mind, enabled by the creative and reconciling presence of the Holy Spirit, is "constituted from above" and has unveiled eyes and unstopped ears to hear what historical inquiry and faculties of reason alone cannot provide.[32] As I argued above, metaphors enable unique access to knowledge, but this knowledge is only accessible by those who understand, and thus participate in an awareness of the metaphor. The invitation inherent in a metaphor necessarily creates bonds between those who participate in a shared understanding of their subjects, and erects barriers between those "in the know" who understand the metaphor, and those "in the dark" who do not.[33] In light of this, we might say that a true understanding of Scripture's metaphors requires an "unveiling" that enables us to see God and his acts in history in truth—in a way that corresponds to his revelatory grace. In this way, metaphor serves as a means through which the Holy Spirit gives us the eyes to see God's gracious activity, and also recognize our prior inability to see and recognize this reality in truth.

Treating Scripture's metaphors as media through which God graciously reveals himself as he speaks into our lives undoubtedly cuts against the grain of much of biblical scholarship. For example, N. T. Wright claims that metaphorical language can be deemed appropriate to "speaking of this god," if indeed the "Jewish and Christian accounts of *humans*, and *human speech*, might turn out to be correct."[34] Note that Wright's view assumes that Scripture's metaphors are primarily a product of a *biblical author's* attempt to express divine attributes or perspectives in human terms, rather than Scripture's metaphors being first and foremost the divine and revealed Word. Instead, I want to investigate below how our

---

32 Torrance, "Can the Truth Be Learned?," 158. I am not arguing, however, that one who does not possess the mind of the Spirit cannot understand anything of Scripture's metaphor. Indeed, anyone could investigate Scripture's metaphors, and especially the models underlying Scripture's metaphors, and reach some relatively sound conclusions regarding some of the implications of these metaphors. However, if metaphors are meant to invite a reader into a shared vision, then they necessarily exclude those who do not share in the vision with the metaphor-maker. See further Cohen, "Some Philosophy: 1."

33 See Cohen, "Some Philosophy: 1," 30; see also Beverly Roberts Gaventa, *Our Mother Saint Paul* (Louisville: Westminster John Knox, 2007), 12.

34 N. T. Wright, *The New Testament and the People of God* (Philadelphia: Fortress, 1992), 130 (emphasis mine).

understanding of God's revelation in Scripture changes *if we view God as the Metaphor-Maker behind the text*, and Scripture's metaphors as a conduit of God's self-revelation. If we view God as Metaphor-Maker, then through the metaphors of Scripture, God self-discloses knowledge of the divine and extends an invitation to the audience of Scripture to view and understand him and his acts in history *in a particular way* and *through a particular lens or framework*. In Scripture's metaphors, God as Metaphor-Maker has condescended to the realm of mundane human experience, taking up and transforming models from the world of the first audience in order to communicate to them attributes of his divine nature and a "sameness of vision" of his divine acts.

So let us take an example from Scripture in order to see the implications for viewing God as Metaphor-Maker and metaphor as a conduit of his self-revelation. My own work on metaphor began in my doctoral studies which focused in part on the *huiothesia* (adoption) metaphor in Galatians, which I think is well suited to a brief examination here. In Galatians 4, Paul writes that at the time appointed by the Father, "God sent his Son, born of a woman, born under the law, in order to redeem those under the law, that we might receive the adoption to sonship" (Gal 4:5). This statement reveals what we might call a "triple condescension" of God.[35] First, this statement picks out the Christ event as a real act in history whereby God condescended to human flesh (Phil 2:1–11) in order to restore and redeem his creation from the effects of sin and death. Second, in the words of Scripture, God condescends once again as a Metaphor-Maker and invites the Galatians to view the Christ event, and their participation in it, through the lens of adoption. Third, if Scripture is God's word to the people of God throughout history, then God condescends also to us in the words of Scripture, inviting all, in and through Christ, to participate in the metaphor through the *phronema tou pneumatos*. However, let us leave aside the third condescension for a moment, and I will revisit it in the final section of the paper.

As you can see, the first two condescensions are, in fact, bound by two distinct sets of cultural and chronological particularities: the historical particularity of Christ's life, death, and resurrection in Jerusalem, and the historical and cultural particularities of the Galatian church sometime

---

35 Perhaps this is somewhat akin to Torrance's discussion of the need for *Horizontverschmeltzung*, except under his paradigm I would see four horizons rather than three (the historical events, the texts to which the historical events refer, the 21st century horizon, and the human horizon in which God is present through the Spirit), "Can the Truth Be Learned?," 158.

between the late 40s and early 50s CE. Since the second condescension is more illustrative of the point I am trying to make, we will focus on it here. As the recipients of Paul's letter, the Galatians are the first invitees and participants in the adoption metaphor in Galatians 4:5, and part of our *a posteriori* investigation into this metaphor here is to give an account of what occurred in this second condescension. From the whole of Galatians, we know that the Galatian believers have accepted Paul's gospel message and received the Spirit by faith (Gal 1:9; 2:15–16; 3:2), and we also know that Judaizing infiltrators are attempting to persuade the Galatian believers to adopt Torah as a completion of their devotion to Christ by arguing that only through adopting Torah can they become true children of Abraham (3:1–9, 15–28). Furthermore, we know that the socio-legal practice of Roman adoption was a common occurrence in the Roman Empire in the first century whereby an adult Roman father would adopt an adult son in order to secure an heir to ensure the preservation of his *familia*. This is thus the most likely candidate for the predominant model underlying the adoption metaphor in Galatians.[36]

This data (and certainly more could be added) gives us a broad sketch of the historical particularity of the adoption metaphor in Galatians 4:5. So, into this particular historical context of the Galatians, rife with questions over the law, Christian identity vis-à-vis Abraham, the experience of the Spirit, and the context of the Roman Empire, God discloses himself through his Word written by the apostle Paul in Scripture. God as Metaphor-Maker, by recounting the acts of Christ in history, and inviting the Galatian believers to view them through the lens of "receiving the adoption to sonship," creates a "sameness of vision" whereby the Galatians are enabled to view themselves, God, and his actions in history from the divine perspective. Through this metaphor, the Galatian believers receive relational knowledge of God as their gracious Father, which is confirmed by the witness of the Spirit (Gal 4:6). Over and against the message promulgated by the false teachers in Galatia, who argue that circumcision is the means by which one becomes a child of Abraham, the adoption metaphor serves as "corrective vision" regarding their spiritual lineage. Through the adoption metaphor, God discloses that in Christ *he already relates to them as children of God*, and since they are children of God, then they are also Abraham's children. It is striking that this one metaphor becomes a lens to view the entirety of Scripture's Grand Narrative, giving the Galatians an

---

36   See chapters 4–5 of my "Light through a Prism."

account of not only their current status in Christ, but also how they relate to God's actions in history as "children of Abraham." Moreover, God's self-disclosure conveys so much more than "objective" knowledge of the Christ event. This metaphor also gives the Galatians a glimpse at God's own perspective of the significance of the Christ event, and of his Fatherly affection for them that has been poured out in Christ. The knowledge conveyed through the adoption metaphor is relational and experiential, and cannot be paraphrased or translated into other "literal" speech. Rather, the knowledge revealed by the Metaphor-Maker is only received through the Galatian believers understanding the metaphor "adoption."

Certainly much could be said about God as Metaphor-Maker and the historical particularity of Scripture's metaphors, but for brevity's sake I will only raise one further issue. If I were to repeat the process above for another adoption metaphor, for example in Romans 9:4 where an adoption metaphor is used of Israel, we would find a different "field of vision" than in Galatians 4:5. As I argued above, metaphorical meaning is bound to particular contexts, and is not wholly transferrable between them. Thus the metaphor in Romans 9:4 conveys different knowledge about God and his acts in history than the adoption metaphor in Galatians 4:5. For example, in Romans 9:4 the adoption metaphor is used to communicate knowledge of God's elective activity that has worked throughout history in order to show mercy (Rom 9:16–28). Although the same underlying model is referenced,[37] the implications of the metaphor in Romans 9:4 are quite different than in Galatians 4:5. Whereas one focuses on God gathering the Galatians into the people of God, the other focuses on God's elective activity and covenant faithfulness toward Israel. Knowing this, we must resist the temptation to flatten these metaphors, or to divorce them from the historical particularities in which they were first revealed.

We can conclude from these few examples that the relational knowledge that comes to us through Scripture's metaphors provides a window into how the Metaphor-Maker sees a particular subject. If we begin with the premise that in Scripture God reveals himself to us through the texts illuminated by the Spirit, then the metaphors in Scripture are a means by which God graciously allows his people epistemic access (albeit through a glass darkly) to his self-revelation. They are media, designed by God's

---

37   The question of the underlying models that a metaphor draws upon is more complex and nuanced, and it is certainly possible for a metaphor to evoke more than one model. This is precisely what is happening in Romans 9:4, which simultaneously evokes models of Roman adoption and Jewish sonship. See chapter 7 of "Light through a Prism" for an extended discussion.

revelatory activity, which serve to enable readers to know and understand God as the Subject to whom the text witnesses. However, as Paul's irruption of praise at the end of Romans 11 affirms, these metaphors, and our understanding of them, give only a fraction of the infinite wisdom and beauty of God. Scripture's metaphors only allow us to take a few cautious steps down paths that are beyond our ability to fully trace out. What is more, as soon as we attempt to take command of God's gracious revelation for ourselves, by reducing Scripture's metaphors into straightforward propositional statements, we risk emptying them of some of their capacity to communicate experiential knowledge, especially if our theological reflection does not attend to both cognitive and affective elements present in Scripture's metaphors.

METAPHOR, REVELATIONS, AND REVELATION

Our examination of the adoption metaphor in Galatians 4:5 demonstrates that in Scriptural metaphors, God's self-revelation descends to the realm of human experience. It is not, as some have suggested, that we assume that biblical authors chose models from human experience and used them to reason their way to the divine. Rather, in Scripture the Divine condescends to our experiences, and thus the "flesh and blood" models underlying Scripture's metaphors act as a conduit of God's self-communication to the first audience. The question that remains is how we are to move from the historically particular "revelations" of Scripture's metaphors to an understanding of Scripture's metaphors as God's revealed word to the church universal. The answer to this question cannot solely rest in our ability as humans to understand correctly what the metaphor "meant" to its first audience (if indeed such a thing were wholly attainable), and then to apply this meaning to contemporary contexts. Implicit in this view is an understanding that the first audience of Scripture's metaphors is the "true" audience, and all other audiences of Scripture's metaphors are not offered an invitation to participate in the metaphor in the same way. If Scripture is God's word for his people in every age, then this decidedly cannot be the case. Instead, we must reckon with what it means for contemporary audiences to participate alongside the Galatian believers, the Roman believers, the people of Israel, and so forth, as part of the community of God's people throughout the ages. In short, we must recognize that the same Metaphor-Maker who discloses himself to

Scripture's first audiences has been at work, and is at work, inviting his people in all times and places to share in Scripture's metaphors.

However, in order to participate alongside the first audiences of Scripture's metaphors, we must also do the hard work of historical inquiry—not to find our way to the divine, but rather to understand the context, the "flesh and blood" model that God chose as his conduit of self-revelation. Our participation in the divine perspective must begin with attention to the historical particularities in which this perspective was revealed—not to understand what the metaphors "meant" to the first audience, but to understand what they "mean" for God's people in all times and places. If we divorce Scripture's metaphors from their under-lying models, then we risk not knowing what it is exactly that we are participating in. Perhaps this kind of theological discourse is akin to get-ting dressed in the dark. We may be able to "put on" the metaphor, but in order to see what it is we're wearing we need to turn on the light of historical context.

The anchoring of theological discourse in the historical context of Scripture's metaphors is thus crucial to enabling the church in all times and places to understand, participate in, and be formed by them. This, I think, is imperative, as Scripture's metaphors are meant to convey rela-tional knowledge of God as the Subject behind the text. Moreover, these metaphors are not intended to facilitate Christians in the quest for "objec-tive" knowledge of God, but rather they are intended for the *formation of God's people* which comes through sharing in the "sameness of vision" created by God's self-revelation in the metaphors of Scripture. Through Scripture's metaphors, God enables his people in every age to under-stand the plight of all of creation in bondage to sin, to view rightly the significance of the Christ event, and to participate in his vision for the redemption of the world.

CHAPTER 7

THE VOICE OF GOD IN HISTORICAL BIBLICAL CRITICISM

JASON MCMARTIN AND TIMOTHY H. PICKAVANCE

THE QUESTION

We're concerned with a particular, highly idealized question: When one is faced with competing testimony from equally competent and equally trusted biblical scholars on some question of exegesis, and one has absolutely no evidence that bears on the question beyond that competing testimony, what is the rational belief state? For example, suppose in developing a lesson on the Ten Commandments, Chris comes across David Clines' denial that Exodus 20:10 ("And God spoke all these words saying . . .") ever took place.[1] That is, Clines holds that it is a false statement. It didn't happen. Then he reads Brevard Childs saying that this verse "points to the direct, unmediated communication of Yahweh himself."[2] Chris takes this claim by Childs to be an affirmation of the truth of the statement of Exodus 20:10. He is faced with contradictory testimony from two biblical experts. What should he believe? To emphasize, the question we're targeting is highly idealized. But we believe proceeding through the idealization will help us in messier, real-world cases. And we'll try to say how this is so in what follows.

---

1   David J. A. Clines, *Interested Parties: The Ideology of Writers and Readers of the Hebrew Bible* (Sheffield: Sheffield Academic, 1995), 27–28.
2   Brevard S. Childs, *The Book of Exodus: A Critical, Theological Commentary* (Louisville: Westminster John Knox, 1974), 397. Clines attempts to undercut this statement by Childs, but that isn't relevant for our example. Chris need only take Childs's view as being that the passage refers to an actual event of divine speech.

The answer to the question is simple: one ought to withhold judgment. This paper is, first, a defense of that answer. Second, though, we try to say why that answer doesn't lead to a basically skeptical condition for average churchgoers about the contents of the Scriptures, given that experts disagree about pretty much every question that can be asked of the Bible. We will develop this skeptical worry and offer two possible responses. Third, we will make some comments about why you should care about all this.

Before we approach those three upshots, we offer two clarifying points about the question. First, the question is not *descriptive*, but *prescriptive*. We are not concerned with what people *in fact* believe in situations where they only have access to competing expert testimony about the content of Scripture. Rather, we are concerned with what people *ought* to believe in those situations, if they are responding rationally to the evidence at their disposal.

Second, the question is idealized, and there are at least three dimensions of that idealization. By this, we mean that we are assuming certain constraints on the situations with which we are primarily concerned. First, we assume that the believer has *absolutely no evidence* beyond the competing expert testimony. There are two sub-assumptions built into this first assumption. The believer has no access to the experts' respective reasons for their views, and the believer has no evidence that is (for him or her) independent of the experts' respective testimonies. Second, we assume that the believer trusts the experts equally. And third, we assume that evidence is the only constraint on rationality. Below, we consider the result of lifting the first two assumptions in some detail, but we largely ignore the third. That is a subject for another day, another paper.

In the idealized case, then, we have in view someone who has literally no evidence bearing on the interpretation of a passage other than disagreeing expert testimony. And we recognize that almost no one is in such a situation. For example, all of us, no matter how naive about a passage, still at least have our common-sense interpretations, and that counts for something. Usually, we have even more than that. At the end of the day, we're concerned with these messier, real-life situations more so than the idealized one. However, proceeding through the idealizations, we hope to show, will help us uncover what rationality demands even in these messier cases. If you are dubious about this, as no doubt many of our readers will be, we ask for your patience, and for an open mind.

We have framed our question as the proper epistemic stance toward instances of disagreement among experts. Contemporary epistemologists have been carrying on a lively discussion concerning disagreement; in this paper, we sketch a prospectus for a research program to bring the resources of the literature on the epistemology of disagreement to bear on questions concerning expert testimony in the field of biblical studies. Our answer to the question takes the first step in the development of this program by considering the case of the ordinary believer. Given that no one finds him or herself in the idealized epistemic position to which we provide an answer, this first step in the research program remains fairly minimal. Nevertheless, the practical implications of this first step will still be substantive. We will also sketch some of the issues that will need resolving in the progression of this research program relating to the lifting of assumptions to particularize the idealized case.

ORIGIN OF THE QUESTION

Our question concerning the competing testimony of biblical scholars in relationship to ordinary churchgoers arises in part from the fragmented state of the academic discipline of biblical studies. In the nineteenth century, a collection of methodologies rose to prominence that now fall under the label of historical biblical criticism, or HBC. Practitioners of this approach to the study of the Bible frequently seek to investigate biblical texts independently from church or theological traditions. It was thought that by shifting to historical inquiry, a non-theological, non-sectarian, and value-neutral exploration of biblical texts could commence.[3] Unlike theology, history was thought to be a scientific discipline that could be engaged in a cohesive manner independently of the scholar's faith tradition. It was thought to be purely descriptive, rather than prescriptive.[4] Sociologically, these methodological machinations gave birth to a split between the academic fields of systematic theology and biblical investigation. J. P. Gabler's oft-cited inaugural address at the University of Altdorf in 1787 concisely "argued for the strict separation of biblical theology and church teaching," following the trends of several other thinkers of the time.[5] Given the birth

---

3   Craig G. Bartholomew, "*Warranted* Biblical Interpretation: Alvin Plantinga's 'Two (or More) Kinds of Scripture Scholarship,'" in *"Behind" the Text: History and Biblical Interpretation*, ed. Craig Bartholomew, et al. (Grand Rapids: Zondervan, 2003).

4   Daniel J. Treier, *Introducing Theological Interpretation of Scripture: Recovering a Christian Practice* (Grand Rapids: Baker Academic, 2008), 13–14.

5   Edward W. Klink III and Darian R. Lockett, *Understanding Biblical Theology: A Comparison of Theory and Practice* (Grand Rapids: Zondervan, 2012), 14. As Klink and Lockett show, ferment also surrounds the relationship of biblical theology to biblical studies and to systematic theology.

of this approach to biblical studies in the modern era, practitioners of HBC frequently employed methodological naturalism. Patterning their study of the Bible after the natural sciences, scholars limited themselves to the deliverances of human reason, broadly construed as ordinary human perceptual and rational capacities. Truths known by faith were set aside.[6]

By self-consciously removing theological tenets from biblical scholarship, the academic disciplines of theology and biblical studies were placed at odds with one another. Since ordinary Christians adhere to the truths of the faith, such methodological posturing also distances believers from the results of biblical scholarship. Another result of these methodological approaches has been increasing divergence among the conclusions scholars draw concerning the content, historicity, and meaning of biblical texts. Academic biblical scholars now regularly dispute or dismiss affirmations held for centuries by the church or believed by Christians in the pew.

Philosophers, theologians, and biblical scholars have, we believe rightly, challenged the epistemological assumptions of HBC. While such disputes frequently concern the correct mode for professional biblical scholars, these discussions frequently implicate non-scholars directly or indirectly. For example, Peter van Inwagen frames his interrogation of HBC by contrasting professional New Testament scholars with "those who regard the New Testament as . . . historically reliable and who are not trained New Testament scholars."[7] Alvin Plantinga launches his criticism on the basis of "traditional Christian belief," without distinguishing among professional biblical scholars and non-professional readers of the text.[8] Several thinkers involved in this discussion fail to distinguish among the proper epistemological approaches to be taken by non-believing biblical scholars, believing biblical scholars, and believing non-scholars. Frequently, the latter two categories are conflated. Plantinga's pivotal piece "Two (or More) Kinds of Scripture Scholarship" and several of the responses to it primarily address Christian biblical scholars of a traditional sort.[9] Others extend the implications of Plantinga's argument to traditional Christians who are not biblical scholars.[10] Although much of the interest may be said

---

6   Alvin Plantinga, *Warranted Christian Belief* (New York: Oxford University Press, 2000), 414–18.

7   Peter van Inwagen, "Do You Want Us to Listen to You?" in *"Behind" the Text*, 101.

8   Plantinga, *Warranted Christian Belief*, 375.

9   The most extended version of this essay may be found as a chapter in *Warranted Christian Belief*.

10   Robert P. Gordon, "A Warranted Version of Historical Biblical Criticism? A Response to Alvin Plantinga," in *"Behind" the Text*, 79–91.

concerning the epistemological disputes among scholars, our focus in this essay will be on proper epistemic stance of non-scholars toward the deliverances of academic debates.

Several Christian philosophers of religion have also suggested that ordinary believers can more or less safely ignore the deliverances of HBC. Alvin Plantinga contends that a "traditional Christian . . . need not be disturbed by the conflict between alleged results of HBC and traditional Christian belief."[11] For example, Plantinga contends that the artificial restriction of a traditional Christian scholar to the canons of one form of HBC "would be a little like trying to mow your lawn with a nail scissors or paint your house with a toothbrush; it might be an interesting experiment if you have time on your hands, but otherwise why limit yourself in this way?"[12] Such a scholar could pay attention to HBC, but only as a player in a game, disconnected from the goal of arriving at truth and concerned only with what would be true under certain assumptions.[13] Peter van Inwagen provocatively asks whether professional New Testament scholars want ordinary believers to listen to them and concludes that "ordinary Christians may therefore ignore any skeptical historical claims made by New Testament scholars with a clear intellectual conscience."[14] Eleonore Stump contrasts Thomas Aquinas' mode of biblical interpretation with what she calls Richard Swinburne's deistic approach. According to Stump, dynamic biblical interpretation (exemplified by Thomas) allows non-expert ordinary believers to access God's communication to them, rather than being dependent on the knowledge of an elite few.[15] Even Brinks, who is generally more friendly to HBC than Plantinga and van Inwagen, seems to concede that HBC should not concern ordinary believers, just as specialized, expert knowledge in any discipline need not be the concern of the person on the street. However, she does believe that criticisms such as Plantinga's may wrongly discourage persons of faith from engaging in biblical scholarship.[16]

The general impression is that ordinary believers can, and probably should, be rather dismissive of the results of HBC. But we wish to affirm

---

11   Plantinga, *Warranted Christian Belief*, 375.
12   Ibid., 417.
13   Ibid., 419.
14   van Inwagen, "Do You Want Us to Listen to You?" 103.
15   Eleonore Stump, "Revelation and Biblical Exegesis: Augustine, Aquinas, and Swinburne," in *Reason and the Christian Religion: Essays in Honour of Richard Swinburne*, ed. Alan Padgett (Oxford: Clarendon, 1994), 161–97.
16   Christina L. Brinks, "On Nail Scissors and Toothbrushes: Responding to the Philosophers' Critiques of Historical Biblical Criticism." *RelS* 49/3 (2013): 357–76.

what Brinks, Gordon, and others have said: HBC does have value for ordinary Christians and not solely those who wish to engage in biblical scholarship. This affirmation runs contrary to the stance that would seem to be implied by philosophical criticisms of HBC and renews the problem those criticisms are meant to forestall. Biblical experts disagree on every substantive question of concern to ordinary Christians, and the evidence they adduce for affirmations contrary to traditional Christianity may lead to a skeptical conundrum.

We will assume without further support that HBC offers valuable insights to traditional believers. Support for that assumption may be found elsewhere.[17] In order for Christians to employ HBC as an aid to hearing the voice of God in Scripture, we must find a way to avoid a skeptical conclusion. We turn now to this task, which first requires sketching a path to that skeptical worry.

DISAGREEMENT, TESTIMONY, AND THE TOTAL EVIDENCE PRINCIPLE

The situations we have in view, in which one has no evidence on a question of exegesis beyond competing expert testimony, bear certain structural similarities with the sorts of situations epistemologists have in view when they discuss the epistemology of disagreement. Further, it turns out that some of the insights found in the disagreement literature are useful for our discussion here. Therefore, we presently supply an overview of that literature, and will highlight four important claims we deploy in order to defend that one ought to abstain in situations like those we have in mind.

The literature on disagreement has largely focused on cases where one finds oneself in a disagreement with an actual or perceived *peer*. A peer, in this literature, is (roughly) someone who shares your evidence and your epistemological abilities. Peers are aware of the same arguments, or see more or less the same scene, or whatever, and they are just as smart, attentive, intellectually virtuous, etc. as you are. The idea is that your peers are just as likely as you to get the truth in the relevant situation. The primary question in the literature on disagreement concerns what one should do when one finds oneself disagreeing with a peer.

---

17   Gordon, "A Warranted Version of Historical Biblical Criticism?" 79–91.

A good bit of the discussion is driven by intuitions about cases. Consider the following case:

> **Restaurant Check.** Suppose that five of us go out to dinner. It's time to pay the check, so the question we're interested in is how much we each owe. We can all see the bill total clearly, we all agree to give a 20 percent tip, and we further agree to split the whole cost evenly, not worrying over who asked for imported water, or skipped dessert, or drank more of the wine. I do the math in my head and become highly confident that our shares are $43 each. Meanwhile, my friend does the math in her head and becomes highly confident that our shares are $45 each.[18]

Many people, when confronted with Restaurant Check, find it really very plausible that one ought to give up one's belief that each of you owes $43, abstaining until one can do some further, more careful checking. Maybe you'll set out to do the math on a napkin, or to get out your calculator.

In light of cases like this (along with other more theoretical reasons) many epistemologists have adopted *Conciliationist* views of disagreement. According to Conciliationism, one is rationally obligated to move one's confidence in the direction of the confidence of one's peer in cases of peer disagreement. In simple cases, in which you believe a proposition while your peer just as confidently disbelieves it, Conciliationism requires that one suspend judgment until further evidence comes to light.

But other cases seem to press our intuitions in a different direction. Consider this case:

> **Lunch Table.** Estelle, Edwin, and I, who have been roommates for the past eight years, were eating lunch together at the dining room table in our apartment. When I asked Edwin to pass the wine to Estelle, he replied, 'Estelle isn't here today'. Prior to this disagreement, neither Edwin nor I had any reason to think that the other is evidentially or cognitively deficient in any way, and we both sincerely avowed our respective conflicting beliefs.[19]

---

18   David Christensen, "Epistemology of Disagreement: The Good News," *The Philosophical Review* 116/2 (2007), 193.

19   Jennifer Lackey, "A Justificationist View of Disagreement's Epistemic Significance," in *Social Epistemology*, ed. A. Haddock, A. Millar, and D. Pritchard (New York: Oxford University Press, 2010), 306.

In this case, many (including Lackey) find dubious the idea that one ought to adjust one's belief in light of one's disagreement with Edwin. In fact, some (not Lackey!) have thought that these sorts of cases reveal that disagreement itself shouldn't impact rationality in any sense at all, and that something else must be going on in explaining our reaction to cases like Restaurant Check. These sorts of views, according to which peer disagreement does not rationally oblige a change in confidence, are *Steadfast* views.

There are a number of dimensions to the dispute between Conciliationists and Steadfasters. Happily, we needn't get into those dimensions here, nor need we take a stand on the more general dispute between Conciliationists and Steadfasters. This reason is simple. The cases of primary concern for us don't revolve around a disagreement between oneself and a peer. Rather, they revolve around disagreements between two people one takes to be one's epistemic superiors. The disagreement is not between oneself and a peer, but rather between two people who aren't you, but whom you look to as epistemic guides.

There is an important fruit of the discussion about peer disagreement that makes raising the conversation helpful for this context. In particular, it has become more clear what types of evidence are involved in cases of disagreement. Take Restaurant Check again. Prior to the disagreement, your evidence that each share is $43 is, we might stipulate, a bit of "mental math." Whatever it is, call that original bit of evidence, E. Importantly, the evidence you have is distinct from the belief you form on the basis of the evidence. On the basis of the same evidence (you know your friend well enough to know that she does mental math in a relevantly similar way to the way you do), your friend believes that each share is $45. You and your friend have the same evidence in spite of conflicting beliefs. When you learn that your friend disagrees and thinks that each share is $45, you get some new evidence, H1. H1 consists of the fact that your friend takes E to support that each share is $45. You also, though, realize that *you* took E to support that each share is $43; call this evidence, H2. And you are antecedently committed to the claim that you and your friend are equally likely to get the right answer. H1 and H2 are distinct from one another and also from E; indeed, they are different in kind from E in a way we will discuss shortly. We might summarize your evidential situations before and after the disagreement as follows:

Evidence Prior to Disagreement	Evidence after Disagreement
E (some mental math)	E
	H1 (on the basis of E, your friend is confident the shares are $45)
	H2 (on the basis of E, you are confident the shares are $43)

There are important differences between E, on the one hand, and H1 and H2, on the other. E is *first-order* evidence, in the sense that it bears directly on the disputed question. H1 and H2 are *higher-order*, in the sense that they do not bear directly on the disputed question, but rather bear on the disputed question by bearing on the question whether some bit of first-order evidence is good evidence about the disputed question. If H1 or H2 bear on whether the shares are $43, they do so by bearing on whether E is good evidence for you that the shares are $43.

Here's a different example to illustrate the first-order/higher-order distinction. Suppose you're looking at a flower, and it seems orange to you. In this case, you have some perceptual evidence that the flower is orange. This perceptual evidence, consisting of a perceptual seeming, a certain sensory experience, is first-order evidence that the flower is orange. But suppose someone then tells you that, not long ago, you drank an elixir that renders your visual perceptual faculties highly unreliable. This new information, that you drank the elixir, doesn't bear directly on the question of whether the flower is orange. Rather, it bears on the question whether your visual perception is reliable, and thus on the question whether that perceptual seeming is a reliable indicator of the color of the flower. Thus, it indirectly bears on whether it's rational for you to believe that the flower is orange on the basis of your perceptual seeming, since it upsets your confidence that your perceptual seemings are a good guide to the color of things. You should become less confident that the flower really is orange, in light of this new evidence. So this higher-order evidence bears on what you should believe about the color of the flower by bearing on your view about the connection between your first-order evidence and the truth of the matter.

There are difficult and delicate questions about the relationship between first-order and higher-order evidence, but we here highlight just one such issue.[20] Sometimes higher-order evidence *screens off* first-order

---

20   See, as a start, Sophie Horowitz, "Epistemic Akrasia," *Nous* 48/4 (2014): 718–44; Sophie

evidence. In the case of the vision-disrupting elixir, the evidence that one drank the elixir renders one's visual perceptual seeming impotent. It's not that one doesn't *have* the evidence of one's senses, or even that it no longer counts as evidence in any interesting sense. Rather, the higher-order evidence prevents the perceptual seeming from making it rational for you to believe that the flower is orange. The higher-order evidence, in that sense, screens off the evidential force of the first-order evidence. In some other cases, higher-order evidence does not seem to screen off first-order evidence. Suppose, in a case very much like Restaurant Check, that you reflect on the fact that you take E to support $43 prior to discovering the disagreement with your friend. That is, suppose you acquire H2 prior to the disagreement. In such a case, H2 would not screen off E at all. Indeed, it seems like H2 has no impact on rationality in such a case.

In the disagreement literature, one issue that drives the discussion is whether the higher-order evidence one acquires in a disagreement screens off the first-order evidence one acquired prior to the disagreement. Certain Conciliationist views are in fact structured around the idea that evidence one acquires from the peer disagreements themselves screen off first-order evidence.[21] Other somewhat Steadfast views (see Lackey 2010) entail that, at least in some cases, the first-order evidence more or less screens off higher-order evidence. Still other views (see Williamson 2011) maintain that higher-order evidence doesn't bear on first-order questions at all; these views "level-split." On these views, one might be rational in believing that *p* on the basis of evidence E, while being just as rational in believing that E doesn't support *p*. We leave open the general question about how first- and higher-order evidence interact.

Almost all parties to the disagreement literature, though, agree that you should believe in a way that comports with your total evidence, even when they disagree about what belief a particular stock of total evidence supports. We call this the Total Evidence Principle:

- **Total Evidence Principle** One ought to believe in a way that is supported by one's total evidence.

Horowitz and Paulina Sliwa, "Respecting all the Evidence," *Philosophical Studies* 172/11 (2015): 2835–58; Thomas Kelly, "Peer Disagreement and Higher-Order Evidence," in *Disagreement*, ed. T. A. Warfield and R. Feldman (New York: Oxford University Press, 2010), 111–74; Maria Lasonen-Aarnio, "Higher-Order Evidence and the Limits of Defeat," *Philosophy and Phenomenological Research* 88/2 (2014): 314–45; Timothy Williamson, "Improbable Knowing," in *Evidentialism and Its Discontents*, ed. T. Dougherty (New York: Oxford University Press, 2011), 147–64.
21   See especially: Adam Elga, "Reflection and Disagreement," *Nous* 41/3 (2007): 478–502.

The Total Evidence Principle is a natural corollary of a kind of Evidentialism:

- **Evidentialism** The only thing relevant to rationality is evidence.

Evidentialism has its detractors, of course, but it is also quite plausible. We don't pretend to defend it.

It's also important for our purposes to recognize that testimony is a legitimate source of evidence:

- **Testimony is Evidence** A's testimony to B that p is (prima facie) evidence for B that p.

Here again, we don't pretend to offer a thorough defense of this claim. However, it's worth noting that a great deal of what each of us knows is known on the basis of testimony. Almost all of the authors' scientific knowledge, for example, is known by the testimony of scientists. But even more intimate things, like one's own name and birthday, are very often known on the basis of the testimony of one's parents. (If you have seen your birth certificate, there is still testimony involved: that of the doctors and nurses present, as well as that of your parents.) Further, Christians have a special reason to take testimony seriously: the Scriptures are testimony from God!

There are at least two ways of understanding the type of evidence that testimony supplies. First, testimony might be a form of fundamental first-order evidence. But testimony might, second, be a kind of higher-order evidence that believing a certain proposition is rational. If the latter, then our idealized case involves two bits of competing higher-order evidence without any first-order evidence. There is, then, a structural similarity to the disagreement cases presented above. The differences are two. First, in the idealized case there is no "E." Second, in the idealized case, both H1 and H2 concern others (rather than one of those two concerning oneself), namely the experts on which one is relying, and their respective reactions to a stock of evidence that you presume they share but that you do not yourself possess. At any rate, we won't be overly concerned with these two ways of understanding how testimony supplies evidence, though it will emerge again briefly below.

One final principle:

- **Evidential Order is Irrelevant** The order in which one acquires a bit of evidence is irrelevant to its impact on rationality.

Say one has two bits of evidence, E1 and E2, for believing something. Maybe E1 is super-strong evidence for believing, and E2 is quite weak evidence against believing. The idea behind Evidential Order is Irrelevant, is that it shouldn't matter whether one got E1 or E2 first. Whatever belief state is made rational by getting E1 first and then E2 should be the belief state made rational by getting E2 first and then E1. Suppose, for example, that you were trying to work out whether it was going to rain. First, you consulted your local meteorologist on the local news broadcast. She says it's gonna rain. So you come to believe that it's gonna rain. But then, just to double-check, you consult Weather Underground, which says it ain't gonna rain. Whatever belief state you wind up in after this second bit of evidence (probably a state of agnosticism), it shouldn't matter that you first consulted the local meteorologist and then Weather Underground. Had you consulted Weather Underground first and then the local meteorologist, you should wind up in just the same state.

That prior point is meant to rely on our intuitive judgments about rationality, but there's an arbitrariness argument for Evidential Order is Irrelevant. Suppose you denied Evidential Order is Irrelevant. Maybe you think that once you've consulted one source of evidence, you ought to stick with that judgment until you get *even better* evidence for a different belief state. So depending on whether you consult the local meteorologist or Weather Underground first, you ought to stick with the resulting belief when you consult the other. (We suggest that this is often how we function as humans.) The trouble with this is that rationality then becomes a kind of luck. Suppose, for example, that your Weather Underground app on your phone just took longer to load than normal, and so the television turned on more quickly than the app opened. Maybe this was because of some quirk in your phone's hardware, or because the software was updating. Who cares. The point is that, whatever the random cause, you consulted the meteorologist first, rather than Weather Underground. Thus, you ought to believe, even after seeing the app, that it's gonna rain. Had things gone normally, had the software not needed updating, you would have rationally believed that it's not gonna rain, even after getting both bits of evidence. That seems weird. Rationality shouldn't depend on such random factors. Together with the intuitive point above, this argument makes Evidential Order is Irrelevant quite plausible.

If you put these four principles together—the Total Evidence Principle, Evidentialism, Testimony is Evidence, and Evidential Order is Irrelevant—one ought to suspend judgment in our target cases. Suppose you were in the kind of case we mentioned at the outset. That is, suppose you're working to settle an interpretive question, and all you have to go on is the testimony of experts, whom you trust equally, but who disagree on the question. Recall Chris's consternation over the conflicting testimony of Clines and Childs concerning the veracity of Exodus 20:10. The testimonial evidence one acquires from these disagreeing experts is equally strong: you trust them equally, after all. So that's two bits of evidence, by Testimony is Evidence, but it's two bits of evidence that cancel out, by Evidential Order is Irrelevant. By Evidentialism, there's nothing else that bears on what the rational belief state is for you. So, by the Total Evidence Principle, you ought to be agnostic about the answer to that interpretive question.

There is also a Conciliationist rationale for the conclusion we're plumping for. The disagreeing experts on whom you are relying ought to end up agnostic if they discovered their disagreement. So they would, post-disagreement, advise you to be agnostic too. Thus, the only evidence one would have would be two experts saying the same thing, namely, be agnostic. It's hard to imagine a better epistemic position to be in when you lack other evidence: you have two experts advising you in precisely the same way!

SKEPTICISM

There's a worry one might have about our argument to this point, namely, a worry about skepticism. If we are right that agnosticism is the proper belief state for folks in the situations we've described, won't many ordinary churchgoers wind up rationally required to be skeptical about almost anything of theological import? There are biblical scholars who disagree about pretty much *everything*, after all. Even about issues of creedal centrality, there are disagreements. Some experts deny that the Scriptures teach that God is triune, or that Jesus was God Incarnate. So the worry is that if we are right, ordinary churchgoers ought to be, more or less, theological skeptics.

We take this worry very seriously. At the end of the day, however, we maintain that it is misplaced. The remainder of this paper will come in two stages. First, in this section and in the next, we will outline some possibilities for avoiding the skeptical conclusion. One way has to do with theological interpretation. The others have to do with lifting the idealizing assumptions articulated in the introduction above. The second stage will set the stage for our final section, in which we outline some pastoral lessons that one can learn from this skeptical worry despite the worry's failure to carry the day.

THEOLOGICAL INTERPRETATION AND THE SKEPTICAL CHALLENGE

One way to deal with this skeptical worry is to adopt some form of theological interpretation of Scripture. Though many differences of approach may be found, proponents of theological exegesis frequently advocate the use of the Rule of Faith as a constraint on interpretation. In the apostolic fathers, the Rule of Faith functioned as an interpretive key for putting the many diverse aspects of Scripture into the proper picture.[22] Given the diversity of the discrete pieces of the biblical witness, varying consistent pictures may be constructed. Irenaeus' combat with heretics would have been readily solved if it had not been the case that his opponents extensively employed Scripture in the formulation of their views.[23] Irenaeus' objection to their views was based on their having used numerous biblical references and biblical language while distorting the essence of the biblical narrative providing cohesion to those discrete bits of Scripture. He used the illustration of the assembly of a mosaic, whose pieces could be used to create varying images, but which needed a key to show the proper assembly of the pieces into the intended image. "The Rule of Faith is like the key . . . which explains how the Scriptures are to be arranged, to render the portrait of the King, whereas the heretics arrange the Scriptures wrongly to form the picture of a dog or fox."[24] The Rule of Faith is a summary statement of God's activity that finds formal representation within the creed and "provides the framework within which the diversity of Scripture can be rightly ordered so that it can be directed towards advancing the apostolic faith in the life, teaching, and worship of the church."[25] The Rule derives from Scripture, forming a non-viciously circular link between text and interpretation.

Use of the Rule of Faith as a criterion for valid interpretations of the biblical text guards against skeptical conclusions concerning the content

---

22   Treier, *Introducing Theological Interpretation of Scripture*, 58–59.
23   Stephen E. Fowl, *The Theological Interpretation of Scripture*, Cascade Companions (Eugene: Cascade, 2009), 28.
24   Kathryn Greene-McCreight, "Rule of Faith" in *DTIB*, ed. Kevin J. Vanhoozer, et al. (Grand Rapids: Baker Academic, 2005), 703.
25   Fowl, *The Theological Interpretation of Scripture*, 29.

of core Christian affirmations, such as those formalized in the creeds. General skepticism concerning the truths of the Christian faith would not result from exposure to the cacophony of expert opinions concerning the Bible, since employment of the Rule of Faith as an interpretive constraint undercuts affirmations contrary to core Christian tenets.

MESSY, REAL-WORLD APPLICATIONS

Beyond adopting a form of theological interpretation, one can also respond to the skeptical worry by noticing that the skeptical conclusion might not follow once one lifts the idealizations with which we began. Recall that we assumed (1) that one has *absolutely no evidence* beyond the competing expert testimony, including access to the reasons those experts have for their views and (2) that one trusts the experts equally. (We assumed Evidentialism as well, but that will stand unchallenged.) We need to lift these assumptions in order to evaluate the force of the skeptical threat for ordinary churchgoers. You might say our idealized scenario needs to be particularized. Sorting out all of the epistemological issues pertaining to the particularizing of our question extends far beyond the scope of this paper. Instead, we'll sketch a trajectory of inquiry by describing some of the issues that will arise when one lifts these idealizations. In doing so, we'll mention some of the theological questions and resources that have been brought to bear on questions such as these.

Lifting the assumption one has no evidence beyond the competing expert testimony. It is unlikely in real world instances that ordinary believers have absolutely no evidence beyond competing expert testimony.

Ordinary believers, first and foremost, often have a stock of evidence independent of that testimony from which to work. In the case we have described, the evidence for the meaning of a particular passage or historicity of events described therein depends solely on what the experts have said about it. But presumably, one's own reading of the passage in question provides an additional kind of evidence. Being an epistemic inferior does not imply the inability to gain evidence on a question, which is independent from that of the expert.[26] Linda Zagzebski has provided an argument that such evidence may be more basic for the ordinary believer than the evidence provided by conflicting expert testimony. She states, "Trust in my faculties is always more basic than any judgment about the evidence and what it supports. Trust in myself is more basic than trust in

---

26   Contrary to Van Harvey. See Plantinga's discussion: *Warranted Christian Belief*, 409.

my judgment of the reliability of myself or anyone else."[27] This does not mean the ordinary believer is in superior evidence, just that the believer does have evidence independent from that of the expert. Theologically, this point is connected to the "clarity" of Scripture.

However, it is worth rehearsing here an observation made above: there are tricky questions to do with the relationship between first-order and higher-order evidence. Suppose that the testimonial evidence one gets from biblical scholars is a kind of higher-order evidence. Given that you take these testifiers to be experts, at least with respect to your own expertise, Zagzebski's view is compatible with the idea that one ought to take their testimony very seriously, maybe even more seriously than you take the evidence you have gathered independently. That is, it may be that your own epistemic situation is such that the expert testimony screens off, in the sense we described earlier, your independent evidence. This can be so *precisely because* you take yourself seriously as an authority, together with the fact that *you yourself* take the experts to be *experts*. What is needed to push this conversation forward is a detailed investigation into the way that testimonial evidence from experts, whether understood as first- or higher-order, interacts with one's own, independent investigations into a question. The prospects for responding to the skeptical challenge when one suspends this dimension of the idealization turns on the results of just such an investigation. Unfortunately, we haven't the space to undertake that investigation thoroughly.

Secondly, though, one might gain access to the reasons those experts have for their views. By so doing, one might come to judge for oneself which way the evidence points. One might, for example, decide that in a particular case an expert you ordinarily trust has made some problematic assumptions, or is influenced by a view with which you disagree and that bears on the way he or she is reading the relevant passage. Chris's conundrum mentioned as an example at the outset would likely have this character. Clines is unusually explicit about his methodological assumptions, and this provides readers with an opportunity to evaluate whether those assumptions are reasonable. (Recall Plantinga's and van Inwagen's worries about HBC discussed above, to which we return shortly.) In such cases, one might come rationally to give more weight to one expert rather than another, and to rely on one's own judgments as well. This also

---

27   Linda Trinkuas Zagzebski, *Epistemic Authority: A Theory of Trust, Authority, and Autonomy in Belief* (New York: Oxford University Press, 2012), 50.

displays that in many cases where one gains access to the experts' respective reasons, one may come to trust them differently as well (on which more below).

Christians believe they have a wide variety of sources of evidence available to them. For example, Plantinga describes two general forms of HBC. The non-Troeltschian variety confines itself to the deliverances of reason alone and disallows anything known by faith. By contrast, "traditional Christians, rightly or wrongly, think they do have sources of warranted belief in addition to reason: divine testimony in Scripture and also faith and the work of the Holy Spirit, or testimony of the Spirit-led church."[28] An ordinary believer may be entitled to think that she has evidence a non-believing practitioner of non-Troeltschian HBC does not have. Certain things count as evidence for the traditional believer that presumably do not count as evidence for a non-believing biblical scholar, including the testimony of the Holy Spirit, the affirmations of the creeds, and the beliefs of the faithful throughout history. Such resources are described by proponents of HBC as theological, in contrast to the non-theological approach espoused by HBC.

Motivation for use of HBC in biblical investigation frequently dismisses these so-called theological resources from an expressed desire to have non-sectarian, "universally agreed rules of evidence and argument."[29] In particular cases, it will often be the case that one person will have access to evidence another does not have. In itself, this is not problematic.[30] Rather, the problem arises when adherents of HBC insist that only certain things count as evidence, and by extension, that so-called theological resources are not evidential. As Plantinga and others have argued, no good reasons for such affirmations are forthcoming. These considerations are relevant to the second aspect of the first dimension of our idealization.

Lifting the assumption one trusts the competing experts equally. Second, our idealized case assumes that one trusts the disagreeing experts equally and that the pronouncements of these experts are in epistemic parity. If, as discussed above, a biblical scholar has limited him or herself to certain kinds of evidence and discounted others an ordinary believer might be entitled to affirm, then the ordinary believer may be disinclined to give

---

28 Plantinga, *Warranted Christian Belief*, 416.
29 Philip R. Davies, *Whose Bible Is It Anyway?* (Sheffield: Sheffield Academic, 1995), 53.
30 Plantinga, *Warranted Christian Belief*, 416–17.

equal weight to a scholar with such epistemic policies. And, as also discussed, there are many cases in which the first idealization fails where these discoveries will be made. Further, one might have other reasons for rationally trusting experts to varying degrees. We won't give a full inventory, but the situation is no different than with other types of testimony. When one has varying confidences in testifiers who disagree, one can avoid the skeptical worry.

IMPLICATIONS FOR ORDINARY CHRISTIANS

Despite many specific instances needing further explication, the upshot of the foregoing is that ordinary churchgoers aren't as obviously threatened with skepticism as it might initially seem. Whether agnosticism is warranted on a given occasion will be a function of exactly what sorts of evidence are in play, and even on the prospects for a certain sort of theological interpretation. Nonetheless, competing expert testimony still ought to impact the confidence we have in our reading of the text of Scripture, even if agnosticism is not rationally required. And in some cases, agnosticism (or something very close to it) will be the rational response. Indeed, it may be the rational response in more cases than we tend to think. This might seem troubling, but we maintain that this can actually function positively in the life of Christians and the church.

Withholding judgment may be psychologically difficult, especially on issues of great existential importance. We tend to resolve cognitive dissonance by finding a place to land. Simply providing the option to churchgoers of suspending judgment on a given question may seem radical. On the part of religious leaders and pastors, such allowance may be perceived as opening a path to disbelief. Yet, not only is such allowance epistemically proper, it also promotes growth toward maturity. For example, the willingness of pastors to refrain from making a judgment on a particular issue from the pulpit or in teaching expresses a trust in the epistemic capacities of congregation members. It implicitly affirms that those parishioners are epistemically capable and thus are being called upon to be epistemically responsible. They, too, have contributions to make to our understanding of Scripture, nor should their epistemic superiors (on questions of biblical scholarship) intimate otherwise.

One aspect of maturity implied by these epistemic policies is the cultivation of virtue. Proponents of the theological interpretation of Scripture have identified two modes in which virtue intersects with the interpretive task.[31] The first is reading and interpreting the Bible toward the end of becoming a virtuous person. Second, the exercise of virtue should be brought to bear in the process of interpreting the Bible. The first reads the Bible to gain virtue. The second uses virtue to gain the meaning of Scripture. Though advocates of theological interpretation disagree, particularly concerning the second of these two links between virtue and interpretation, the two modes should be seen as mutually reinforcing.[32] Both modes identify the goal of theology and of biblical interpretation as the end of becoming a certain kind of person.[33]

Primary among the virtues linked to our discussion is the virtue of intellectual humility. That's not a new or revolutionary thought, but it may be given new impetus by the epistemic situation we have sketched. A humble stance includes directedness toward Christ as the object of confidence (Mark 1:7–8; 1 Cor 2:1–5). Since humility involves accurate self-representation, it may mean that church leaders learn to avoid the immense pressure to represent themselves as knowing more than they do. It encompasses a stance of openness toward Christians of differing theological or denominational persuasions. It does not require capitulation to every contrary view one comes across, but a willingness to find truth where it may be found. Humility also means coming to see that ordinary believers are often more competent epistemic agents than they believe themselves to be.

Summarizing, we think that not only is a bit of epistemic caution called for from the point of view of rationality, but more broadly epistemological and pastoral concerns are served by such caution as well. How much caution is an issue with which philosophers and theologians ought to wrestle in order to better hear the voice of God in Scripture.

---

31 Stephen E. Fowl, "Virtue," in *DTIB*, ed. Kevin J. Vanhoozer, et al. (Grand Rapids: Baker Academic, 2005), 837–39.

32 Treier, *Introducing Theological Interpretation of Scripture*, 96.

33 Fowl, *The Theological Interpretation of Scripture*, 13–15; Ellen T. Charry, *By the Renewing of Your Minds: The Pastoral Function of Christian Doctrine* (New York: Oxford University Press, 1997).

CHAPTER 8

POST(MODERN) BIBLICAL HISTORIOGRAPHY: AN INTERIM REPORT FROM THE FRONT LINES[1]

WILLIAM J. ABRAHAM

THIS PAPER FALLS INTO FOUR PARTS. In part one I identify crucial elements of postmodernity as they relate to historical investigation and indicate briefly how we should handle the deep tensions that lie within the canon of postmodern materials as I perceive them. In part two I transition to Alvin Plantinga's response to Ernst Troeltsch's vision of historical inquiry, treating Troeltsch, contrary to the standard disjunction between postmodernity and modernity, as identifying significant elements in postmodern commentary on history. In the third part I raise a network of

1   In the Fall of 2015 I co-taught a course on Post(modern) Biblical Historiography with my colleague Professor Susanne Scholz. This was a challenging and exhilarating experience and I am extremely grateful to Professor Scholz for sharing in this enterprise and for being such a splendid colleague. I am also extremely grateful to the students who were such a vital part of the course. At the end of the course Professor Scholz argued in a fascinating paper that in fact we are now in a post-postmodern world. There is no space here to take this move into account.

critical problems in Plantinga's response and briefly call for a fresh appropriation of some of the formal but not material insights to be found in Troeltsch. In the fourth and final part I take stock of where we are and suggest that it is time we took a hard look at the invention of biblical studies as the foundation of our theological work.

CRUCIAL ELEMENTS OF POSTMODERNITY

It is commonplace to note that postmodernity is hard to pin down and thus extremely difficult to evaluate. Some critics see this state of affairs as intentional. Rational criticism necessarily involves an initial effort to understand what proposals postmodern writers are actually advancing and what arguments are deployed in their favor. However, given the incessant deferral of meaning[2] and given the death of the author,[3] this assumption no longer holds; so the evaluation, whether negative or positive, cannot get off the ground. There are no claims to assess and no authors to praise or blame. Hence the critic is disarmed from the outset. A crucial condition of rational assessment is missing and no amount of repetition as regards "différance" or the death of the author can resolve the difficulty. This repetition, however, does not appear to be accidental; the postmodern theorist has rigged the game from the beginning. A semantics of radical instability stops serious assessment in its tracks.

We can reach a similar conclusion from another angle. On a very natural reading of the literature, postmodern materials come across as a jumble of contradictory proposals that seem to hang together by means of mere association in the mind. Alternatively, we can see the jumble of ideas as constructed from a loose canon of diverse texts that are offered as the core body of theory and reflection. The problem that immediately arises is one of coherence. It is difficult to see how the diverse range of claims forms a coherent network of reflection and theory.[4] Again one

---

2   On this score the relevant authority to which appeal is made is Jacques Derrida in his deconstruction of poststructuralism. One source that develops this line is his seminal work, *Writing and Difference* (London; New York: Routledge, 2005).

3   The relevant text on this issue, Roland Barthes short paper, "The Death of the Author." It is available at http://artsites.ucsc.edu/faculty/Gustafson/FILM%20162.W10/readings/barthes. death.pdf. Barthes sees the death of the author as a necessary follow-through to the death of God announced by Nietzsche. "In precisely this way literature (it would be better from now on to say *writing*), by refusing to assign a 'secret', liberates what may be called an anti-theological activity, an activity that is truly revolutionary since to refuse to fix meaning is, in the end, to refuse God and his hypostases—reason, science, law." Ibid., 147.

4   It is easy to cover up this difficulty by laying claim to the benefits of integration as found in inter-disciplinary work. However, this only goes so far, for, as the old saying goes, you can't

suspects that some adherents of postmodernity readily admit the charge; they do not want to be hostage to yet one more condition of rationality as championed in modernity. Once more the critic is disarmed at the outset. Complaints about incoherence miss their mark if there is no intention to be coherent from the beginning. Again, it looks as if the game has been rigged at the outset. A crucial but very modest criterion of rationality is set aside and this commitment stops serious assessment in its tracks. As James Barr expressed the issue in his inimitable manner: ". . . to me, to utter the word 'postmodern' is equivalent to saying 'I am now going to start talking nonsense'."[5]

On a more substantial reading of the literature, one can begin to piece together a network of extremely interesting philosophical proposals. Thus there is a pretty passionate rejection of foundationalism, a resistance to privileging natural science as the paradigm of knowledge, a readiness to contest claims that propose we can get access to reality independently of our conceptual commitments, a call for other perspectives to be heard rather than suppressed (especially oppressed and marginalized voices), and a reiterated demand that considerations of power and social location be taken into account in understanding and assessing any claim to truth. Indeed claims to truth are highly suspect, but this is surely a natural corollary of the claim that there is no independent access to reality out there that would adjudicate between competing portrayals of reality.[6]

When it comes to historical investigation we can detect a variety of claims that keep showing up. Thus the rejection of metanarrative means the rejection of any effort to place historical events in any kind of wider cosmic, theological, or, say, national narrative. Equally it can mean the rejection of the claim that we can provide objective criteria of assessment for historical claims. Whatever we make of historical investigation, it does not provide us with any kind of neutral, objective description or explanation of the past.[7] The most radical version of this thesis is that there is no

integrate what you ain't got in the first place.

5   James Barr, *History and Ideology in the Old Testament* (Oxford: Oxford University Press, 2000), 30.

6   It would take me too far afield to bring out the significance of the fascinating work of Edith Wyschogrod's *Saints and Postmodernism, Revisioning Moral Philosophy* (Chicago: University of Chicago Press, 1990). This is a remarkable book which uses the particularity of the moral challenge represented by the lives of diverse saints to call into question the claims of general moral theory beloved of many analytic philosophers. There are several strands within postmodernity that she usefully distinguishes and evaluates.

7   The crucial relevant authority on this score is Hayden White. See especially his *Metahistory, The Historical Imagination in Nineteenth Century Europe* (Baltimore; London: Johns Hopkins University Press, 1973). White's work is worthy of extended reflection and reflection for those interested in

essential difference between history and fiction, between history and literature, between history and aesthetics, and between history and poetics. Historical facts are constructed all the way to the bottom; there is no significant distinction between fact and interpretation. More modestly we get the claim that all historical writing is biased, prejudiced, and ineradicably subjective. It is decidedly not scientific but relative to the presuppositions of its practitioners. Hence there can be no final, authoritative account of the past; there are only histories written from the perspectives of historians. The concerns in this catalogue are essentially epistemological rather than semantic in character.

We might call the aforementioned summation the deconstructive element in postmodern theory and discourse. Yet there are at least four other elements in the literature that run radically counter to these expressions of skepticism and relativism.

First, there is *ab initio* the sharp contrast between modern and postmodern developments in thinking through the cultural changes over the last hundred years or so.[8] In this phase of the presentation we are expected to accept as relatively accurate a narrative of our recent history.[9] It is far from clear how this is to be reconciled with the claim that we have no access to the truth about the past or that there is no way of adjudicating rival accounts of the recent past.

Second, in presenting the case for postmodernity it is not uncommon to come across uncompromising straight talk about the world we currently occupy. For my part, in so far as I will use the standard disjunction or even schema of modernity and postmodernity, I am perfectly happy to see myself as unapologetically premodern.[10] I am even happy to correlate this sorry condition with my initial social location in the bogs of Ireland; I represent an intellectual backwater that should long have disappeared off the face of the earth. However, this kind of move will be countered with

---

the analytic philosophy of history. He has in fact paid his dues in the debates that show up in the analytic philosophy of history.

8   For a helpful point of entry into the contrast as it applies to biblical studies see George Aichele, Peter Miscall, Richard Walsh, "An Elephant in the Room: Historical-Critical and Postmodern Interpretation of the Bible," *JBL* 128 (2009): 383–404.

9   Aside from the odd disjunctive or binary set up (a matter usually excoriated by postmodern thinkers), one of the shortcomings of this schema is its failure to come to terms with the place of Romanticism in the nineteenth century. For a seminal treatment of this movement as offering a critique of modernity see Isaiah Berlin, *The Roots of Romanticism* (Princeton: Princeton University Press, 1999). Much of the Berlin corpus is devoted to the retrieval and understanding of the opposition to modernity and the Enlightenment.

10   I deliberately deploy this strategy to destabilize the limiting of standard options to that of modernity and postmodernity. The reality is much more complicated, of course.

the assertion that we are all postmodern whether we like it or not. This is the world we now inhabit, we are told, whatever one may say to challenge this. Not to recognize this reality is to be subject to self-deception. Turned on its head and stated positively, we all know that we live in a postmodern world; those who do not recognize it should wake up and get over it.[11] It would be difficult to think of a more naïve form of realism than this; we simply should see the relevant cultural reality and its attendant analysis and that is the end of the matter. The dogmatism at this point is deafening for those with ears to hear.

To be sure, the dogmatism is initially presented as the result of argument, but the very language in which the claim is couched quickly gives the critic little chance of answering back; the critic is deprived of any serious agency. Consider this set of assertions by Keith Jenkins:

> As I have argued elsewhere on another occasion, I think we live today within the general socio-economic and political conditions of postmodernity. I don't think we have a choice about this. For postmodernity is not an ideology or position we can choose to subscribe to or not, postmodernity is precisely our condition: it is our historical fate to be living now. As to how we should read the details of this moment—as, say, a period, of post-Fordist flexible accumulation as opposed to modernist Fordism; as a period of capitalist de-differentiation; as a period of late capital; as part of general time-space compression involving spatial reorganizations or as a combination of all these and other factors—is subject to much debate. But I would like to leave such details for now, important as they are, and argue more generally that the condition of postmodernity and the postmodern theoretical expressions concomitant with it are due to the overall failure of the experiment in social living we can term "modernity." That is, the general failure, as measured in its own terms, or the attempt, from the eighteenth century in Europe, to bring through the application of reason, science and technology, a level of social and political well-being within social formations which, legislating for increasingly generous emancipation of their subjects/citizens, we might characterize by saying that they were trying, at best, to become "human rights communities."[12]

We have here a clear commitment to argue a case but this is soon cancelled out; at the end of the day we do not have any choice in the matter.

---

11   This was often the strategy deployed in the nineteen sixties to bring recalcitrant theological students into line with modernity.
12   Keith Jenkins, ed., *The Postmodern History Reader* (London; New York: Routledge, 1997), 3–4.

We are doomed to be postmodern whatever we may say in response to the arguments on offer. Oliver O'Donovan has neatly described this kind of bogus argument as a "philosophical strong-arm tactic."[13]

Third, there is no hesitation in both assuming the reality of authors and the attribution of stable meaning to their texts when these authors and their texts are seen as representing the illusory project of modernism that is to be replaced by postmodern thinking and intellectual practices. Equally, it is difficult to rid the world of authors and their texts when we are invited to become good and faithful postmoderns. We are invited to read a canon of diverse and often very confusing texts. The relevant texts are not created by discourse or by language; they are produced by real live agents who really exist and have a history that we can explore by means, say, of their biographies. Moreover, we cannot avoid the common recourse to understanding the relevant intellectual and social context of these texts if we are to come to terms with their content. Genealogy and not just conceptual analysis really matter at this point.[14]

Fourth, the constant referral to the place of power dynamics in play in interpreting and assessing this or that historical proposal (or more radically any proposal whatsoever) assumes a causal account of reality without which the claims about power and dominant discourse are simply empty of content. Thus when we seek to show that a particular historical construction is the mirror of this or that political or social location we willy-nilly are assuming a causal connection between the construction and its originating causal conditions.[15] Philosophers after Hume are acutely aware of the challenge of making sense of causation, but this does not stop either the ordinary citizen or the postmodern theorist from reaching for causal stories that are presented and meant to be received as reality depicting.

Fifth, one of the hallmarks of postmodern material is the aggressive moral language that readily shows up. Thus modernist proposals, say, about history, are said to be dangerous and harmful proposals, even more so when they are cloaked in the language of objectivity and neutrality. They exclude marginal and oppressed voices and are therefore unjust.

---

13   Oliver O'Donovan, "Reflections on Pluralism," in *The Kuyper Center Review, 1, Politics, Religion, and Sphere Sovereignty*, ed. Gordon Graham (Grand Rapids: Eerdmans, 2010), 9.

14   The importance of genealogy is, of course, brought out by the crucial place of Foucault (and before him of Nietzsche) in the postmodern canon. Precisely because of the wealth of historical learning that he brings to the table his work is well worth pondering.

15   For a neat deployment of this strategy to explain the varieties of history of ancient history see Keith W. Whitelam, *The Invention of Ancient Israel, The silencing of Palestinian History* (London; New York: Routledge, 1996), especially ch. 3.

They are ideological in the pejorative sense that they are really expressions of interests that are profoundly harmful to minorities. They reflect shameful colonial oppression of subject peoples that must be rooted out and replaced by emancipatory forms of discourse that bring liberty and justice to the oppressed.[16] The irony of this element in postmodernity is worth noting in that we can surely read the emphasis on the ethical over against the religious as one of the great legacies of modernity as visible, for example, in Immanuel Kant. A crucial element in modernity is peeping through at this point. However, this is not generally noticed. Postmoderns have readily pressed the accusation that Kant is complicit in anti-Semitism and in various colonial enterprises and thus they see themselves as on a radically different page from that supplied by Kant.[17]

One way to think of these deep tensions within postmodern materials is to see them as essentially political in orientation. Thus the semantic elements in postmodern theory can be seen as a first shot at the clearing of the decks. It is an effort to provide a network of nuclear strikes that effectively destabilizes the opposition by undermining crucial dimensions of what we might call standard rational discourse. Thus there are no authors and no stable meanings that can be attributed to the texts that express their theories or judgments. If this fails to work then the epistemological elements can be brought in as a back-up strategy. There is no truth. There are no objective standards for evaluating claims to truth. There is no world out there that can act as a rational constraint of assertability. There are no secure, infallible foundations on which to build an agreed or accurate account of reality. We might call these the skeptical assault on the opposition. The goal, intentional or otherwise, is to wrong-foot the prevailing orthodoxy wherever it may be found in the academy.

The effect is often to disarm the critic at the outset and then take possession of the field. In my experience there is limited desire in sorting through the difficult philosophical issues on the table. The semantics and epistemology are certainly identified and flagged as crucially important but there is little or no interest in following up these matters or consulting the massive body of material that deal with them in contemporary

---

16   This element is especially prominent in the worries about the perlocutionary effects of histories of ancient Israel on the current Palestinian-Israeli conflict. See, for example, James G. Crossley, "Christian Origins, 'The Land', and the Ideological Scholarly Apparatus," in Emmanuel Pfoh and Keith W. Whitelam, eds., *The Politics of Israel's Past, The Bible, Archaeology and Nation-Building* (Sheffield: Sheffield Phoenix, 2013), 89–101.

17   See, for example, the treatment of Kant in J. Kameron Carter, *Race, A Theological Account* (New York: Oxford University Press), 2008.

philosophy.[18] In these circumstances it is no accident that the go-to ancillary discipline is no longer philosophy but cultural studies.[19] In so far as philosophical arguments and materials are deployed they are often underdeveloped or not even recognized as in need of careful, critical examination.[20]

What really matters is the complex ethical and emancipatory political program that is really in play once the decks have been cleared, once the initial semantic and epistemological nuclear strikes have been delivered. It is surely no accident that the relevant political program turns out to be a variation on Marxist and revisionary Marxist agendas. At one level this is an entirely one-sided affair in that the focus of attention is the failures of empire, most conspicuously the neo-liberal, consumerist, capitalist empire led by the United States of America. Often the alternative is left underdeveloped, at least in the short term. There are good tactical reasons for this way of proceeding. However, this is the least of the worries a philosopher will have. What is really left out is the massive body of material offered up in moral and political philosophy that seeks to sort through carefully and critically the tangled issues that have to be addressed. Once again cultural studies come to the rescue as the crucial partner that does the heavy-lifting in the materials. What is at issue here is not commitment to this or that political agenda but the effort to clarify and evaluate competing philosophical claims as they show up in our political commitments.

The tensions between the semantic-epistemological elements and the ethical-emancipatory elements are visible in the vehement and often witty rejections of the former by socialist or Marxist scholars. One thinks

---

18   For a devastating analysis of the semantic and hermeneutical shortcomings of postmodernity see John M. Ellis, *Against Deconstruction* (Princeton: Princeton University Press, 1989). For the best treatment of the epistemological issues that show up in postmodernity I have not found anything better than Alvin I. Goldman, *Knowledge in a Social World* (Oxford: Clarendon, 1999), ch. 1. The whole of part 1 is worth consulting. Even so I have an open mind about the insights that may be available within postmodern philosophy. Much of the trouble here stems from radically different ways of tackling philosophical issues with very different historical genealogies and very different conceptual resources.

19   Even then "cultural studies" is a carefully restricted if not invented "discipline" that cuts itself loose from more expansive conceptions of cultural studies. On this see Roger Scruton, *Modern Culture* (London: Bloomsbury, 1998). While it looks as if one is appealing to a body of expertise or specialized learning, it becomes clear on closer inspection that one is dealing with the creation of a sub-discipline in the contemporary academy designed to deliver a settled response to certain thoroughly contested questions about contemporary culture.

20   This is certainly the verdict to be rendered of Jean-Francois Lyotard's *The Condition of Postmodernity: A Report on Knowledge* (Minneapolis: University of Minnesota Press, 1984). The very first sentence is enough to set the serious epistemologist's teeth on edge. Lyotard confuses discourse about knowledge as available in the debates within epistemology with the proposed claims about the content of knowledge now transmitted through technology.

immediately of the work of E. P. Thompson[21] and Terry Eagleton.[22] Moreover, it is no surprise that analytic philosophers and their friends in theology readily give up on the debate and move on to greener pastures. They worry that those who advance the relevant semantic and epistemological elements are, if not outright dishonest, then simply incompetent. In their response to the advocates of postmodernity they remind me of the comment made informally by a Presbyterian theologian when he said that talking to a Methodist theologian was like talking to a giggly adolescent female. They have next to no clue about the complexity of the issues involved in semantics and epistemology; in the nature of the case the competence needed to sort out what is involved is lacking; worse still, this is not even recognized.

In the end I think that many of the semantic-epistemological elements that show up in the current debate can and will readily be jettisoned; they really are subordinate to other more salient considerations. This does not mean that I think they are as easily disposed of as may appear on first sight. They embody worries, say, about historical investigation that are genuine and need to be addressed. Nowhere is this more visible than in the long-standing debate about the significance of historical investigation for Christian theology. Historical investigation is inescapable in Christian theology and most especially in biblical studies. Thus it is no surprise that analytic philosophers recognize the need to enter the fray on this front. They rightly recognize that jettisoning the historical elements of Christianity mean the end of Christianity. Yet at this point many biblical scholars get nervous because they are not sure they want to take on board the theological baggage that comes with the intervention of the analytic philosopher. In some cases they would even prefer the company of postmodernists as an alternative. After all, softer versions of postmodernity create space for any and every perspective, it would seem, so why not take a deflationary view of one's theological and historical proposals and dance at the postmodern ball of inclusion and diversity. So let's now enter that thicket of issues.

PLANTINGA'S RESPONSE TO TROELTSCH

One favorite target of both theologians and philosophers is the proposals put forward by the famous nineteenth century polymath Ernst

---

21   See his *The Poverty of Theory* (London: Merlin Press, 1995).
22   See his *The Illusions of Postmodernism* (Oxford: Blackwell, 1996).

Troeltsch. Troeltsch matters in part because of the impact of his work over the last century and a half. He also matters because he actually embodies many of the concerns of postmodern writers on what they call metahistory even though he is taken to be the poster child of modern biblical criticism.[23] On this score I think that Troeltsch actually calls into question the claim that many postmoderns make about the nature of so-called modern or historical biblical criticism. In this respect the term "modernity" as applied to biblical studies is often deployed as a construction in the pejorative sense of that term, that is, it is an effort to construct and invent a straw opponent who can be set up as the fitting bad guy over against the good gal or guy of postmodernity. To use the jargon of postmodernity I want to use Troeltsch as a site of investigation that will problematize the debate. And I want to use the response of Alvin Plantinga to the work of Troeltsch to problematize the response of one network of analytic philosophers. I will begin this exercise back to front by starting with the work of Plantinga.

The crucial unit of interest in Plantinga can be found in chapter twelve of his magisterial *Warranted Christian Belief.*[24] He begins by insisting that on his account of the epistemology of theology the ordinary Christian can *know* the great truths of the Scripture without paying any attention to the work of historical scholarship.[25] This is so, first of all, because Scripture is perspicuous in the main lines of its teaching (creation, sin, incarnation, atonement, resurrection, eternal, and life). Thus it "can be understood and grasped and properly accepted by any one of normal intelligence and ordinary training."[26] It is so, second, because of the internal instigation of the Holy Spirit/faith.

> By virtue of this process, an ordinary Christian, one quite innocent of historical studies, the ancient languages, the intricacies of textual

---

23   I follow the stipulated definition developed by Philip R. Davis in "Whose History? Whose Israel? Whose Bible? Biblical Histories, Ancient and Modern," in his *Rethinking Biblical Scholarship* (Durham: Acumen, 2014), 23–24.

24   *Warranted Christian Belief* (New York: Oxford University Press, 2000).

25   Whether this is in fact what Plantinga established given the astonishingly modest account of what he has accomplished in the extraordinary last paragraph of *Warranted Christian Belief*, I leave aside for now. The crucial problem is this. In order to secure knowledge, we need to know that *p* is true and that *p* is warranted. What Plantinga claims to show at the end is that if Christian belief is true, it is warranted. Here, in chapter twelve, he clearly thinks that the inner instigation of the Spirit and the gift of faith give not just warrant but also truth. There is work here for Reformed epistemologists to take up and resolve. They cannot help themselves to knowledge without an independently secured account of the truth of scripture that does not appeal to the account of warrant supplied by Plantinga.

26   *Warranted Christian Belief*, 374.

criticism, the depths of theology, and all the rest *can nevertheless come to know that these things are, indeed true*; furthermore his knowledge need not trace back (by way of testimony, for example) to knowledge on the part of someone who does have the special training. Neither the Christian community nor the ordinary Christian is at the mercy of the expert here: *they can know these truths directly.*[27]

On the surface this is a startling and radical claim, yet it fits with many of Plantinga's hermeneutical, theological, and epistemological assumptions. On the theological and epistemological front, Plantinga's position involves a strong claim about the origin of Scripture: Scripture is divinely inspired. But note what this means. It really means that Scripture is identical with divine revelation, that Scripture is a volume of divine discourse, that it is authored by God, and that it is a matter of God speaking to us.[28] Consequently, whatever it teaches is true. "Once it is clear, therefore, what the teaching of a given bit of teaching of Scripture is, the question of truth is settled."[29] So the picture is something like this. Through the internal instigation of the Holy Spirit and the gift of faith, the believer knows that the great truths of the Bible and the intended teaching of God, the principal author, in any particular text are true independently of consulting any kind of scholarship, including historical scholarship. The task of the interpreter is to discern what the Lord intends to teach the reader; and once this is discerned the believer has access to the truth given by God.

On the hermeneutical front, given that God is the principal author of Scripture, what is said in one place can be used to interpret what is said in another place; and inferences from sets of texts that interpret each other can also by inference be taken to be taken as divine teaching. Moreover, given divine authorship, the meaning of the text is not confined to the meaning available through interpretation of the human author. It is the former meaning, that of the divine author, that the biblical scholar tries to discern. For Plantinga, this is more or less what traditional Christian biblical commentary has been providing from the days of John Chrysostom even up to and including the work of Karl Barth.

Given this prior commitment, it is easy to take care of the problems thrown up by historical biblical criticism. Objections to this view that

---

27   Ibid. The emphasis is mine.
28   These are the substitute terms for divine inspiration that show up again and again in his work.
29   *Warranted Christian Belief,* 383.

arise because of the nature of biblical criticism are to be seen as defeaters, so the task in hand is to defeat the defeaters. The default position is that we already know that what Scripture teaches is true; objections therefore are to be taken as potential defeaters and treated accordingly. Happily for Plantinga as he sees the relevant landscape, there are no such defeaters once we uncover the assumptions that lie at the base of the varieties of biblical criticism that he identifies.

My intention here is not to examine the waterfront as Plantinga has mapped it. There is much in what he has to say that I find apt, convincing, and deftly presented. It is not difficult for a philosopher with Plantinga's gifts to lift the lid of biblical and theological criticism and have a field day with the bizarre results that have been presented across the years. What interests me is what he has to say about Troeltsch.[30] Beyond that I want to draw attention to the conceptual muddle that lies at the heart of his initial theological commitments and the tendentious way in which he conceals these confessional commitments from critical scrutiny because of his lack of interest in critical historical investigation.

Plantinga's reading of Troeltsch can be briefly summarized here. He rightly points out that Troeltsch was committed to the principles of criticism, analogy, and correlation. He thinks that these principles are either toothless if not platitudinous, and thus can readily be accommodated by the traditional biblical commentator; or they are nested in a wider set of assumptions which are intellectually unsecured. Thus they presuppose that God does not perform miracles, or raise Jesus from the dead, or speak as already indicated in and through Scripture as its author. In the latter case, they pose no problem whatsoever in that they are a matter of prior assumption brought to the evaluation of the text rather than something derived from a study of the text. The traditional believer, on Plantinga's account, already knows that these claims are either possible or indeed true. So he or she will need much more than platitudinous principles or prior assumptions to have any kind of defeater on their hands. Hence they can with integrity ignore the results of Troeltschian biblical criticism. It is a matter of game, set, and match for the traditional believer.

---

30   Even so, Plantinga has been careful to draw a distinction between Troeltsch and some of his interpreters. Despite this he shows no real interest in listening to the subtlety of Troeltsch's remarks about the nature of historical investigation. This dovetails with his lack of interest in working on the historical etiology of his own ontology of scripture; he simply assumes that there is a traditional or classical position that has been displaced by historical biblical criticism.

CRITICAL PROBLEMS IN PLANTINGA'S RESPONSE

This is a deeply inadequate reading and assessment of Troeltsch.[31] To be sure, Troeltsch is committed to criticism, analogy, and correlation. However, he is also committed to at least three other insights in his account of historical investigation. First, he insists that, while the historian may have all sorts of other interests, his first interest is to find out what really happened in the past. In this respect postmodern readings of history either conveniently ignore Troeltsch altogether, or provide merely a flat-footed reading of his work and thus fail to take account of the careful way in which he handles the role of interests in our study of the past. In fact, if postmoderns had paid attention to Troeltsch's subtle account of interests of the first and second degree they would have saved themselves from some of the obvious fallacies they make about subjectivity and objectivity in historical investigation. As far as Plantinga is concerned, he appears to have no interest in the importance of this insight in the development of historical investigation. Somehow, it can be shoveled aside as of no interest or significance for theology even though in his own way he wants to help himself to the results of historical investigation when it suits him.

Second, Troeltsch was well aware of the metaphysical and theological assumptions he was relying on when he made evaluations of what happened in the past. He was not all committed to some version of empiricism; he was an idealist who was convinced that there was a divine mind at work in, with, and through human and natural events. More to the point, he supplies a serious set of proposals as to how his metaphysical and theological proposals were to be defended epistemologically. The issue here is not whether Troeltsch is right or wrong materially on these issues; the point is that he saw how important they were in principle and insisted that they be taken with the utmost seriousness.

Third, it was these latter assumptions that were in play when he assumed that God does not intervene directly in history or causally bring the Scriptures into existence as a matter of divine authorship or divine speaking. These assumptions did the heavy-lifting for him when it came to his application of criticism and analogy. Yet on Plantinga's account he comes across as somehow naïve and self-serving intellectually. Hence

---

31   In what follows I stand by the interpretation and evaluation of Troeltsch in ch. 5 of *Divine Revelation and the Limits of Historical Criticism* (Oxford: Oxford University Press, 1982). The relevant and much neglected material in Troeltsch is laid out there, so I shall not cite it here.

the whole tone of his treatment, in part fueled by a reading of Troeltsch through a network of other scholars and interpreters, is one of disdain and condescension.

The deeper problem here is that Plantinga is not sufficiently interested in probing the deeper elements in Troeltsch's position. He is on a fishing expedition looking for defeaters; given his impoverished reading of Troeltsch, he has no difficulty defeating the defeaters. There is as a result a gross failure to tackle the complex story behind the development of biblical criticism. This should not in the least surprise us for the same problem shows up in his summary of traditional biblical commentary. Again, I have great sympathy with Plantinga in that he readily represents a synthesis of historical, philosophical, and theological materials that will have enormous salience in conservative Christian circles. Moreover, with him I want to articulate and defend a robust vision of Christian theology. To do so will require a lot more work than has been done to date or that I can even begin to sketch here. However, let me pursue some of the issues by way of a series of telegrams.

First, the ontology of Scripture presented by Plantinga has a long pedigree, yet it is surely conceptually confused to construe divine inspiration along the lines of divine revelation, divine authorship of Scripture, divine speaking, and other related action predicates. The story behind this development is complicated of course; I have told it already elsewhere and I will tell it again elsewhere in due course.

Second, it is this confusion that lies behind the inference that whatever Scripture says (rightly interpreted, of course), God says. Without this assumption there is no need to work up the story of double authorship that deploys the standard idea of divine concurrence, borrowed, say, from Aquinas. Nor should we accept the old adage that we can use a text from this part of Scripture to interpret another text of Scripture. This too stems from a story that confuses divine inspiration with divine authorship.

Third, it is surely an obvious fallacy to claim that whatever God says or authors should automatically be construed as true. Even when we make all the relevant qualifications about genre, context, and "all the accoutrements academics have come to know and love and demand,"[32] then for all we know in advance God may have supplied us with wonderful myths, tall tales, parables, and other materials that are not true assertions at all. It is simply false to argue from God says *p*, to *p* is true. Even Bultmann could

---

32 *Warranted Christian Belief*, 381.

have accepted that God dictated all of Scripture and have still maintained that the resurrection of Jesus is really a story of the rise of faith in the early disciples; this was God's way of telling ancient believers and us what happened in a way that was spiritually fruitful.

Fourth, Plantinga's whole appeal to the internal instigation of the Holy Spirit, more commonly referred to as the inner witness of the Holy Spirit, has next to nothing to do with the Spirit causing us to believe the great truths of the Gospel or believe that this or that bit of Scripture is true or that these texts and not these are canonical.[33] In its original setting in Paul it has to do with our filial relation to God wherein we gain assurance of the forgiveness of our sins and our adoption as children of God.[34] To be sure, this is not the end of the story as regards the working of the Spirit; but to tell that story will require careful historical readings of, say, the Gospel of John, and the way in which these texts were appropriated in the history of theology.

Fifth, the same could be said about the use of the appeal to traditional biblical commentaries. This notion flattens what has been in play across the centuries in the interpretation and evaluation of Scripture. One only has to compare, say, Origen and Barth to see how inept this generalization is. They have radically different ontologies of Scripture and different strategies for overcoming the difficulties they find in the texts before them. Again, only careful historical work where the interest of the first degree is to find out what they were doing historically in their context will get us within earshot of what is needed.

THE INVENTION OF BIBLICAL STUDIES AS THE FOUNDATION OF OUR THEOLOGICAL WORK

At this point we can return to Troeltsch and to postmodernity. What Plantinga is effectively doing is asking us to adopt a vision of Scripture where the text should, with minor reservations, be read ahistorically. He is partially right about the history behind this vision. There was a broad consensus that Scripture was authored by God; one knew this for a variety of reasons, including reasons supposedly derived from the work of the Holy Spirit. It was then inferred that whatever Scripture says, God

33 Plantinga is leery of this last move; but his work can readily be deployed to shore it up. See Michael J. Kruger, *Canon Revisited, Establishing the Origins and Authority of the New Testament Books* (Wheaton, IL: Crossway, 2012).
34 See Rom 8:14–17.

says; and whatever God says is true. There was no need to worry about historical investigation and the problems it might present. Plantinga has effectively updated this vision of Scripture; this is one reason why biblical scholars are and should be nervous. This is especially the case among those who have made him into something of a cult figure in contemporary Christian philosophy, a fate he would be the first to excoriate.

It is this vision of Scripture that fell apart on both theological and hermeneutical grounds in modern theology. Theologically, this vision involved freezing in place and then updating a network of conceptual, hermeneutical, and epistemological claims that really involved interesting innovation rather than simply restating what was presented across the centuries.[35] In fact, this would be one way to read what Plantinga has done; he is not the first and he will not be the last, for the traditional understanding of Scripture as authored by God runs so deep it is virtually ineradicable. More importantly, hermeneutically, the traditional view failed because once we shifted to the crucial role of the human authors in the production, editing, and compilation of Scripture, the findings across a wide spectrum of competing theological traditions did not correlate with the doctrines of inerrancy and infallibility that were the contingent outcome of the so-called traditional commentary on Scripture. Troeltsch saw this with uncanny insight, as did John Henry Newman in a very different world. While I have no interest in microwaving Troeltsch's material metaphysical or theological proposals, I think he was right on target in much that he has to say in terms of the logic and nature of historical investigation. In particular, his distinction between interests of the first degree and interests of the second degree in writing history, and his insistence that prior theological, epistemological, and metaphysical commitments are inescapable in doing good historical evaluation of our sources is right on track.

While it would be ridiculously false to say that historical biblical criticism is dead and gone, the attack on historical criticism by postmoderns changes the landscape. Postmoderns readily reject the first insight. Depending on which version of postmodernity one consults, it is self-delusional, as they generally see it, to make such a distinction. In the end it is really interests in and around claims about exclusion and power, governed by a hasty ethics of justice, that carry the day. Moreover, their caricatures

---

35 I have argued this case as it applies to Benjamin Warfield in my *Canon and Criterion in Christian Theology* (Oxford: Clarendon, 1998), ch. 12.

of nineteenth century historical investigation lead them to miss the second insight. They fail to note Troeltsch's crucial claims about the place of causal assumptions in making decisions about the past, even as they deploy highly contested causal claims in their own proposals about authority and power. Just as there is no presuppositionless exegesis and translation, there is no presuppositionless historical inquiry. Postmoderns have made much of this, but it is nothing new on the horizon. What is new is the presuppositions they want to make central in the current study of Scripture. In so far as they are open to articulating and defending their presuppositions, then there is hope we can move forward into a more fruitful conversation. A positive way to read Plantinga is to see him as doing exactly this kind of work across a lifetime of extraordinary and original philosophical reflection. He has effectively outlined how one might restate a traditional vision of the ontology of Scripture and render harmless the logic and results of historical inquiry, except where they confirm what is already known to be true independently of historical investigation. Yet that work falls short precisely when it comes to critically examining the historical origins of his own theological commitments and in exploring in its own right the logic and nature of historical investigation.

Working in the intersection of philosophy of history, biblical studies, the epistemology and theology are not for the faint-hearted. Plantinga is right to unpack and excoriate the theologically alienating presuppositions that lie at the heart of much that passes for historical biblical criticism. He is also right to draw attention to the array of bizarre and contradictory results that we have been offered across the years. Postmoderns have been right to insist afresh on the crucial place of prior assumptions in translating, exegeting, and evaluating our sacred Scriptures. They are now avidly adding to the array of bizarre and contradictory results that show up across the academy.

We have come to a crossroads. The invention of biblical studies was an interesting phenomenon. On the one hand, those who shared something akin to Plantinga's ontology of Scripture brought it into existence because they had come to see that they needed expert historical investigation to read the texts from which they derived their confessional and dogmatic commitments. On the other hand, more secular and theologically revisionist thinkers invented the historical study of Scripture in order to cope with the manifold moral, theological, and historical problems they found when they read the text closely and were driven to read it apart from or over against traditional theological commitments. In the invention of biblical studies, we had an odd shotgun wedding between defenders of orthodoxy and critics of orthodoxy; the outcome is a motley crew of fecund and radically different children and grandchildren.[36]

Given our traditional curricular arrangements within Protestantism and their implicit adoption within Roman Catholicism, systematic theologians are between a rock and a hard place. We invented biblical studies with help from our enemies in hopes of having secure resources from which to operate; there are no such secure resources, however we summarize the results, or however we identify the logic and nature of historical investigation. The situation is a critical one for theology, for biblical studies has long been the backbone and foundation of the curriculum. I suggest it is time we reviewed that invention. We may even need to rework the curriculum in ways that, without neglecting the crucial role of history in theological studies, finds a new and better future for our theological work together.

---

36   For two interesting but ultimately unsatisfactory readings of crucial aspects of the history see Jonathan Sheehan, *The Enlightenment Bible, Translation, Scholarship, Culture* (Princeton: Princeton University Press, 2005) and Stephen D. Moore and Yvonne Sherwood, *The Invention of the Biblical Scholar: A Critical Manifesto* (Minneapolis: Fortress, 2011).

CHAPTER 9

READING SCRIPTURE IN OUR CONTEXT: DOUBLE PARTICULARITY IN KARL BARTH'S ACTUALISTIC VIEW OF SCRIPTURE

DANIEL D. LEE

IN THEIR BOOK *The Bible in a World Context*, Walter Dietrich and Ulrich Luz surmise that "Western biblical scholarship suffers most from being 'without context'" resulting in "abstract results and truths" detached from the present situation and the lives of ordinary people.[1] What they are referring to is the problematic illusion of objectivity and the lack of contextual awareness that have plagued the Western theological tradition in the modern era. Dietrich and Luz look to non-Western scholars for that needed contextual self-awareness in reading Scripture. This call for non-Western voices, especially from the margins, is an increasingly common

---

1   Walter Dietrich and Ulrich Luz, eds., *The Bible in a World Context: An Experiment in Contextual Hermeneutics* (Grand Rapids: Eerdmans, 2002), ix.

one, whether it be early liberation theologies or the present postcolonial contributions.[2] These voices would challenge "the hegemony of European and North American biblical interpretations" that has been accepted as normality and universal by highlighting subaltern perspectives.[3] However, we will be amiss if we perceive this growing contextual awareness as limited only to liberationist or postcolonial concerns. James Brownson argues for the pressing need of a missional hermeneutic for the post-Christendom church in the West.[4] His concern is the challenge of bringing "the gospel to bear upon Western culture itself, a culture that has become, in many ways, powerfully resistant to Christian faith."[5] As Brownson points out, reasons for a contextual reading of Scripture are not only liberationalist or postcolonial, but also missiological and ecclesiological.

In this exploration of contextual hermeneutics, looking to Karl Barth might seem unconventional to some. While early Barth studies with its neo-orthodox rubric was largely blind to his contextual aspects, Bruce McCormack with his watershed study inaugurated a more accurate and situationally engaged portrayal of Barth.[6] In his posthumously published letter in *The South East Asian Journal of Theology*, Barth himself offers the clearest admission of his own situatedness and contextual limitations, all the while exhorting non-Western theologians to engage in the task of theology concretely with their own cultural, philosophical tools for their "new, different, and special situation[s]."[7] However, Barth also warns that theology should be free from all "Babylonian captivities," that is, cultural or contextual strictures upon divine freedom.[8]

Everyone who has read Barth's Romans commentary knows that it is no abstract, universalized reading devoid of context. Now to be sure, Barth in his historical situation was suspicious of anything labeled "contextual" with very good reasons. When "contextual" means an ideological

---

2   See for example, John R. Levison and Priscilla Pope-Levison, eds., *Return to Babel: Global Perspectives on the Bible* (Louisville: Westminster John Knox, 1999).

3   Levison and Priscilla Pope-Levison, *Return to Babel*, 2.

4   James V. Brownson, *Speaking the Truth in Love: New Testament Resources for a Missional Hermeneutic* (Harrisburg, PA: Trinity Press International, 1998).

5   Brownson, *Speaking the Truth in Love*, 4–5.

6   See Bruce L. McCormack, *Karl Barth's Critically Realistic Dialectical Theology: Its Genesis and Development, 1909–1936* (Oxford: Clarendon, 1995).

7   Karl Barth, "No Boring Theology! A Letter from Karl Barth," *The South East Asian Journal of Theology* 11 (Autumn 1969): 3–5. This letter was technically penned by Eberhard Busch, Barth's last assistant, but personally approved by Barth. See Eberhard Busch, *Meine Zeit mit Karl Barth: Tagebuch, 1965–1968* (Göttingen, Germany: Vandenhoeck und Ruprecht, 2011), 677.

8   Barth, "No Boring Theology!," 4.

co-opting of the gospel as has occurred during Nazi Germany, a theologically or *contextually* appropriate response must be a call to ignore the context and let the Word speak.[9] His *Nein!* to natural theology of every form, whether it be *analogia entis*, point of contact, or Tillichian correlation, still stands and it must if we are to do Barth justice.[10] In fact, his rejection of Babylonian captivities in the midst of his contextuality is exactly why we could benefit from thinking after (*nachdenken*) and thinking with (*mitdenken*) Barth for our time.[11] While Barth does not exactly frame his thoughts as I am doing now, nor ask the specific questions that I am asking, he was passionate about reading Scripture and encountering the living God in his context.

In what follows, I will explore Barth's theological and contextually self-aware hermeneutics for contemporary insights by making explicit what I believe to be his implicit ideas. In a way, we can think of this as an exercise in connecting the dots that Barth left behind. First, we will look at Barth's actualistic view of Scripture and how it serves as the basis of a participatory hermeneutic, where the reader must participate in the subject matter of the Bible to gain its meaning. As we will see, this actualistic perspective is another way of saying that the Scripture is alive, or more accurately that the living God encounters us in the Bible. Next, the dynamics of double particularity in our reading of Scripture will serve as the heart of my proposal. This double particularity refers to the scriptural particularity of *there and then*, and our particularity of *here and now* and the living Jesus Christ who is present in both. Third and lastly, a summary of concrete implications of this double particularity and its dynamics for our reading of Scripture will be laid out.

Actualistic Ontology of Holy Scripture

In this section, I will briefly explain what actualism or actualistic ontology means in Barth's theology, its origins in Christology and the incarnation, and its significance for the doctrine of Scripture.

---

9   Hancock explains that Barth's counsel to ignore the context in his *Homiletics* lectures is a *contextual* response to his political situation that instrumentalized the Bible and sermons for ideological purposes. Angela Dienhart Hancock, *Karl Barth's Emergency Homiletic, 1932–1933: A Summons to Prophetic Witness at the Dawn of the Third Reich* (Grand Rapids: Eerdmans, 2013).

10   Eberhard Busch, *The Great Passion: An Introduction to Karl Barth's Theology*, trans. by Geoffrey Bromiley (Grand Rapids: Eerdmans, 2004), 71–72.

11   To think after (*nachdenken*) and think with (*mitdenken*) the authors are how Barth admonishes us to interpret the Bible.

I begin by noting that Barth "never once uses the term," actualism or actualistic ontology.[12] Yet, it is ubiquitous in his writings in "the language of occurrence, happening, event, history, decisions, and act."[13] Indeed, actualism is been considered one of the most distinctive and difficult aspects of Barth's theology.[14] Barth "thinks primarily in terms of events and relationships rather than monadic or self-contained substances" or in "static or inactive terms."[15] As with everything else in Barth, the basis for this actualism is found in his understanding of God's being.

This deep feature of Barth's theology is grounded in the doctrine of the incarnation with "the being-in-becoming of the God-human," not from some abstract, external philosophical commitments. Rejecting metaphysical speculation about the being of God, Barth takes revelation in Jesus Christ as the source of our knowledge of God. If God's being lies beyond the person of Jesus Christ, then we still are left without a real knowledge of God.[16] However, if in Christ, God has truly revealed Godself to us, then God's being is in God's become flesh. Barth rejects as speculation any knowledge of "a God who could be known and whose divine essence could be defined on some other basis than in and from the perception of His presence and action as incarnate Word."[17] In fact, "God is who He is in His works."[18] The incarnation does not mean God merely expressing God's being in flesh, but rather making creation and history constitutive of God's being, without losing divine freedom or transcendence.[19]

---

12   Paul T. Nimmo, *Being in Action: The Theological Shape of Barth's Ethical Vision* (New York: T&T Clark, 2007), 5. I used the terms actualism and actualistic ontology interchangeably here with an understanding that McCormack's exposition of Barth's actualistic ontology is a more precise definition of what actualism means. See Bruce L. McCormack, "Grace and Being: The Role of God's Gracious Election in Karl Barth's Theological Ontology," in *The Cambridge Companion to Karl Barth*, ed. John Webster (Cambridge: Cambridge University Press, 2000), 92–110.

13   George Hunsinger, *How to Read Karl Barth: The Shape of His Theology* (New York: Oxford University Press, 1991), 30.

14   Hunsinger, *How to Read Karl Barth*, 30.

15   Ibid.

16   Barth argues that apart from "Jesus of Nazareth and with the people which He represents . . . God would be a different, an alien God. According to the Christian perception He would not be God at all." Karl Barth, *The Doctrine of God*, II/2 in *Church Dogmatics* (Edinburgh: T&T Clark, 1957), 7. Hereafter, references to the *Church Dogmatics* will take the form: Barth, *CD* II/2, 7.

17   Barth, *CD* IV/1, 181.

18   Barth, *CD* II/1, 260.

19   McCormack argues convincingly that the implication of Barth's doctrine of election, where Jesus Christ is the Subject of election, leads to no abstract understanding of God apart from the human race. However, unlike Hegel's view, this divine historicization is a free act of God's gracious decision, not a necessary process for God to become complete. Bruce L. McCormack, *Orthodox and Modern: Studies in the Theology of Karl Barth* (Grand Rapids: Baker Academic, 2008), 190–91.

In his typical fashion, Barth begins with the particular witness of Scripture and then thinks outward to broader implications.[20] Of course, this kind of methodological sensibility is why Thomas Torrance describes him as a biblical and evangelical theologian.[21] Extending out of his Christocentricity, this actualism frames Barth's conception of "Trinity, election, theological anthropology and, yes, Scripture as well."[22]

We should clarify that actualistic ontology is not process theology: God's being is in its becoming, *not* God's being is becoming.[23] The former actualism simply means that God gives himself in a particular localized event such as the incarnation, or Holy Scriptures. The latter process theology expresses "change, growth or development" in God's being as though God's being is incomplete, discounting divine aseity.[24]

In the person of Jesus Christ, we have God's revelation, but veiled in human flesh. God became flesh, but we do not have direct access to this knowledge. Rather, the knowledge of God must be actively revealed by God (Matt 11:27). In Barth's mind, actualism functions closely connected to the dialectical idea of *indirect identity*, which is a dynamic interpretation of Chalcedonian Christology and the hypostatic union of divine and human natures.[25]

On the one hand, in the event of revelation God allows the divine self to become indirectly *identical* with a particular human being, meaning God is present in the medium.[26] The divine nature remains divine and the human nature remains human. The human medium does not become divinized, or become some *tertium quid* (a third thing) neither God nor man. However, in this identity, God becomes an object for us to behold with our human faculties. Without this identity, we would not truly encounter the living God in Christ, but merely a representation, a symbol with the true being of God still eluding us.[27] This identity invites

---

20   Hunsinger, *How to Read Karl Barth*, 32–35.

21   See Thomas F. Torrance, *Karl Barth: Biblical and Evangelical Theologian* (Edinburgh: T. & T. Clark, 1990).

22   Bruce L. McCormack, "The Being of Holy Scripture Is in Becoming: Karl Barth in Conversation with American Evangelical Criticism," in *Evangelicals and Scripture: Tradition, Authority and Hermeneutics*, ed. Vincent E. Bacote, Laura C. Miguélez, Dennis L. Okholm (Downers Grove, IL: InterVarsity Press, 2004), 64.

23   Ibid., 65.

24   Ibid., 65, n.13.

25   See how Barth uses the concept of indirect identity here: "the human nature of Christ (and especially in this connexion His corporality and therefore His spatiality), in its unity with the deity of the Son (unconfused with it, but also undivided from it, in real indirect identity), is revelation." Barth, *CD* II/1, 486.

26   McCormack, *Orthodox and Modern*, 110.

27   Barth rejects the idea that there is a "hidden fourth" or some other way of understanding

us to be oriented towards *revelation itself* and not merely *our experience* of the revelation. Contra Ludwig Feuerbach we are not simply left with our projections of God, or with our pietistic experiences of God.

On the other hand, this identity is *indirect*, meaning that God's revelation is veiled, and that it is not immediately available for all. God in this human medium is hidden and can only be perceived by the eyes of faith, which of course is a gift of God. In other words, the creaturely medium *in and of itself* cannot mediate God's presence to us; rather, God actively *makes* this event of revelation happen by lifting the veil and giving us the spiritual ability to discern this presence. The point here is that God is always Lord even in his revelation and we are only "unworthy servants" desperately in need of God's grace (Luke 17:10).[28]

This lordship of God in his revelation is why Barth distinguishes revelation and history. It is not that revelation is not historical, but knowing history in of itself does not give us access to revelation. This indirectness explains Barth's reticence towards apologetics, if that means seeking a direct path to God's revelation through reason.[29] This search would be a form of revelatory legalism or works righteousness that try to bypass God's sovereign grace. This indirectness critiques the conservative or evangelical positivism and rationalism.[30]

Turning to Barth's understanding of Scripture, this same actualistic dialectic of indirect identity is at work.[31] In his threefold form of the Word of God, Barth relates and distinguishes Scripture from the Word in indirect identity. The reason for this unity-in-differentiation of Jesus Christ the living Word, Scripture, and preaching is to explain how we truly encounter the living God.

Although Scripture is human words, it becomes God's Word by God's gracious act. In reading the Bible we are always at God's mercy. Just like how we must encounter God in Jesus Christ and cannot bypass this historical person to some direct revelation, the Bible is where God has promised

---

God's being behind the revealed triune God. Barth, *CD* I/1, 355.

28   As McCormack explains the "principle consequence of this concept of an indirect revelation for theological epistemology is that God is the Subject of the knowledge of God." McCormack, *Orthodox and Modern*, 110.

29   See McCormack's coinage "dynamic infallibilism" as a way of describing the trustworthiness of scripture in Barthian fashion. McCormack, "The Being of Holy Scripture Is in Becoming," 73.

30   See Dorrien's critique of early evangelicals as "antimodernist modernizers." Gary Dorrien, *The Remaking of Evangelical Theology* (Louisville: Westminster John Knox, 1998).

31   Barth, *CD* I/2, 499–500. The hypostatic union serves as a metaphor for the nature of scripture. See the discussion in McCormack, "The Being of Holy Scripture Is in Becoming," 68.

to speak to us. Through preaching that is rooted in Scripture and witnesses to the Word, God reveals Godself and speaks to us here and now.

Early in his career, Barth concludes that knowing Scripture is not the same thing as encountering God in Scripture. There is an indirectness or a distinction that has to be made even in the identity of the Bible being the Word of God.[32] Another way of describing this distinction is the Bible as a *source* as opposed to a *witness*. Scripture is not a source of knowledge about God's past acts, but rather a witness to the living God who speaks to us. In stating *Deus dixit* as a way of describing revelation in Scripture and preaching, Barth states that the Latin perfect tense denotes "an eternal perfect" in that God spoke and continues to speaks.[33]

Barth means that the Scripture is an address. The act of reading Scripture is not only learning about spiritual wisdom, about God's work in the lives of those in the past, or even learning about God. To Barth, the "presupposition of the Bible is not that God is but that he spoke" and still speaks.[34] In fact what "makes scripture holy scripture is . . . the I-Thou encounter, person to person . . . Only within this I-Thou relation, in which one speaks and another is spoken to, in which there is communication and reception, only in full *action* is revelation."[35]

In sum, Barth's actualistic view of Scripture means that in the Bible we are dealing with the living God who actually speaks, and that we are at God's mercy for this encounter. God's living Word demands that Scripture must be engaged contemporaneously and not just historically.[36] While the life and works of Jesus Christ are the basis of God's contemporary presence, we are not studying a dead Savior, but a living One who is with us in the power of the Spirit.

With the Bible as a witness to the living God who speaks and meets us in its pages, we now explore the dynamic of double particularity in our contextual reading of Scripture.

---

32   Richard E. Burnett, *Karl Barth's Theological Exegesis: The Hermeneutical Principles of the Römerbrief Period* (Grand Rapids: Eerdmans, 2004), 223.

33   Karl Barth, *The Göttingen Dogmatics: Instruction in the Christian Religion* (Grand Rapids: Eerdmans, 1991), 1:59.

34   Ibid., 1:58.

35   Ibid.

36   In distinguishing himself from Bultmann, Barth argues that "calls for constant new understanding and exposition" of scripture is not "the 'cradle' of the language, the thought-forms, etc., in which the message is enshrined" but rather the living message itself. Karl Barth, "Bultmann—An Attempt to Understand Him," in *Kerygma and Myth, A Theological Debate Volume II,* ed. Hans-Werner Bartsch, trans. Reginald H. Fuller (London: SPCK, 1962), 87.

DOUBLE PARTICULARITY OF SCRIPTURAL READING

Expanding upon the actualistic idea of Scripture as the locus of our encounter with the living God, a contextual hermeneutic could be explained through the language of *double particularity*.[37] The primary particularity is found in the one event of divine revelation in the person of Jesus Christ and the witness of Scripture *there* and *then*. The secondary particularity is found in the presence of the living Christ encountering the identity and the situation of the reader *here* and *now*. Put differently, this double particularity refers to the particular *text* that witnesses to the living Christ, and our particular *context* that hears the living Christ.

These two particularities together comprise what Barth calls the "living context" where God speaks and encounters us.[38] By living context, Barth means that there is "a simultaneity which heals the past of its dumbness and the present of its deafness, which enables that past to speak and the present to hear."[39] This simultaneity is founded upon the living Jesus Christ, who unifies the past and the present.[40] Barth also talks about "a twofold contingency" of Christ's contemporaneity, in which "a contingent *illic et tunc* [there and then]" and "a contingent *hic et nunc* [here and now]" come together as a divinely orchestrated event.[41] In more traditional terms, Barth views the Holy Spirit's "inspiration as a single, timeless—or rather, contemporary—act of God (its communication, too, is really an act) in both the biblical authors *and* ourselves."[42]

This double particularity presents a dialectical and dialogical reading of Scripture. I will unpack these ideas in three main points.

First, for Barth reading Scripture is "always a combination of taking and giving, of reading out and reading in," of exegesis and eisegesis.[43] There is a real dialogue between the text and the context, back and forth. Barth proposed this practice of eisegesis early and defended it throughout his career.[44] With this statement he is not claiming "reading

---

37   As the features of my argument show I am deeply indebted to Burnett's excellent work throughout this paper. Richard E. Burnett, *Karl Barth's Theological Exegesis: The Hermeneutical Principles of the Römerbrief Period* (Grand Rapids: Eerdmans, 2004).

38   Burnett, *Karl Barth's Theological Exegesis*, 101, 284.

39   Karl Barth, *The Epistle to the Romans* (London: Oxford University Press, 1933), 145.

40   Burnett, *Karl Barth's Theological Exegesis*, 108.

41   Barth, *CD* I/1, 149.

42   Barth, *The Göttingen Dogmatics*, 225.

43   Barth, *CD* I/1, 106.

44   Burnett, *Karl Barth's Theological Exegesis*, 112.

in" per se as a goal, nor the impossibility of "reading out." Rather Barth is acknowledging that we have presuppositions, in that "none of us can study scripture without accompanying with our own thoughts that we establish more and less without prejudice, without doing so even in the very process of establishing it."[45] We cannot avoid eisegesis and its dangers by appealing to "a definitive and decisive teaching office in the Church" as in Roman Catholicism, or to "a historico-critical scholarship" as in Protestantism.[46]

Of course, Barth offers words of caution regarding this eisegesis, because it can be arbitrary and wayward. In a sense, admitting the inevitability of presuppositions enables us to consciously name them and not be deluded with a false sense of objectivity. Barth quips that we "should at least honestly admit" our presuppositions, and "be kind enough to give the child its right name."[47] However, we must not only admit them but be willing to question them as well, being critical with our critical thoughts so as to not hamper the freedom of the Word.[48] Our assumptions must be open to criticism again and again in the process of opening ourselves up to the voice of God.

Now while there is no sure escape from our capricious thoughts, Barth believes that tradition can help so that we do not wander too far.[49] While tradition has "no independent value and authority beside that of the Word of God," it can in the form of the church fathers, the creeds, and the confessions, challenge our presuppositions and guide our reading of Scripture.[50] The church fathers should be thought of as our "older and more experienced fellow-pupils" in dealing with the Word.[51] Through their instruction, we avoid becoming in bondage to the present and its ideas.[52]

While many dangers persist, the living context of Scripture where we encounter the living God also *requires* this eisegesis.[53] Reading Scripture means active participation in its subject-matter, not neutral passive detachment. Thus, we must come to the text with "one's whole self, with the full

---

45   Barth, *The Göttingen Dogmatics*, 258.
46   Barth, *CD* I/1, 106.
47   Barth, *The Göttingen Dogmatics*, 259.
48   Burnett, *Karl Barth's Theological Exegesis*, 198.
49   Barth, *The Göttingen Dogmatics*, 260.
50   Barth, *CD* I/2, 828.
51   Ibid., 607.
52   Ibid.
53   Burnett, *Karl Barth's Theological Exegesis*, 114.

depth and weight of one's problems, questions, and concerns, including the fundamental questions of one's existence."[54] Barth avers that "we not only cannot detach ourselves from ourselves and our situation; we ought not to do so. We have to come to ourselves—with God and from God. We have to be there. For this concerns us."[55] Again, this is a crucial aspect of God's Word as address, an I-Thou encounter. What is required of us is that we hear the Word of God and "take it up into our own particular situation, seeing that in Holy Scripture it has, in fact, already entered into our situation."[56]

Second and correspondingly, Barth rejects the "bifurcated, two-stage, dualistic 'double-entry bookkeeping'" approach to biblical interpretation where what was meant is fundamentally distinguished from what it means.[57] There is no two-step process where we first figure out what the text means "according to its grammatical, literary, and historical sense" and then ascertain its meaning "according its theological sense" for us.[58] To be sure, the theological meaning must be understood in light of the grammatical, historical sense. Also, there is no difference between what the text meant then and what it means now. However, apart from the theological understanding there is no getting at a genuine historical meaning either.

For Barth, there are numerous reasons why the two meanings cannot be separated distinctly. To begin with there is no neutral place to scientifically and objectively approach the text. True engagement with the text would require openness to the living God, and our active participation in the subject-matter. Also, what the Scripture is communicating was not something "dead or frozen" that can be taken apart with the tools of historical criticism.[59] The subject-matter of the Bible is not ancient spiritual wisdom, but God, God who spoke and speaks today.

While Barth does not use this analogy, such a separation between the historical and the theological sense of Scripture would be akin to the problematic search for the historical Jesus distinct from the God-man. While our theological understanding of Jesus is rooted in historical study, there is no getting at an objectively historical Jesus.

---

54 Ibid., 111.
55 Barth, *The Göttingen Dogmatics*, 255.
56 Barth, *CD* I/2, 699.
57 Burnett, *Karl Barth's Theological Exegesis*, 85.
58 Ibid., 84.
59 Ibid., 244.

For Barth a proper reading of Scripture means that we not direct our attention *behind* the text towards the author, nor in *front* of the text towards ourselves the reader. Barth's dialectical approach is not about historical criticism, nor a "reader response" theory of interpretation.[60] Of course, we must attend to the historical particularities of the biblical author and Barth never denies that. Historical-critical method is a significant "preparation" that serves "the broader, deeper and more important" task of apprehending the theological meaning of the text.[61]

Instead of *behind* or in *front*, for Barth, scriptural meaning is *in*, or more precisely *with*, the text. Barth states that to understand the biblical author means that we "*stand with him*, to take each of his works in earnest, . . . to participate with him in the subject matter, in order to interpret him from the inside out."[62] Even though a great ugly historical and cultural ditch divides the biblical authors from us, we share with them the same subject matter; we both encounter the living God. We do not truly apprehend the text "until Paul speaks there and [the reader] hears here, until the conversation between document and reader is concentrated entirely on the *subject matter* (which *cannot* be different here and there!)."[63]

See how Barth describes this conversation between text and reader in the example of Calvin's exegesis:

> History is indeed being studied, but it is also being made. . . . [S]omething is happening in it, . . . a fruitful dialogue and living dialogue is in fact taking place here across the cleft of the centuries. We are in the 1st century but we are equally in the 16th. We hear Paul, and we also hear Calvin. The voices merge into one another so that we can hardly distinguish them. . . . This relevance of Calvin's exposition, quite apart from specific applications, means that it still speaks and teaches and persuades today. We believe Calvin the more readily because he is not deliberately trying to make us believe but simply setting out what he finds in Paul, yet not, of course, without being able or even trying to hide the fact that he himself believes it. This quiet kinship between the apostle and the exegete speaks for itself.[64]

---

60 Bruce L. McCormack, "Significance of Karl Barth's Theological Exegesis," in *Epistle to the Philippians*, 40th Anniversary Edition by Karl Barth, v–xxv (Louisville: Westminster John Knox, 2002), xiv, n.29.

61 Barth, *The Epistle to the Romans*, 1.

62 Burnett, *Karl Barth's Theological Exegesis*, 281.

63 Burnett, *Karl Barth's Theological Exegesis*, 118, quoting and translating Karl Barth, *Der Römerbrief, 1922* (Zürich: Evangelischer Verlag Zürich, 1954), xi.

64 Karl Barth, *The Theology of John Calvin* (Grand Rapids: Eerdmans, 1995), 392.

This conversation or kinship does not mean that there are no right or wrong interpretations of the text. Barth notes that we should not separate between the thoughts of the authors and their writings as though their Scripture has a life of its own apart from them.[65] God uses human authors and their writings with their human particularities and limitations and we cannot bypass this creaturely medium directly to the Spirit through a mystical experience. We must attend to the text to discover the meaning. Yet, because of its subject matter, our interpretation will always be "provisional" at best and require us to return to the biblical text again and again.[66]

Third and lastly, Barth rejects the notion of a "general anthropology, a common, universally intuitable core of humanity" that would serve as a connection between the biblical writers and us.[67] In the liberal empathic hermeneutical tradition of Friedrich Schleiermacher and Wilhelm Dilthey, the reader understands the meaning of the text by deeply empathizing with the inner lived experience of the author. Thus, even though greatly divided by time, culture, and individualities, this interpretive approach assumes the existence of a common basic human nature shared by the author and the reader.[68]

After Barth's break with liberalism, he rejects this common human core because he realizes this approach focuses on the spiritual experience of author and not the subject matter of Scripture.[69] Moreover, with this focus on the common human core, the individualities of the authors are limited or truncated so that we only see what we expect, in other words only reflections of ourselves. However, if the subject matter of the Bible is "wholly other," this truncation would serve to tame God to our expectations. Barth proposes that instead of a common human core, the author and the reader shared a common subject matter in which they both participate.

Barth's affirmation of human particularity is rooted in his doctrine of election and Christology, in the very Jewishness of Jesus Christ. Reconciliation is founded upon the Jewish flesh of Jesus of Nazareth and the people who are in him.[70] Only in this Jewish flesh is Jesus Christ the

---

65   Barth, *CD* I/2, 505.
66   Burnett, *Karl Barth's Theological Exegesis*, 245, referring to Barth, *Der Römerbrief, 1922*, xiii–xiv.
67   Burnett, *Karl Barth's Theological Exegesis*, 187.
68   Ibid., 164.
69   Ibid., 189.
70   Mark R. Lindsay, *Covenanted Solidarity: The Theological Basis of Karl Barth's Opposition to Nazi Antisemitism and the Holocaust* (New York: 2001), 214. See *CD* II/2, 8.

Savior because this Jewishness confirmed God's faithfulness to Israel.[71] Extending this idea, Scripture's historic particularity is a vital part of its being.

Moreover, even our own contextual particularities are the "divinely intended creative substance of [our] existence."[72] In fact, "it is not accidentally or in vain but meaningfully and purposively that God has called [us] to serve [God] in this determination and this outlook, background and origin."[73] Thus, we must "handle our human contextual particularities critically but positively, gently and with love."[74] Barth makes it clear that this space of contextual particularities is where we encounter the Word of God:

> [We] cannot try to live . . . [a] Christian life which is private and neutral in face of its past and present. [We] must affirm the presuppositions and its past and at [our] own place and time take up and genuinely share the problems of its future. In not refusing to do this, but doing it, [we] will hear and obey the command of God. [We] will respect the freedom of God's Word under this historical determination of [ours], and exercise [our] own freedom in the constraint thereby imposed.[75]

There is no neutral space to read the text and we should not try or pretend to.

Of course, as always with Barth, there is the other side of the dialectic. While we cannot and must not deny our contextual particularities, we cannot make it an idol either. These particularities must be "absolutely subordinate" to the freedom of God's Word.[76] Barth states his chief concern thusly: "The command of God must be *master*, and all historical interpretations and notions, all other considerations, all economic, political, social, cultural and even religious evaluations of the situation must *be mastered and not try to play the master.*"[77]

Not only theologically, but contextually, there are reasons why the context cannot be dominant. Foreshadowing contemporary postmodern and postcolonial theorists, Barth argues that aspects of our cultural context

---

71 Lindsay, *Covenanted Solidarity*, 212. See *CD* IV/1, 168, 170, and Karl Barth, *Evangelical Theology: An Introduction* (London: Collins, 1965), 27–28.

72 John G. Flett, *The Witness of God: The Trinity, Missio Dei, Karl Barth, and the Nature of Christian Community* (Grand Rapids: Eerdmans, 2010), 117.

73 Barth, *CD* III/4, 292–93.

74 Ibid., 293.

75 Ibid., 295.

76 Ibid., 290.

77 Ibid., 296. Emphasis added.

are reversible, fluid, and removable.[78] In other words, these contextual particularities are not *essentializing*, but *hybridic* in postcolonial terms. An essentialized identity assumes the existence of a pure authentic essence of a particular group with a set of fixed and distinguishing properties. A hybridic identity, on the other hand, rejects this notion of purity for a fusion or a mixture with indefinite or dynamic features.

Barth rejects the construction of "precise" or essentialized identities by recalling the second commandment: "Thou shalt make no image, no abstraction, including none of *the* American, *the* Swiss, *the* German, etc.!"[79] So consequently Barth states that:

> Christians will always be Christians first, and only then members of a specific culture or state or class or the like. . . . Christianity exists in Germany and Switzerland and Africa, but there is no such thing as a German or Swiss or African Christianity.[80]

Therefore these contextual identities cannot become the criteria, a Procrustean bed into which the Word of God must neatly fit. While we always read Scripture in our particular contexts leading to our particular insights, there cannot be an ideological domestication of our reading for the sake of relevance.

READING SCRIPTURE IN OUR CONTEXT

In this final section, I will summarize the concrete and practical implications of this double particularity, organizing the above insights together in four main themes.

First, the primary particularity, or the particularity of the subject matter, grounds our conceptions of God and Scripture. There is no teasing out the abstract divinity from the scandal of particularity in divine revelation. We cannot go behind this particularity to grasp the subject matter philosophically as the ground of Being, or theologically as justification by faith, gospel, or grace, or politically as liberation or freedom.[81] The

---

78 Ibid., 299–301. See for example the resonances between Barth and Tanner's descriptions of postmodern notions of culture. Kathryn Tanner, *Theories of Culture: A New Agenda for Theology* (Minneapolis: Fortress, 1997).

79 Karl Barth, *Evangelical Theology: An Introduction* (Grand Rapids: Eerdmans, 1979), viii.

80 Barth is stressing his concern over allegiance to nationalism and other ideologies. His comments should not be understood as proposing that there is a way to be Christian in some abstract and neutral way beyond human particularities. Barth, *CD* IV/1, 703.

81 See Tillich's conception of God as the ground of Being in Paul Tillich, *Systematic Theology*, vol. 1 (Chicago: University of Chicago Press, 1951). See Bonhoeffer's critique of grace as a godless

fullness of God is revealed in the Jewish Jesus of Nazareth in the first century.[82]

Moreover, this primary particularity in Scripture means that we use all the critical tools at hand to acknowledge the particularity of the scriptural authors, knowing that our understanding of them will always be provisional, that we must come to the text with fresh eyes again and again. The God that we encounter in Scripture and the biblical authors who witness to this God are strange and different, totally other. This otherness cannot be glossed over with glib assumptions of comprehension that often arise out of our self-projections.

Second, the secondary particularity, or the particularity of our context exposes or affirms our full humanity as readers. There is no room for a false sense of objectivity, with illusions of an abstract general personhood. If we do not own up to our particularity, it will remain invisible to us with all its "givens" as normative. This is how patriarchy, racism, capitalism, individualism, modernism, Constantinianism, colonialism, and Western hegemony operated in the shadows of our mind and so often in our hermeneutics. Thus, Scripture becomes captive albeit rather unconsciously and unintentionally.

Positively, we do and must bring our thoughts, questions, and our struggles to understand the text. Our hearing of God in the text is an I-Thou encounter. We must not objectify God or reduce ourselves into an *It*, as in an I-It interaction. We cannot reduce ourselves to a passive "yes-man or woman" so that God is merely speaking to Godself, as in an I-I sense.[83] In the I-Thou encounter, we approach the text as God's covenant partners.

Third, the asymmetry between the particularities, specifically the precedence of the biblical particularity over the contextual particularity, guards against various kinds of Babylonian captivities. The double particularity has a functional trajectory with the telos in service of the text. As

---

abstraction, "grace without the living, incarnate Jesus." Dietrich Bonhoeffer, *Dietrich Bonhoeffer Works*, vol. 4 in *Discipleship* (Minneapolis: Augsburg Fortress, 2001), 44. Barth clarifies how Jesus Christ cannot be lost in the concept of grace: "The last word that I have to say as a theologian or politician is not a concept like grace but a name: Jesus Christ." Karl Barth, *Final Testimonies* (Grand Rapids: Eerdmans, 1977), 29.

82 "In the Christ of Israel this Word has become *particular*, that is, Jewish flesh. It is in the particularity of the flesh that it applies *universally* to all men. The Christ of Israel is the Saviour of the world." Karl Barth, *Evangelical Theology*, 23.

83 See Brueggemann's description of how in a genuine covenant interaction with God we cannot be "yes-men and women." Walter Brueggemann, *The Psalms and the Life of Faith* (Minneapolis: Fortress, 1995), 102–4.

we noted above, we bring our whole selves with all of our presuppositions to the text, but we must be open to be critiqued by the Word.[84] In the name of contextuality, our hermeneutic must not become captivity to an ideology of feminism, socialism, postcolonialism or any national, racial, ethnic, or cultural identities. A reading of Scripture that takes our context seriously does not mean a justification of an ideological reading.

Furthermore, as readers of Scripture, we must remember to serve "only one Spirit, one Lord, one God" and "belong to the one people of God, to the one Church of Jesus Christ, to the one communion of the Holy Spirit."[85] Reading Scripture as part of this one ecumenical community means that we learn from and contribute to the collective wisdom or tradition. This community spans boundaries of history and geography, as well as those of racial, ethnic, cultural, social, political, and economic distinctions. Without this broader and diverse community, we would be captive to our own conditions assuming that they are normative and universal.

Fourth and finally, this double particularity makes our need for prayer more than just a pietistic sentimentality. For Barth, prayer is essential for the task of theology, as part of theological methodology. In fact, for Barth "[t]he first and basic act of theological work is *prayer*" even before study and before service.[86] Because "[t]he object of theological work is not some thing but some *one*" we must appeal to God and God's grace to reveal the divine self to us. Of course, we need God's grace to perceive ourselves clearly as well. We must learn from Anselm who gazing upon himself prayed: "*Revela me de me ad te! Da mih, ut intelligam!* (Reveal me from myself to thee! Grant that I may understand!) And gazing upon God: *Redde te mihi! Da te ipsum mihi, Deus meus!* (Restore thyself to me! Give thyself to me, my God!)"[87]

CONCLUSION

Our context is one of global, multiethnic, transnational, overlapping identities and currents, a world of systemic racism and black lives matter, of ISIS, Syrian refugees, and impassioned debates about immigration

---

84 See Bonhoeffer's assessment of American Christianity as one that does not understand the critique of the Word. Dietrich Bonhoeffer, "Protestantism without the Reformation," in *No Rusty Swords: Letters, Lectures and Notes, 1928–1936*, ed. Edwin H. Robertson, trans. Edwin H. Robertson and John Bowden (London: Collins, 1965), 92–118.
85 Barth, "No Boring Theology!," 5.
86 Barth, *Evangelical Theology*, 159.
87 Ibid., 169.

policies, a world with questions about if Muslims worship the same God as Christians, about Lesbian, Gay, Bisexual, Transgender, Intersex, and Asexual (LGBTQIA) identities, just to list some examples.

In this context, we read Scripture, participating in its living context and encountering the living God in an I-Thou manner. Our context matters in our reading of Scripture not merely for historical, cultural, or sociopolitical reasons, but for doctrinal ones as well. Barth offers these doctrinal reasons and also guides us to navigate through their dangers while retaining theological integrity.

Barth continued throughout his career to listen to God's Word and to be corrected by it. With his actualism and contextual sensibility, Barth strove to not become a "Barthian," to not be boxed in by his own theology, but to be open to God's Word and to be corrected by it again and again.[88] It is this theological sensibility of his, this attitude towards Scripture, that we can still appreciate and learn from today.

88　Karl Barth, *Letters 1961–1968* (Grand Rapids: Eerdmans, 1981), 255.

CHAPTER 10

"FOR THE LOVE OF GOD": SCRIPTURE AND THE FORMATION OF HUMAN IDENTITY

Ryan S. Peterson

Knowing the telos of Scripture helps the hearer receive God's message. Given the diversity and complexity of the biblical texts, however, explaining Scripture's telos is not easy. So, a number of analogies have been employed for this purpose. The analogy one uses to illuminate Scripture's telos has important implications for the way Scripture is read and how its authority is construed. For example, if Scripture is primarily understood in terms of "realistic narrative," as it is in George Lindbeck's *The Nature of Doctrine*, then the telos of Scripture is to help believers interpret themselves in light of the literary identities described therein.[1] Reading Scripture, in this case, is similar to reading a novel, albeit a non-fictional one.[2] Scripture shapes the cultural-linguistic understanding of the reader and conforms her to its patterns.

There are stronger ways of construing the telos of Scripture on the

---

1   See George A. Lindbeck, *The Nature of Doctrine: Religion and Theology in a Postliberal Age* (Louisville: Westminster John Knox, 1984), 120–21.
2   David Kelsey, *The Uses of Scripture in Recent Theology* (Minneapolis: Fortress, 1975), 48. Cited by Lindbeck, *Nature of Doctrine*, 121.

basis of the narrative analogy. Robert Jenson takes up the analogy and radicalizes it.

> The persons who appear in Scripture as the character of the divine story—Father, Son, and Spirit—and the plotlines between them simply are Scripture's God. The persons Father, Son, and Spirit are the doers not only of our life but of God's; and the plotlines of this action between Father, Son, Spirit—the Father's finding himself in the Son or the Spirit's liberation of both to love each other—constitute the drama of God not just with us but for himself.[3]

In this case, Scripture does not merely provide a narrative by which one can better understand oneself and the world. Rather, Scripture's story "*is itself* the truth about God."[4] Again, it is not that Scripture can be used to interpret one's own story. Such a view would limit Scripture's import too severely. Jenson asserts, "Scripture's story is not part of some larger narrative; it is itself the larger narrative of which all other true narratives are parts."[5] The telos of Scripture, for Jenson, is the proclamation of divine-human history, as well as a word from the Lord inviting participation since Scripture "tells a story about God and us that we are even now living."[6] Jenson uses both "narrative" and "drama" to describe Scripture's role.

Kevin Vanhoozer has developed more extensively the analogy of drama, describing Scripture as the church's script. Drawing upon Hans Urs von Balthasar's three-volume work, *Theo-drama*, Vanhoozer makes the following comparison between narrative and drama: "Narratives require narrators and recount their tales in the first or third person. Dramas, by contrast, *show* rather than tell. Moreover, in drama, the words are part of the action. Drama, more so than narrative, provides a salient reminder that we should not draw too fine a distinction between 'word' and 'act.'"[7] Vanhoozer uses the metaphor compellingly to demonstrate that Scripture both describes divine action and is itself a part of God's action.[8] Scripture contains God's speech-acts, and these serve as the church's script for acting out faithful worship and wisdom on the stage of the world.

---

3   Robert W. Jenson, "Scripture's Authority in the Church," in *The Art of Reading Scripture*, ed. Ellen F. Davis and Richard B. Hays (Grand Rapids: Eerdmans, 2003), 33.

4   Ibid.

5   Ibid., 34.

6   Ibid., 30.

7   Kevin Vanhoozer, *The Drama of Doctrine: A Canonical-Linguistic Approach to Christian Theology* (Louisville: Westminster John Knox, 2005), 48.

8   Ibid., 70.

The drama analogy situates Scripture in an action-oriented context. This move is illuminating of the relationship between God's people (the actors) and Scripture (the script). While it makes clear the holistic way humans participate in the divine drama, it is not natural to this analogy to explain human knowledge of God. For this theologically crucial piece, Vanhoozer incorporates another analogy—that of map-making. "Theological cartography is a dramatic exercise of holy reason," he says.[9] And such cartography makes sense, as C. S. Lewis notes in *Mere Christianity*, when one is meant to proceed on a journey.[10]

While neither the narrative nor drama analogies do enough in terms of explaining participatory knowledge of God, the journey analogy comes to our aid. Augustine, in *De doctrina christiana*, asks us to think of ourselves as travelers who require assistance for our journey in fellowship with God. Augustine's analogy provides the context for an exceptional analysis of Scripture's telos on the basis of God's invitation for humans to know and love God and so participate in the divine life. My goal in this chapter is to recover Augustine's analogy for contemporary appropriation. So, in the following sections of my paper, I will (1) trace the logic of Augustine's analogy and its implications for the doctrine of Scripture, (2) analyze the doctrinal convictions needed for the analogy's success, and (3) draw implications for the doctrine of Scripture on the basis of these doctrinal convictions. I will not try to prove that the journey analogy, over against others, is the best one. Rather, I hope to show the unique ways this analogy illuminates Scripture's telos, uncovering a compelling vision of the relationship of God and humanity.

READING FOR THE JOURNEY

Early in Book 1 of Augustine's *De doctrina christiana*, he asks us to join him on a thought experiment. He says:

> Suppose we were travellers who could live happily only in our homeland, and because our absence made us unhappy we wished to put an end to our misery and return there: we would need transport by land or sea which we could use to travel to our homeland, the object of our enjoyment. But if we were fascinated by the delights of the journey and the actual travelling, we would be perversely enjoying things that

---

9   Ibid., 301.
10   C. S. Lewis, *Mere Christianity* (New York: Touchstone, 1996), 135–38.

we should be using; and we would be reluctant to finish our journey quickly, being ensnared in the wrong kind of pleasure and estranged from the homeland whose pleasures could make us happy.[11]

As Augustine moves his argument forward, it becomes clear that this analogy is much more than a thought experiment. In fact, it sets the context for Augustine's entire approach to Scripture. Augustine draws the following connections:

> So in this mortal life we are like travellers away from our Lord [2 Cor 5:6]: if we wish to return to the homeland where we can be happy we must use this world [cf. 1 Cor 7:31], not enjoy it, in order to discern "the invisible attributes of God, which are understood through what has been made" [Rom 1:20] or, in other words, to derive eternal and spiritual value from corporeal and temporal things.[12]

The distinction between *uti* (to use) and *frui* (to enjoy) is foundational for Augustine's theology of creation and also for his profound ethical analyses. But here the distinction is made for the sake of those who wish to become wise readers of Scripture. In this context, Augustine makes it clear that all creation is meant to bring us to love and enjoyment of God:

> To enjoy something is to hold fast to it in love for its own sake. To use something is to apply whatever it may be to the purpose of obtaining what you love. . . . The things which are to be enjoyed, then, are the Father and the Son and the Holy Spirit.[13]

Life in fellowship with God is the homeland that makes us happy.

Other humans, both friends and enemies, ought to be loved for God's sake.[14] We ought even to love ourselves for God's sake.[15] Augustine has the "double love" of God and neighbor in view here: "You shall love the Lord your God with all your heart, and with all your soul, and with all your mind. This is the great and first commandment. And a second is like it: You shall love your neighbor as yourself. On these two commandments hang all the Law and the Prophets" (Matt 22:37–39).[16] Jesus's summation of the law implies three loves: love of God, love of neighbor, and love of

---

11 Augustine, *On Christian Teaching*, trans. R. P. H. Green (Oxford: Oxford University Press, 1997), 9–10.
12 Ibid., 10.
13 Ibid., 9–10.
14 Ibid., 16–17.
15 Ibid., 17.
16 Ibid., 17, 27. Unless otherwise noted, English translations in this essay are taken from the ESV.

self. We are meant to enjoy God along with others, who are directed to the same end. We love others and ourselves by moving, with others, into deeper love of and fellowship with God. This movement is the relational journey ordained by God for human happiness and fulfillment.

By enjoying God, we actually receive God. Lest anyone think God is selfish in his desire to be loved, Augustine explains that "it is God who wants himself to be loved, not in order to gain any reward for himself but to give to those who love him an eternal reward—namely himself, the object of their love."[17] Again, Augustine clarifies the end toward which rightly ordered loves are aimed: "This reward is the supreme reward—that we may thoroughly enjoy him and that all of us who enjoy him may enjoy one another in him."[18] Human flourishing is dependent upon rightly ordered love of God and neighbor since true happiness is located in, ordered by, and given through God's own life.

Just so, rightly ordered loves lead to genuine happiness and satisfaction. Note that Augustine has introduced this account of rightly ordered loves on the basis of the divine life. Scripture has been used to support this account. But he has not yet provided a doctrine of Scripture per se. When Augustine turns his attention to Scripture, he says that:

> The chief purpose of all that we have been saying in our discussion of things is to make it understood that the fulfillment and end of the law [cf. Rom 13:10; 1 Tim 1:5] and all the divine scriptures is to love the thing which must be enjoyed and the thing which together with us can enjoy that thing (since there is no need for a commandment to love oneself). To enlighten us and enable us, the whole temporal dispensation was set up by divine providence for our salvation. We must make use of this, not with a permanent love and enjoyment of it, but with a transient love and enjoyment of our journey . . . so that we love the means of transport only because of our destination. So anyone who thinks that he has understood the divine scriptures or any part of them, but cannot by his understanding build up this double love of God and neighbor, has not yet succeeded in understanding them.[19]

So, Scripture itself is seen to be a creature, as something to be used for the sake of learning love of God and neighbor. Scripture is a "means of transport" that, when read and received properly, shapes the loves of

---

17 Ibid., 22.
18 Ibid., 25.
19 Ibid., 27.

the reader so that the reader is moved toward the "destination," which is God himself.

Augustine's account of Scripture is dependent upon two anthropological presuppositions. First, humanity is meant to enjoy God by participating in the divine life. Second, humanity can grow progressively into this participation through the virtuous formation of the soul enacted by the work of the Holy Spirit. For Augustine, these ideas can be presupposed because of the doctrine of the *imago Dei*—humans are made in God's image. God's purpose for humanity conditions the purpose of Scripture; and God's purpose for humanity is what motivates God to create Scripture as the love-shaping, love-producing text that it is. Building on Augustine's account in *De doctrina christiana*, therefore, I will now explore the theological and anthropological presuppositions needed for its success.

HUMAN IDENTITY AND HOLY SCRIPTURE

Given its importance for understanding the telos of Scripture, I will offer an interpretation of the *imago Dei* that situates knowing and loving God in the context of human identity. I will not trace Augustine's interpretation of the *imago Dei* here, but my own. The question I wish to investigate is whether Scripture, and not only Augustine's analogy, indicates that humanity is on a journey into fuller participation in the divine life. If Scripture indicates this, then the nature of this journey will have significance for our doctrine of Scripture.

Being made in God's image, humans are created representatives of God in the world.[20] Since it is fitting to the nature of creation, humans are made to develop diachronically and dynamically into mature representatives of God. Knowing and loving God constitutes a dual movement that propels humans forward in this development toward godliness. The human journey into knowing and loving God fuels growth in God's image because of its participation in the knowing and loving proper to the triune life of God. God's self-knowing and self-loving is the very substance of the divine life. Therefore, when humanity is invited to know and love God, this is an invitation into creaturely participation in the divine nature (2 Pet 1:4). As we participate in knowing and loving God, we are progressively conformed to that knowledge and love, and therefore are conformed also to God.

---

20 For a more detailed exploration of the meaning of the *imago Dei*, see Ryan S. Peterson, *The Imago Dei as Human Identity: A Theological Interpretation* (Winona Lake: Eisenbrauns, 2016).

Intentional journeying into the knowledge and love of God is uniquely fitting to humanity's existence as God's earthly image. Growing participation in the divine life constitutes growing realization of the *imago Dei*. However, according to Genesis 1:26–28, humanity was made in God's image prior to any intentional imitation of God:

> Then God said, "Let us make man in our image, after our likeness. And let them have dominion over the fish of the sea and over the birds of the heavens and over the livestock and over all the earth and over every creeping thing that creeps upon the earth."
> So God created humankind in his image,
> in the image of God he created them;
> male and female he created them.

The *imago Dei* appears to be a settled fact about humanity rather than something progressively developed. At first glance, this appears to conflict with the journey analogy. So, further consideration of Genesis 1 is required if we are to sustain the connections I have been making between the image of God and creaturely participation in the divine life. I will offer exegetical comments on Genesis 1 here, showing how the text, when read theologically, invites and motivates one's journey in relational fellowship with God.

Genesis 1 helps the hearer contemplate God's identity and the nature of God's world. God is revealed as creator of all things, having dominion over the environments in which creatures move (Days 1–3) and the creatures that move in those environments (Days 4–6).[21] In this context, a paradigmatic relation between God's action and human imitation is established. Since humanity is created to be an earthly image of God, it is granted creaturely dominion over the world's other living creatures. For the same reason, human dominion is patterned upon divine dominion. Human dominion is not independent of God; rather, human dominion is constituted by its participation in God's dominion.

In order for humans to exercise dominion in a way that is patterned upon God's dominion, humans must know God and imitate God's character in creaturely ways. Such imitation requires participation in God's wisdom and love. Humans must share in God's wisdom in order to know

---

21   See Henri Blocher, *In the Beginning: The Opening Chapters of Genesis* (Downers Grove, IL: InterVarsity Press, 1984), 51–52, for a discussion of the literary balance of Genesis 1.

the good of creation and share in God's love in order to desire the good for creation. In Genesis 1, therefore, humanity is shown to have a divine Father who invites fellowship through revelation (by his Word) and conformation (by his Spirit).

The cultivation of wisdom and love requires additional knowledge of God, knowledge that exceeds the teaching provided in Genesis 1. As Athanasius argues in *On the Incarnation*, humans are intended to contemplate God for guidance in wisdom rather than turning to creation for direction.[22] The assignment to rule over the earth's other creatures reveals humanity's identity as the creature intended for willing participation in the knowing and loving of God.

But why do we need to call human knowledge and love of God "participation in the divine life"? Humans know and love God only because God shares his self-knowledge and self-love with us. The nature of human participation in the divine life can be clarified through reflection on the movement from God's self-knowledge and self-love to human knowing and loving of God. The triune life is a life of knowing. God knows himself. Concerning the Son's knowing of the Father, Matthew 11:27 indicates that "no one knows the Son except the Father, and no one knows the Father except the Son." With respect to the Spirit's knowing of the Father and the Son, 1 Corinthians 2:10–11 explains: "For the Spirit searches everything, even the depths of God. For who knows a person's thoughts except the spirit of that person, which is in him? So also no one comprehends the thoughts of God except the Spirit of God."

God's self-knowing is his wisdom.[23] So, Paul identifies the incarnate Christ as "the power of God and the wisdom of God" (1 Cor 1:24). The divine economy, in which Christ "became to us" wisdom from God (1 Cor 1:30), makes known the eternal truth that the Son is the wisdom of God since he is the Father's Image and Word. The Spirit of God is the Spirit of wisdom (Eph 1:17) because he is the Spirit *of* the Father and the Son. As Kyle Strobel and Adam Johnson explain, "Jesus is wisdom incarnate, acting on our behalf, and through him we received the Spirit of wisdom (Isa 11:2; Acts 2:33), such that the wisdom we receive is the wisdom that is had only through participation in the divine life of Wisdom."[24]

---

22   See Athanasius, *On the Incarnation*, §4.
23   See Augustine, *De Trinitate*, VII.1.
24   Kyle Strobel and Adam J. Johnson, "Atoning Wisdom: The Wisdom of God in the Way of Salvation" in *Locating Atonement: Explorations in Constructive Dogmatics* (Grand Rapids: Zondervan, 2015), 92.

On the basis of God's self-knowledge, God makes himself known to humanity. Returning to Matthew 11:27, we see that the exclusive knowledge of the Father possessed by the Son is revealed to others: "no one knows the Son except the Father, and no one knows the Father except the Son and anyone to whom the Son chooses to reveal him." Summarizing Augustine, Matthew Levering observes that "Wisdom Himself" has taught us how to enjoy God, "in the humility of Christ Jesus, who is both the 'end' and the 'Way.'"[25] For the human creature made in God's image, knowing God leads to wisdom. By contemplating God through the divine economy, humans develop a true understanding of what is good. In Christ, humanity is "renewed in knowledge after the image of its creator" (Col 3:10) and "created after the likeness of God in true righteousness and holiness" (Eph 4:24). Discerning the will of God for life—wisdom—comes from the knowledge of God that transforms us "by the renewal of [our] mind[s]" (Rom 12:2). This journey into God's wisdom comes through participation in knowing that belongs to the divine life.

Just as God is in himself wisdom, "God is love" (1 John 4:8, 14). God is not merely loving; God has not arbitrarily willed to express love toward creation. Rather, love characterizes eternally the divine life *ad intra*. The fact that God is love is the ontological basis for God's loving acts *ad extra*. If "[w]e love because he first loved us" (1 John 4:19), God first loved us because God loves himself; God is love in the world because God's triune life is a life of love.

God's love is made known through God's loving action. The divine economy is the epistemological basis for our knowledge of God's love. I noted above that God's love for humanity and for creation as a whole is revealed in Genesis 1. The intensity of God's love is expressed in the incarnation. "For God so loved the world that he gave his only Son" (John 3:16). Again, "In this is love, not that we loved God but that he loved us and sent his Son as an atoning sacrifice for our sins" (1 John 4:10 NIV).

Fellowship with God produces love. "[W]hoever loves has been born of God and knows God" (1 John 4:7). And the production of love in those born of God should be expressed representatively in the world. "Beloved, let us love one another, because love is from God" (1 John 4:7). Ephesians 5:1–2 picks up the theme of imitation directly: "Therefore be imitators of God, as beloved children. And walk in love, as Christ loved us and gave

---

25   Matthew Levering, *Paticipatory Biblical Exegesis: A Theology of Biblical Interpretation* (Notre Dame: University of Notre Dame Press, 2008), 66.

himself up for us." Modeling ourselves on the revelation of God in Christ, we should grow progressively in God's love: "No one has ever seen God; if we love one another, God lives in us, and God's love is perfected in us" (1 John 4:12).

When God's own inner life of love is considered alongside the "dual love" found in Jesus's summation of the law and the prophets, love's significance for our understanding of human identity is amplified. In fact, Karl Barth's best observation regarding the *imago Dei*—that both in God's own life and in humanity there is "a genuine but harmonious self-encounter and self-discovery; a free co-existence and co-operation; an open confrontation and reciprocity"—is another way of saying that love is central to the meaning of the *imago Dei*.[26] Barth points out that "the analogy between God and man, is simply the existence of the I and the Thou in confrontation. . . . To remove it is tantamount to removing the divine from God as well as the human from man." The possibility for loving relationship is the condition of genuine covenantal fellowship between God and humanity so that "In this way He wills and creates man as a partner who is capable of entering into covenant-relationship with Himself—for all the disparity in and therefore the differentiation between man as a creature and his Creator."[27] Humanity is made by, and for, love.

The invitation to know and love God, then, is rooted in God's own self-knowing and self-loving and is fitting because humans are made in God's image. Humanity's identity as God's image is a fact that invites a journey of representative creaturely conformation to and imitation of God. The rest of Scripture presumes this relationship between God and humanity. For example, sin must lead to death because the refusal of God's wisdom and love is the refusal of God, who is also the source of life. And given humanity's identity as God's image, life without the wisdom and love of God is no *human* life at all. As a contradiction of God's own life, sin is a contradiction of human identity and therefore an effort to destroy it. So, humanity's sin is literally self-destructive. God's work of redemption is the gathering of humanity back into the divine life, through the radical work of the incarnation. The cross reconciles humanity to God through the recapitulating obedience of Jesus Christ and his sacrifice unto death. The resurrection is the victory over death and the establishment of new life lived in the knowledge and love of God.

---

26   Karl Barth, *Church Dogmatics* III/1, 185.
27   Ibid.

Through all of this, human identity as God's image remains fixed. Subjective participation in the realization of that identity is dependent upon active movement into the divine life by the work of the Holy Spirit who unites a believer with Christ and moves her to identify with God's self-revelation and covenantal history. To put it in terms of Augustine's analogy, all humans are considered travelers on the way to their homeland, but only those who love their homeland and identify with it, subjecting other loves and other identities that would otherwise divert their travels, will make it home.

Scripture as Love-Producing and Love-Shaping

Scripture provides guidance for this journey. Because of God's interest in the realization of human identity—that is, participation in and creaturely expression of the divine life—God gives his people Holy Scripture. Interpreting Augustine, Levering notes the theological connection of Scripture to knowing and loving God: "[U]nderstanding the texts [of Scripture] has as its purpose the encounter with Love—none other than incarnate Wisdom, Jesus Christ—teaching through them, so that we might be caught up into Love's wise pattern for our lives."[28] Scripture's *raison d'etre* is the facilitation of human knowing and loving of God. Scripture makes known the crucial realities concerning God, humanity, and the world, and it trains us to assimilate to those realities. Through this assimilation to the realities revealed in Scripture, God draws the reader into participation in the divine life.

"God's aim in Scripture," Timothy Ward maintains, "is to lead us to true devotion to Christ, and obedience to him and love for him, impinging on every area of life and thought."[29] "Impinging" is an unfortunate word here. God's aim in Scripture is to train the reader in wisdom and love by reconfiguring her perspective on every area of life and thought. Scripture casts an all-encompassing vision that reorients the reader toward the reality of God in view of her true identity.

Herman Bavinck, whom Ward engages fruitfully throughout his account, sets his definition of Scripture in the context of the revelation of a new world, a new reality. "The revelation of Scripture makes known to

---

28   Levering, *Participatory Biblical Exegesis*, 67.
29   Timothy Ward, *Words of Life: Scripture as the Living and Active Word of God* (Downers Grove, IL: IVP Academic, 2009), 73.

us another world, a world of holiness and glory. This other world descends into this fallen world not just as a doctrine but also as a divine power . . . [which leads this world] out of the state of sin, through the state of grace, to the state of glory."[30] Scripture is, as Bavinck has it here, revelation of another world. Into the fallen and dysfunctional realities of this world, Scripture reveals the possibility of a world without sin, of fellowship with God, of God's redeeming work that brings this fellowship into reality, and of a world in which everything will be made new and where God will be at home with his people. This other world, and its new life dynamics, is tangibly different from the fallen world currently experienced.

But in other ways, Scripture reveals not another world but the reality of this world. And all humans are included in God's account of this world. God's action in history is relevant to all people. Insightfully, Robert Jenson describes the life of the church as one which is "*inside* the story Scripture tells."[31] More than this: all humanity is inside the story Scripture tells.

This is true of the account of humanity in Genesis 1, and it is true of the rest of Scripture. Consider God's promise to Abraham in Genesis 22:17–18: "I will surely bless you, and I will surely multiply your offspring as the stars of heaven and as the sand that is on the seashore. And your offspring shall possess the gate of his enemies, and in your offspring shall all the nations of the earth be blessed, because you have obeyed my voice." Through this promise to Abraham humanity receives a loving word from the Father in the Son by the power of the Holy Spirit. Jesus Christ is promised as a blessing to all nations, and not only for Abraham's physical lineage. Since this blessing is for all nations but is given through this family, the subsequent stories of Israel are, therefore, stories that belong to all nations. So, when the attention of Scripture moves from creation to covenant, the implications are no less universal. Theologically, since the triune God is the only true God, then Israel's encounters with God belong to all people. Rather than putting distance between us and Israel's history, Scripture draws all people into that history.

In this way, all people who hear or read Scripture are invited to take part in the realities revealed therein. Prior self-understandings are relativized by the larger story of Scripture. A new orientation is established, and new landmarks appear from the perspective of that orientation. These

---

30   Herman Bavinck, *Reformed Dogmatics*, vol. 1 in *Prolegomena*, ed. John Bolt; trans. John Vriend (Grand Rapids: Baker Academic, 2003), 380–81. As cited by Ward, *Words of Life*, 73.
31   Jenson, "Scripture's Authority in the Church," 30 (emphasis original).

new landmarks are set by God's covenant fellowship with humanity, and they set the course for the journey of faith. One's loves are re-ordered through identification with God's revelation in Scripture. One joins the history of God's covenant fellowship. Abraham becomes one's own ancestor (by faith), Israel's history one's own history, Jesus one's own savior, and the church one's own people. One's orientation to God finds its bearing with respect to these landmarks. They shape the identity of the reader so that she is re-oriented to the journey of life with God.

Scripture reveals the truth of God. So, Levering argues that:

> From a modern perspective, distanced from the view of scriptural reading as a mode of participation in *sacra doctrina*, Augustine's and Aquinas's exegetical practices seem to be inevitably eisegetical. But from a perspective that in faith centers on the divine Teacher and the dynamics of mediated divine teaching, their approach is required to account for even the linear-historical complexity of the biblical texts. God is alive and historical realities cannot be understood outside of human relationships with him.[32]

Scripture refers away from itself to the very life of God. Yet, contemplation of God through Scripture is contemplation of God himself. Through Scripture God gives us the opportunity to contemplate God through his works, draw inferences about God's character, stoke the desire to imitate that character in our own lives, improvise upon these understandings to create renewed relational realities in the world, and become habituated thereby into being the people of God remade after his image. Moreover, Scripture models this practice. The biblical authors contemplate God and draw inferences about God's character. They describe the human imitation of divine attributes, such as love, mercy, justice, etc. They show us what reconfigured relational realities ought to look like. And they condemn deformed relational realities that keep us from imaging God's character in the world. They provide for us the habits of thought that enable us to be transformed by the renewing of our minds. Through this process, human identities are subjectively reconciled to God's vision for humanity, which is derived from God's knowledge of himself as the model, God's knowledge of humanity as his creature, and God's knowledge of the world as the context for that vision to be made real.

---

32   Levering, *Participatory Biblical Exegesis*, 77.

THE TRUTHFULNESS OF SCRIPTURE IN LIGHT OF ITS TELOS

Scripture serves to reorient our understanding of divine and human identities for the sake of fellowship with God, for a journey of participation in and conformation to God's life. Toward this end, God condescends to make himself known in human terms. Augustine finds in the incarnation both the revelation of God's love and the ultimate pattern for our love of others:

> Let us consider this process of cleansing as a trek, or a voyage, to our homeland; though progress towards the one who is ever present is not made through space, but through integrity of purpose and character. This we would be unable to do, if wisdom itself had not deigned to adapt itself to our great weakness and offered us a pattern for living; and it has actually done so in human form because we too are human.[33]

Scripture, too, is accommodated to human form. Scripture's diachronic account of God's action is fitting to humanity's diachronic experience of history, for it is through consistent and faithful action that one's character is revealed. So, God uses concrete historical events, and a particular interpretation of those events, to shape the larger story of history, to reveal himself in the world, and to shape the people of God according to his revelation.

Scripture can serve the purpose outlined above only if it is entirely true. Taking his cues from the divine life, Scott Swain argues that Scripture's truthfulness is a consequence of the fact that "The triune God is a God of truth. The Father's Word is truth (Jn 17.17). The Son is the Father's true Word (Jn 1.1; 14.6). The Holy Spirit is 'the Spirit of truth,' the one who hears and declares the true Word of God (Jn 16.13)."[34] Because of the divine authorship of Scripture, "the Bible is neither deceived nor deceiving when it speaks. . . . [A]s the Word of God written, the Bible speaks truth and only truth when it speaks."[35]

Moreover, the divine authorship of Scripture is what enables it to "bear a unified message."[36] Scripture's unified message of the identity of God, human identity, and the historical unfolding of the relationship of God with humanity, is the context for understanding the journey of faith. If the landmarks were misplaced or if there were misdirection regarding

---

33 Augustine, *On Christian Teaching*, 13.
34 Scott R. Swain, *Trinity, Revelation, and Reading: A Theological Introduction to the Bible and Its Interpretation* (New York: T&T Clark, 2011), 77.
35 Ibid., 78.
36 Ibid., 80.

the destination, success on the journey would be made impossible and Scripture would be made impotent with respect to its telos. But this is not the case. Scripture is, in fact, "living and active, sharper than any two-edged sword, piercing to the division of soul and of spirit, of joints and of marrow, and discerning the thoughts and intentions of the heart" (Heb 4:12). And it is able, by the power of the Holy Spirit, to reform those thoughts and intentions according to the image of God.

At this point, a potential criticism of my account can be addressed. Barth and others have worried that such a strong account of divine revelation in Scripture would make God's revelation subject to human manipulation.[37] Indeed, the subjection of God's revelation to human control would be a real problem. The journey analogy and its theological underpinnings do not allow for such power over Scripture, however. Here, I can offer a brief three-part reply to this concern. First, one must have willingly joined the journey of participation in the divine life in order to receive Scripture's love-producing, love-shaping effects. Merely reading Scripture is not sufficient for laying hold of the end. Second, human willing is subject to the work of the Holy Spirit. Since God is Lord over the will, one does not possess God or God's love simply by possessing the words of Scripture. Third, for Scripture to have its intended effect, not only is both human and divine willing necessary, but so is submission to the word of God. Just as a map can help only the reader who is willing to submit to its instruction, Scripture only truly belongs to those who let Scripture direct their path. For these reasons, any hubristic effort to control Scripture will remain a strictly human power play, and it will possess none of the reality of God.

Scripture is true in its witness—to events, interpretation of those events, and in the fruit produced in the hearer. God ensures the truthfulness of Scripture because of its telos, because the hearer is invited into a new reality anchored by God's action in the world. For Scripture to serve its end, it must be true, since Scripture refers the hearer to God's triune life, and it is this very life into which we are welcomed as hearers of the Word.

Conclusion

Recovery of Augustine's journey analogy has proven helpful for articulating a doctrine of Scripture supported by the realities of God's identity,

---

37 This concern arises regularly in Barth's *Church Dogmatics* I/2.

human identity, and the divine-human relationship. Humanity is made in God's image and is intended, by knowing and loving God, to be conformed to the contours of the divine life. The telos of Scripture is determined by that relationship. Through Scripture, God reveals that we are made for a journey into the knowledge and love of God, invites us to move intentionally and willingly forward in that journey, and facilitates successful movement in that journey. Scripture produces and shapes love in the believer when it is used for enjoying God, who generously encourages our enjoyment and in whose life of love we are at home.[38]

38 Thanks to Seokhee Garcia, Adewale Giwa, Garrett Kono, Richard Moua, Joshua Nordstrom, Brede Parker, and Paul Switz for their helpful comments on an earlier draft of this paper.

Scripture Index

Subject Index

Marxist, 153
maturity. See, formation
Melchizidek, 56
memory, 31
metaphor, God is, 78
    and theological method, 112–26
midrash, 99
millennials, 62
mind, of the Spirit, 121
minorities, harmful to, 152
miracles, 157
modernism, 151, 178
modernity, 148, 149, 150, 152
    the term, 155
monotheism, 37
moral theology, 33, 36–37
Moses: Jesus and, 51, 52
    testified to, 47
myths, 159

nations, teachings of the other, 88
naturalism, 130
natural law, so-called, 88
natural theology, 166
    wisdom as, 89–91
new covenant, 31, 36, 98
New Testament, appeals to the
        Scriptures, 68
    attests to the Logos, 30
    and the Old, 26, 31, 52, 103
Nicene Creed, 66

obedience, 48, 56
objectivity, 158
    false sense of, 178
Old Testament, the: anticipates the
        new, 31
    as Christian Scripture, 23
    in Hebrews, 97, 98
    and historical criticism, 60, 61
    interpretation of, 66
    in light of the New, 103
    and the Logos, 29–30
    and New Testament, 52
ontology, actualistic, 166, 167
    of the reader, 109

of Scripture, 162
orality, Scripture's, 33, 34
original grace, 86
orthodoxy, defenders of, 163

parachurches, 25
particularity, 166, 170, 171
    of our context, 178
    human, 175–76
    of the subject, 177–78
Passover, 116
patriarchy, 178
peers, disagreement with, 132, 133, 134
philosophical categories, 34
philosophy, no longer, 153
    of history, 162
positivism, 169
postcolonialism, 73–75, 179
postmodern, doomed to be, 151
    the word, 148
postmodernity, 160
    adherents of, 148, 149, 150 154
    elements of, 146, 147
    shortcomings of, 153
postmoderns, readily reject, 161, 162
post-postmodern world, 146
poststructuralism, 147
prayer, is the way, 72
    need for, 179
presuppositions, 162, 172, 178
priesthood, change of the, 36
    Christ's, 56
primary particularity, 177–78
process theology, 168
prophecy, evaluation of, 70
prophets, 43, 44, 52, 88
Protestant, mainline, 24
    in solidarity with, 23. See also,
        Protestantism
Protestantism, 163, 172
punishment, of the attackers, 68

racism, 178
rationalism, 169
rationality, 138, 148. See also, reason
reader, responsibility as, 120

Author Index